PASTORAL
LIFE AND PRACTICE
IN THE EARLY CHURCH

PASTORAL LIFE AND PRACTICE
IN THE EARLY CHURCH

CARL A. VOLZ

Augsburg • Minneapolis

Pastoral Life and Practice in the Early Church

Scripture quotations, unless otherwise noted, are from the Revised Standard Version of the Bible, copyright © 1946, 1952, and 1971 by the Division of Christian Education of the National Council of Churches.

Library of Congress Cataloging-in-Publication Data
Volz, Carl A.
    Pastoral life and practice in the early church / Carl A. Volz.
        p.   cm.
    Bibliography: p.
    ISBN 0-8066-2446-9
    1. Pastoral theology—History of doctrines—Early church, ca.
30–600.   2. Women in church work—History.   I. Title.
BR195.P36V64   1990
262'.1'09015—dc20   89-15118
                                                                                                    CIP

The paper used in this publication meets the minimum requirements of American National Standard for Information Sciences—Permanence of Paper for Printed Library Materials, ANSI Z39.48-1984.   ∞™

Manufactured in the U.S.A.   AF 9-2446

94   93   92   91   90   1   2   3   4   5   6   7   8   9   10

TO LYDIA
Loving Wife, and Mother of
Carol, Martin, Stephen, Katherine, Michael

Contents

Preface

From the time of the apostles the Christian church has always been served by leaders, however they varied in status, title, or function. Although the Sacrament of Holy Baptism consecrates every Christian to a life of ministry, from earliest times the community of the baptized has set apart some individuals to function as leaders of the communities of faith. In time these individuals became known collectively as clergy (Greek = a portion), referring either to those few selected to lead, or to the portion of the faithful each one was to lead. This book describes the development of the pastoral role in the early church. The focus is primarily upon the office of parish pastor (presbyter)— that is, those individuals who were chosen to lead early Christian congregations. Of necessity the study includes bishops, who were the earliest pastors, and deacons, who were ordained to assist them.

In recent years there has been considerable discussion over the role and function of the clergy, especially their relationship with the baptized community and their identity as ordained servants of God's word. This book does not presume to offer answers to contemporary issues, but it describes the evolution of the ordained ministry during the formative years of the church. By so doing it offers the context in which the clerical office developed, which may assist contemporary discussions. In this context there are elements both of continuity and change; continuity in that clergy have always been engaged in the proclamation of God's word and in presiding at the sacraments, change in the influence of the culture that has shaped the role and identity of the clergy. In the early church the most significant such change came about when the clergy became officials of the Roman government and assumed positions previously reserved for leaders of the Roman cults.

The designation "early church" is admittedly ambiguous, and its limits arbitrary. For this study the *terminus ad quem* is the fifth century, for this time the basic outlines of pastoral life and practice had reached a level of uniformity that would remain until the expansion of Christianity beyond the Mediterranean. As new people were brought into the church's orbit, the pastoral office would take on new forms as it was shaped by its culture, but this takes us into that epoch commonly associated with medieval. In some instances the time has been extended into the sixth century—that is, Gregory's *Pastoral Rule* in the discussion of pastoral care.

"The Pastoral Office" (chap. 1) is a description of the changes that occurred from the loosely organized Pauline churches with leaders who emerged primarily on the basis of their charisms, to the ante-Nicene period when churches came under the leadership of clergy who were selected by them and received ordination. Under the imperial church, there was considerable legislation governing the pastoral office as well as pastoral authority, and the clerical hierarchy assumes a more definite form.

"Pastor and People" (chap. 2) outlines the nature of early Christian congregations, the problems relating to persecution, and the frequent internal tensions of the churches. The pastor functioned primarily as the leader of communal worship and as one who was "called to be holy." Here we also find a description of the pastoral duties with respect to charity, hospitality, and adjudication.

"Pastor and Proclamation" (chap. 3) refers to the office of teaching, primarily in catechesis, and to the development of the Christian sermon—prophetic, liturgical, and exegetical. Both classical rhetoric and Jewish antecedents had a decisive influence on early Christian homilies. Under the imperial church the sermons, sometimes delivered in large basilicas, became major events. This discussion concludes with examples of homilies by the most celebrated preacher of antiquity, John of Antioch (Chrysostom) together with a review of Augustine as preacher.

"The Care of Souls" (chap. 4) describes this aspect of pastoral life in terms of counseling, guiding, and sustaining the faithful. Then, as now, such care focused on the bereaved, the indifferent, the sinners, the proud, and the timid. The literature of consolation includes most of the expected comforts associated with this genre together with some unexpected and (to our mind) highly unconventional counsel, conditioned by the assumptions of the time. Examples are also given of reconciling the penitent, and the nonclerical role of spiritual director is discussed. The chapter concludes with a discussion of Gregory's *Pastoral Rule*, for which we are in debt to Thomas C. Oden's masterful analysis, in which he indicates that Gregory anticipated many of the techniques and assumptions we have come to associate with contemporary pastoral care.

"The Pastoral Role of Women" (chap. 5) rehearses primarily the ministry of widows, virgins, and deaconesses. Although these women were not included in the offices of presbyter or bishop, their ministry was highly significant in the early church. In outlining this book a decision had to be made regarding the placement of women's ministry, whether their service should be included within each chapter or in a separate section. To do the former would not have been feasible, for women did not serve as pastors of congregations. It seemed best to include such ministry in a separate section, and because the pastoral functions of women accelerated with the passing of time, reaching its culmination in later centuries, it seemed appropriate to conclude the work with this treatment of the often neglected pastoral role of women in the early church.

In any discussion of an institution that spans two millennia, there are always pitfalls to be avoided. The most obvious one is the temptation to portray the early church as a mirror of our times and to find our own legitimation in their precedent. Throughout this research I have tried to avoid painting their portrait by using contemporary models. There is sufficient distance in time and culture to recognize the early church as living in a context far removed from the present. On the other hand, there are sufficient continuities in pastoral life and practice between the ancient church and our times for the reader to identify with these early practitioners of the pastoral office.

I am in debt to the insights of many seminarians who have been my colleagues in studying the history of pastoral life. I am also grateful to Luther Northwestern Theological Seminary in St. Paul, Minnesota, for the time granted for this study, as well as to the University of Chicago School of Divinity for offering me a fellowship to complete this work. The libraries of the University of Chicago and of the Lutheran School of Theology at Chicago were most helpful, and the hospitality of colleagues at both institutions was warm and genuine. Lisa Strandjord typed the completed manuscript, for which I am in her debt. I am also grateful to Michelle Rowell whose careful reading of the manuscript produced the index.

1 The Pastoral Office

Pastoral office refers to a position of leadership recognized as such within the Christian community, with a degree of permanence and status. This chapter addresses the development of positions of leadership in the early church. The first century did not have clergy as we understand that role today in terms of salary, recognition, authority, selection, education, or societal and political status. Here we shall trace the development of pastoral office from the time of Jesus' disciples to that of Augustine (A.D. 420), addressing the question, How did leadership develop in the early church?

Ministry in the New Testament

The New Testament has no exclusive form or terminology for ministry. Some churches have bishops and deacons, and others do not. Some have presbyters, while other officials are called prophets, teachers, pastors, and evangelists (Eph. 4:11-12). Paul and Barnabas, referred to as apostles, are commissioned by prophets and teachers in Antioch (Acts 13:1ff.). Bishops appear to be synonymous with elders (Titus 1:5-7) and to these leaders are added workers of miracles, healers, helpers, administrators, and speakers in tongues (1 Cor. 12:28). The all-inclusive term that describes every gift of leadership is that of ministry (*diakonia*). All are "ministers of the new covenant" (2 Cor. 3:6), or "ministers of Christ" (2 Cor. 11:23), or "ministers of the church" (Col. 1:25). Correspondence is sometimes addressed simply to "the church of God" (1 Cor. 1:2), or "to the saints" (Eph. 1:2), implying that no single leader was recognized. The New Testament literature leads us to believe that the primitive church was not yet highly organized or stratified into various types of clergy and laity. Rather than offices, we find persons who possessed gifts or functions of service, which Paul refers to as "varieties of ministry" (1 Cor. 12:5). All these gifts of service were understood to be given by the Spirit, who apportioned "to each one individually as he wills" (1 Cor. 12:11).

Despite this diversity of gifts, from the beginning one group is prominent in a leadership role, and that is the Twelve, a relatively stable group of disciples whom Jesus called "to be with him" (Mark 3:13-14). This is clearly a symbolic title that calls to mind the twelve patriarchs and tribes of Israel, signifying the church as the New Israel. They were witnesses of the life, death, and resurrection of the Lord (Acts 1:4-11), and after Judas's defection they were careful to maintain their number by appointing Mathias, but further vacancies were not filled. The later writings of the New Testament tend to speak of apostles rather than the Twelve as direct envoys of Jesus.[1]

The term "apostle" comes from the Jewish concept of ambassador, with the person so designated having full responsibility for representing the one who sent him. "The ambassador of man is like the man himself."[2] In the New Testament the apostles included the Twelve in addition to others who had seen the risen Lord and had been commissioned by him through the Spirit. As many as seventeen are named apostles, including Paul, Barnabas, Silvanus, and James, the Lord's brother. They were primarily missionaries, though James seems to have remained in Jerusalem. Paul never suggested he should be considered one of the Twelve, but he insisted vigorously he was to be counted among the apostles (1 Cor. 15:8-10). The apostles not only proclaimed God's word, but they acted with authority even over sickness and demons (Matt. 10:1). Because the Twelve and the apostles were directly associated with Christ's earthly ministry and called by him, there could be no replacements for them. They had their own disciples, but they were not apostles.

The Twelve and the apostles were the earliest leaders of the primitive church. The original twelve attempted to maintain the guidance of the church from Jerusalem until the Roman destruction of the city in

A.D. 70. Paul as apostle communicated with the churches he founded as one possessing authority. He speaks of "daily pressure because of my anxiety for all the churches" (1 Cor. 11:28). He was called on to settle disputes, answer questions about sex, reconcile quarreling factions, deal with masters and slaves, and a host of other issues. Yet the distinction among early Christian leaders remains ambiguous. "Though there was development in ministry in the first century, it was not unilinear. It is historically more exact and eventually more instructive theologically to respect the differences in structuring the ministry that existed simultaneously in different churches."[3] The mission of the Twelve and the apostles was identical with that of all believers, to proclaim the gospel and to announce the coming of God's kingdom in Christ.

By the time Paul wrote to the Corinthians two new offices of leadership appear in addition to that of the apostles, those of prophet and teacher. He wrote, "God has appointed in the church first apostles, second prophets, third teachers" (1 Cor. 12:28). By carefully enumerating these ministries in a hierarchical pattern, Paul gives evidence of the earliest triad of church leadership. After the apostles came prophets and teachers. As with the apostolate, these other ministries were perceived as gifts of the Spirit for the purpose of building up the community. Prophets, and sometimes teachers, were itinerants who served the church-at-large; their sphere was not limited to a single locality. They were identified in their leadership roles through the self-authenticating gifts of the Spirit. They were not elected to their "office" nor was there an ecclesiastical ceremony to set them apart.

Whereas the apostles were missionaries who established Christian communities, the prophets nurtured these new congregations. Because of their itinerant nature, prophets were not always present in a local community, but they came and went at their pleasure. Following the example of the Old Testament, prophets emerged in Jewish Christian communities (Acts 11:27; 15:32). They were also found in mixed (Jewish/gentile) congregations and in purely gentile churches (Acts 11:27; Rom. 12:6-7). Some prophets mentioned are Agabus, Barnabas, Saul, Symeon Niger, Lucius of Cyrene, Judas, and Silas. In addition to these there were numerous prophetesses, such as the four daughters of Phillip (Acts 21:9). Prophecy appears frequently in the primitive church down to the close of the second century.

The content of prophecy was insight into the relationship between God and humanity. In addition to the gift of proclaiming God's word, the prophet played a special role in church discipline and in reconciling penitents. Some sins were believed to be so grievous that only the voice of God through the prophet could offer absolution. Given such wide-ranging authority, it is not surprising that the prophets assumed a commanding role in the primitive church. In some cases they declared who should fill the offices of leadership for the congregations, and they arbitrated disputes among the faithful. Nor is it surprising that such authority was occasionally abused and practiced by charlatans who traded on the credulity of the Christians. There are numerous warnings against "false prophets" (Matt. 7:15; 24:11), and the need to "test" the prophets (1 John 4:1). The test given them had to do with the consistency of their message with that which had already been received, and with their manner of life (1 Cor. 12:3; 1 John 4:1).

Teachers formed the third class of charismatic ministries, after the apostles and prophets. In many ways they appear to function the same as prophets, and the line between them is not easy to draw. A prophet was sometimes a teacher and a teacher the prophet, with extensive overlapping. These gifts were functions in the church as compared with defined offices. Paul (Acts 13:1-3) was both prophet and teacher. It was the prophets and teachers of Antioch who decided that Paul and Barnabas should undertake a mission to Cyprus and who "laid hands on them and sent them off" (Acts 13:1-3). A distinctive feature of teachers was preparing catechumens for baptism, and for providing advanced instruction in the faith. Paul gave them a "pattern of teaching" (Rom. 6:17) for their instructions. The function of teacher apparently outlived that of prophet, as we find numerous teachers well into the fourth century. Justin the Martyr and Tatian are prominent in the second century, and in Alexandria we find Clement and Origen in the third century. Eusebius refers to "the presbyters and teachers of the brethren in the villages" in the fourth century.[4]

Alongside the triad of apostles, prophets, and teachers, there is another cluster of ministries, that of bishops, presbyters, and deacons. At first the bishops and presbyters (elders) appear to be interchangeable (Titus 1:5). The bishop (*episkopos*) probably emerged from Greek congregations; as such "overseers" were common functionaries in the

Hellenic world and were attached to social institutions as administrators. *Episkopoi* were administrators of burial associations, athletic clubs, and other special interest groups, including municipal governments. The office was simply one of overseer or general manager. When Paul greets the *episkopoi* and deacons of Philippi (Phil. 1:1), he is using a commonly accepted term for leaders. It is interesting that in this case he employs the plural of bishop, implying there was more than one bishop in that congregation, unless the term included the elders as well. Although the title of bishop was borrowed from the culture, the church invested the office with spiritual meaning and authority. Paul in his speech at Miletus said bishops were those whom "the Holy Spirit had appointed to tend the church of God" (Acts 20:28).

Elders (*presbyteroi*) appear for the first time with the collection for famine relief among the Jewish Christians of Jerusalem (Acts 11:30). The term was undoubtedly borrowed from contemporary Judaism. Each synagogue had its seat of elders (sanhedrin), which functioned as a court and governing body. They were among the "rulers, scribes, and high priests" (Acts 4:5, 8, 23). They administered the famine relief sent by Antioch, and the gift was received by the elders in Jerusalem and not by the Twelve, who at this time may have been scattered due to persecution. A few years later at the Council of Jerusalem we again meet the elders as leaders with the Twelve. After that we find them mentioned in the Pastorals (1 Tim. 3:2, Titus 1:7) indicating the office was now part of the Greek Christian congregation as well as Jewish Christian. It appears that all bishops were at first presbyters who were selected to chair the council of elders who governed each church.

The ministry of the Seven represents an advance in the concept of office in the New Testament in that a new position was established by the church and not directly by the Spirit. The "body of disciples" was told by the Twelve to "pick out from among you seven men of good repute, full of Spirit" (Acts 6:3). Inasmuch as the "brethren" selected them, we can assume they were chosen by some form of democratic process, after which the apostles laid their hands on them and offered prayers. Although *diakonia* is the generic term for ministry of all kinds, the deacons as officeholders were selected for the service of "waiting at tables." That included the distribution of alms and the maintenance of the physical properties of the church. In pre-Nicene times they commonly read (or chanted) the epistle and gospel at the

Eucharist, received the offerings, and assisted at the distribution of Holy Communion. The archdeacon became the bishop's chief administrative officer.

In the Pauline churches we read of other forms of ministry in addition to those already mentioned. Corinth had charisms of miracle-working, healing, helping, administration, and speaking in tongues (1 Cor. 12:28). The list of ministries in Romans 12:6-8 outlines similar gifts that can be divided between those of the word and those of service. Elsewhere Paul refers to fellow workers (2 Cor. 8:23) and those who "are over you in the Lord" (1 Thess. 5:12). In Ephesians and Colossians there are ministries with fixed forms. They are apostles, prophets, evangelists, pastors, and teachers (Eph. 4:11-12). Colossians refers to Paul as a minister (*diakonos*) according to the divine office (1:25); Epaphras and Tychicus are called ministers as well (1:7; 4:7).

The clearest expression of a church order among the Catholic Epistles is 1 Peter. There it is said that each member of the community has received a charism (4:10), which is to be employed for one another, but the only charismata mentioned are those of speaking (*lalein*) and serving (*diakonein*). There is also a fixed circle of presbyters (5:1) who are engaged in an ordered ministry that consists of "shepherding" (5:2-4). This ministry is to be carried out on behalf of Christ who is the chief shepherd and bishop. James refers to presbyters (5:14) who have a shepherding function, including prayers for the sick.

This brief survey of the New Testament indicates a gradual development from an earlier period of a multiplicity of varied ministries, validated by the Spirit and centered on functions, to that of the Pastorals where we find the existence of fixed offices.

The issue of ministry in the New Testament has been dominated by questions posed by Rudolph Sohm and Adolph Harnack in the early part of this century.[5] Sohm thought of the church as a body of Spirit-endowed persons characterized by deep spiritual and religious experiences. There was no official ministry or order in the beginning, only "charismatic organization." With the passage of time, such Spirit-filled leadership was replaced by elected officeholders (clergy), and this development Sohm considered unfortunate. Harnack contended that the church as a social organization required more order simply to exist. He popularized the two-triad theory of early Christian ministry, setting the charismatic apostle, prophet, and teacher against the institutional bishop, presbyter, and deacon of later years.[6] The distinction is useful and represents the literature from the period, but critics fault Harnack for making too rigid a separation between the charismatic and institutional ministries. It is certain that by the end of the first century the Pauline multiplicity of ministries given by the Spirit has developed into the threefold offices of bishop, presbyter, and deacon. Yet there was considerable overlap between the two triads and within them.

Clement of Rome's letter to the Corinthians, a document contemporary with the Pastorals at the end of the first century, indicates the direction in which events are moving. He rebukes the Corinthians for having removed from office a presbyter who stood in a line of succession from the apostles, and who had "in a blameless and holy manner offered the gifts" (i.e., Eucharist).[7] Clement cites the Old Testament hierarchy of high priest, priest, and Levite to justify order in the church, although in Corinth it was the presbyter who had been removed from office, who may also have been a bishop. In the context of establishing this hierarchy, Clement for the first time in early Christian literature suggests a distinction between clergy and laity. "A layman (*laikos*) is bound by the ordinances of the laity."[8]

The development of the pastoral office is associated with the means of selecting clergy and the method of installation (ordination). The Twelve were called directly by Jesus, and the other apostles claim to have been commissioned by the risen Lord through appearances to them (Acts 1:21). In 1 Cor. 12:28 Paul states that "God has appointed" apostles, prophets, and teachers. The church at Antioch had been advised by the Holy Spirit to "set apart Paul and Barnabas" (Acts 13:2), and then hands were laid on them by prophets and teachers, accompanied with fasting and prayer. There is no mention of a gift conveyed to Paul through the laying on of hands. Indeed, hands were laid on him by Ananias in connection with the removal of his blindness, and Ananias expressed the hope that he might also be filled with the Holy Spirit (Acts 19:9). It seems doubtful that either of these impositions of hands corresponds to later ordination, as Paul insists he was chosen by God and not by men. Certainly his conversion experience gave him greater confidence in his ministry than the imposition of hands either by Ananias or the prophets and teachers of Antioch.

With the Seven we first encounter an election followed by the imposition of hands. Again it may be questioned whether this constituted an ordination in the later sense of the term, inasmuch as the gift of the Spirit was a precondition for the laying on of hands rather than an accompanying gift. The imposition of hands seems to have been a ratification and acknowledgment by the Twelve in their selection.

We do not know how the various ministers in the Pauline churches were selected for their roles, except to suggest that in some cases there must have been empirical proof of their having special gifts (i.e., miracle-working, administration, healing). There is no mention of any special induction into their office; it seems more appropriate to speak of these ministries as functions rather than offices. At one time Paul and Barnabas appointed presbyters (Acts 14:21-23) and inducted them into office simply with prayer and fasting. At Corinth, Paul laid hands on twelve "disciples" who then received the glossalalia, but this cannot be understood as induction into an office.

The Pastorals reflect a situation in the Pauline field shortly after the apostle's death, where we find bishops, presbyters, and deacons in place. The imposition of hands is now definitely associated with the conferral of the charism necessary to the discharge of one's office. "Do not neglect the gift you have, which was given you by prophetic utterance when the council of elders laid their hands upon you" (1 Tim. 4:14); "Rekindle the gift of God that is within you through the laying on of my hands (2 Tim. 1:6).[9] For Timothy the imposition of hands is so closely associated with induction to office as to be synonymous with it, when he writes, "Do not be hasty in the laying on of hands" (1 Tim. 5:22). The precise meaning of the act or its efficacy, and whether there is a transmission of charism from God directly or through the ordinator, or whether the act is simply a bestowal of office (i.e., inauguration of a president), remains undefined.

The New Testament does not offer us a clear or unified picture on the selection of church leaders. Even Paul's "appointment" of elders can be translated to mean "select by election." In some churches Paul and Barnabas appoint such leaders and in others they do not. Imposition of hands was not universal, and it was not limited to clerical induction. There seems to be no single administrator of hands—at one time it is Paul, or the presbyters, or prophets and teachers, or the Twelve.

The practice of laying on of hands rests on Jewish precedent as the rite of induction into office. Moses laid hands on Joshua and thus appointed him his successor (Deut. 34:9).[10] As a result of this act

Joshua is endued with the powers necessary to the discharge of his office. This took place before the assembled congregation to give public legitimacy to the transfer of power. Following the Moses/Joshua model and with express appeal to it, the rabbis developed their own practices of ordination. When a student had achieved the required proficiency in his studies, he was ordained by his teacher and two assistants. This took place in the presence of witnesses, and its intent was to indicate that the "chain of tradition reaching back to Moses would be lengthened by the addition of another link, the gift of wisdom being imparted to the authorized scholar by his teacher."[11] This could be done only in Palestine, and it was nonrepeatable.

There is frequent reference to the laying on of hands in the accounts of healing the sick by Jesus. These accounts are numerous, and we can sum them up with Luke's statement: "All those who had any who were sick with various diseases brought them to him, and he laid his hands on every one of them and healed them" (Luke 4:40). This healing ministry was continued by the apostles, also through the laying on of hands. Whether these actions should be associated with magic, Gerhard Kittel makes this observation: "There is no magical practice of healing in the New Testament records. The decisive elements are the Word of Jesus and the faith that is put in him. The healing power of Jesus is not bound up with any means or mode of transfer. His Word can operate even from afar (Matt. 8:8, 13; Luke 7:7; John 4:50-52)."[12] This observation is significant in terms of the imposition of hands in ordination, for in later years the church will speak of special charisms conferred in the rite.

Hands are also imposed in blessing (e.g., the children in Mark 10:13) and in connection with baptism (Acts 8:17; 19:6). It was understood that in baptism, the hands conferred the Spirit, and it was with this understanding that the imposition of hands was used in the installation of clergy. The church also borrowed from rabbinical practices. Since Num. 27:15-23 served as a basis for the rabbinate, the intentional borrowing from the pericope in Acts 6:1-6 is designated to show that the institution of the Seven is meant as a type of ordination following the Jewish model. In both Jewish and Christian practices the rite was given only to those who had already proven themselves capable of leadership. But more was involved than competence. It was also a sign of continuity in rabbinic/apostolic teaching, with a major difference being the conferral of the gift of the Spirit by the

Christians. Timothy's caution against hasty induction to office indicates that certain preconditions were expected of candidates, and he gives us a long list of such expectations (1 Timothy 3). Likewise, the Seven were to be "men of good repute, full of the Spirit and of wisdom" (Acts 6:3). Apparently the induction into office was as much a recognition by the community of the proven virtues/gifts of the candidate as it was the conferral of new charisms. This question, the meaning of the imposition of hands and its attendant gifts, continues to engage theological reflection in the church today.

With Clement of Rome we see the association of pastoral authority and legitimacy associated with the concept of order. The selection of presbyters is to be made by those "of proper standing," and it is to be done only "with the consent of the whole church" (44:3), which refers to the local congregation. Clergy are not irremovable, but in the case of Corinth the congregation was culpable because the elders were "blameless." Clement does not tell us how elders were installed into office, but insofar as authority depended on a line of succession from the apostles we may reasonably assume there was a laying on of hands, although Clement does not appeal to it. Indeed, he does not associate the clerical office with any charism or Spirit-filled context, but he is solely concerned with right order for the sake of peace.

The Ante-Nicene Church

Early in the second century it is apparent that a distinction between the two triads of ministry was recognized in the church. After the apostles, prophets and teachers continued working as evangelists, usually traveling from place to place visiting the churches. In the *Didache* we find some reserve toward unknown prophets who claimed to be inspired by the Spirit. If such prophets appeared in a community, they must be tested as to their lives and teachings. If they are found to be orthodox and beyond reproach, they are to be given precedence over the local ministry of the bishop for the time they remain in the community. "Not everyone who speaks in the spirit [in tongues?] is a prophet; he is only a prophet if he has the ways of the Lord. The false and genuine prophet will be known therefore by their ways. Every genuine prophet who desires to settle among you has a right to his support. . . . Let prophets give thanks as they will."[13] The author continues by saying, "You must elect for yourselves bishops and deacons . . . for their ministry to you is identical with that of the prophets and teachers. You must therefore not despise them." It is clear that the prophets and teachers were held in higher regard than the bishops and deacons. But the administrative and spiritual needs of the churches could not wait for sporadic and intermittent appearances of charismatic leaders, and the local ministries of bishops, elders, and deacons were bound to gain in prominence as being more stable, reliable, and in touch with the local community. The transition from the prophetic to the presbyterial ministry cannot be seen as a retrogression but as a natural and mostly beneficial development.

The Pastoral Epistles reflect the emerging prominence of the local ministries, but far more emphatic in support of the bishop, elder, and deacon are the seven letters of Ignatius (110). In the face of threatening heresy and to maintain the unity of the church, the bishop serves as the hub of the community. He alone leads worship and dispenses the sacraments. "I advise you, be eager to act always in godly concord; with the bishop presiding as the counterpart of God, the presbyters as the counterpart of the apostles, and the deacons. . . . Be united with the bishop and those who preside. You must do nothing without the bishop and the presbyters."[14] Ignatius tells his readers to "follow the bishop as Jesus followed the Father." The authority of the ministers is not derived from apostolicity but from the idea that their offices are the earthly type of a heavenly pattern.[15] Despite his enthusiasm for the ministerial offices, Ignatius does not appeal to his role as bishop to validate his teaching but to his coming martyrdom—that is, to a charismatic rather than institutional authority. It is necessary to keep in mind that in the second century the bishop was the pastor of a local congregation, assisted by a group of elders and deacons. None of these officials was salaried as we know it today; they maintained themselves through their own occupations, although they were entitled to some of the "firstfruits" offered by the congregation. The emergence of a single bishop as leader in each local community is known as the monepiscopate (monarchical episcopate) signalizing the unity of the church around one recognized leader.

Toward the end of the second century we encounter the dual challenges of Montanism and Gnosticism, each of which contributed significantly to the development of the clerical office. The Montanist challenge represented a revival of the prophetic ministry against the developing institutions of bishop, presbyter, and deacon. It therefore posed the question of the legitimacy of leadership in the church. The challenge of Gnosticism was more serious in that it claimed to possess authentic (divine) revelation apart from and opposed to that which was accepted as orthodox by the churches. In responding to these challenges, the church found it necessary to distinguish the true from the false prophet and teacher. Montanism found itself discredited, due to its excesses and the appearance of charlatans and self-seeking opportunists among the prophets, who were not accountable to any authority. Lucian, pagan critic, ridiculed the Christians' credulity in a diatribe, *The Death of Peregrinus*, in which the hero, a criminal who had escaped from prison, found a church which gave him the honors of a prophet. He displayed his prison scars as having been received for confessing the faith, but then he was apprehended by the Roman officials and suffered death ostensibly as a martyr, though he was not a Christian. Yet his followers revered him as a saint after his death. The story illustrates the abuses that were possible in a free-lance ministry without ecclesiastical oversight.

With Gnosticism we find independent teachers who were suspect because of their autonomy from the ecclesiastical orthodoxy and teachings at odds with the received tradition. Neither prophecy nor teaching declined, but they were absorbed by the episcopal/presbyterial office. The church's reaction to the gnostic threat was to insist on continuity of teaching with that of the apostles—that is, apostolicity. Clement of Rome insisted on a linear succession of office bearers for the sake of order. "Jesus Christ was sent from God. Thus Christ is from God, and the apostles from Christ."[16] An orderly procedure depends on God's will. There has been an orderly succession of leaders, and this is all in keeping with universal order and harmony. "We view it as a breach of justice to remove from their ministry those who were appointed either by them [i.e., apostles] or later on and with the whole church's consent, by others of proper standing."[17]

Irenaeus was more interested in a succession of apostolic teaching, which he found to be guaranteed through a demonstrable chain of elders leading back to the apostles, something the Gnostics could not produce. "By this order and succession, the tradition of the apostles in the church and the preaching of the truth have come down to us."[18] Therefore one must listen to the elders in the church who hold the teaching succession from the apostles. In his polemic, Irenaeus coins the phrase "charism of truth" (*charisma veritatis; Against Heresies,* 4:26:2) as that which presbyters and bishops (he uses both terms) possess. In using this concept he was borrowing an ideal already in vogue among the Gnostics themselves, whose teachers validated their message through a chain of transmission from philosophers and philosophical schools. Irenaeus followed the Gnostic and Jewish models of transmission to validate authenticity, but the source of truth, the charism of truth, had to be demonstrably apostolic and public. In this sense the charism refers to authentic apostolic teaching and not to the later "indelible character" of Augustine.

Irenaeus never mentions ordination, nor does he associate any such rite with legitimate ministry. Tertullian claimed that all churches that taught as the apostles taught enjoyed apostolic succession. "Because they agree in the same faith, they are reckoned to be no less apostolic through their kinship in doctrine."[19] By the beginning of the third century the test of apostolicity came to be applied as the criterion of orthodoxy. This referred to apostolic literature (i.e., New Testament canon), apostolic creeds (Rules of Faith), and an apostolic ministry. It was a development largely in reaction to the threat of Gnosticism and its vagaries.

The second century also witnessed the activities of Polycarp, Hermas, and Justin. Polycarp, the bishop of Smyrna, is known especially for his letter to the Philippians, filled with exhortations to steadfastness and fidelity to the gospel. Irenaeus states that Polycarp had received his tradition of faith directly from the apostle John, and that he had been appointed to his bishopric by "apostles in Asia."[20] Hermas does not add significant material on the pastoral office, other than the fact that the prophetic ministry is still very much alive in the mid-second century, and he offers tantalizing information of corruption both among the prophets and the established clergy. Justin's First Apology (160) gives evidence of the liturgical role of the pastor, whom he refers to as the "president," and of the office of a reader in the services. It is the president who receives and distributes the alms of the faithful and is responsible for the care of all who are in need, which indicates the close relationship between works of mercy and the emergence of the monepiscopate. The need to preserve uniformity of teaching led to a greater involvement by sister churches in mutual consultations and selection of clergy, though at the beginning of the third century the Christian church was still a loose federation of autonomous churches.

By this time (200) there was an emerging consensus on the selection of clergy. The church looked for those who gave evidence of an aptitude for ministerial functions, which included a virtuous life as well as fidelity to the apostolic tradition. The possession of these gifts was acknowledged through ordination. Whether or not a "grace of vocation" accompanied the laying on of hands, a precondition for the rite was a demonstrable aptitude for the office. It was also the rule that every community elect its own bishop/presbyter, but election alone did not confer authority. "The process [of selection] was not completed until he had received the acceptance, approval, and ordination of at least one (preferably more) of his fellow bishops."[21] At the beginning of the third century the authority of the pastor did not derive from his office or the rite of ordination, but it was largely associated with interior qualities of aptitude, moral example, and the natural endowments (gifts of the Spirit) of the holder. The ordination rite was a recognition of these gifts.

Early in the third century the *Apostolic Tradition* of Hippolytus gives us more information on the development of the pastoral office. Hippolytus was a presbyter in Rome and the most important theologian of that church in the third century. When Origen visited the city (c. 212) he heard Hippolytus preach, which indicates that even in Rome the homily was not reserved to the bishop. The *Apostolic Tradition* is a detailed description of practices in Rome at the turn of the third century, and offers us a description of the pastoral role in terms of ordination. Hippolytus writes:

Let the bishop be ordained after he has been chosen by all the people. When he has been named and shall please all, let him, with the presbytery and such bishops as may be present, assemble with the people on a Sunday. While all give their assent, the bishops shall lay their hands upon him, and the presbytery shall stand by in silence. All shall keep silent, praying in their heart for the descent of the Spirit. Then one of the bishops who are present shall, at the request of all, lay his hand on him who is ordained bishop, and shall pray as follows.[22]

Two actions are significant: (1) The bishop has been chosen by all the people (i.e., the local community); and (2) ordination is by laying on of hands by one of the bishops. All in attendance pray for the gift of the Spirit. The prayer by the ordainer includes these petitions: "Pour forth now that power, which is thine, of thy royal Spirit . . . which he bestowed upon his holy apostles . . . to have authority to remit sins according to the authority which thou gavest to thy apostles." The prayer requests the Spirit who had empowered the apostles and refers to the forgiveness of sins, one of the earliest associations of absolution (Matt. 16:19) with the episcopacy. "And when he is made bishop, all shall offer him the kiss of peace, for he has been made worthy (*axios*)." Hippolytus does not explain the meaning of the hands, but he is explicit about receiving the Spirit through prayer.

In the ordination of a presbyter, the *Apostolic Tradition* prescribes that the bishop lay his hands on the candidate while the presbyters merely touch him, though later they also lay on hands. The bishop prays for the Spirit. In the ordination of a deacon, only the bishop imposes hands, because the deacon "does not receive that Spirit which is possessed by the presbyter." Presbyters may only receive and not give, which strongly implies that the laying on of hands confers something palpable and substantive. On the other hand, against Hippolytus, there is considerable evidence from this period that presbyters also ordained bishops as well as fellow presbyters. This is because of the synonymity of presbyters with bishops and the interchangeable nature of the terms.

[23]Hippolytus continues by saying that a confessor (one who had suffered under persecution) receives the honor of the presbyterate by virtue of his confession, without the laying on of hands, but if he is to advance to bishop he requires the hands. Through his fortitude under persecution, the confessor has given evidence of being Spirit-filled, and he does not require the imposition of hands, but as bishop he does require it. It seems probable that episcopal consecration is not for the reception of a special charism but for the sake of order in the church—that is to say, for the sake of his pastoral office. If every confessor/presbyter claimed episcopal rights, there would be confusion, something which Cyprian and the church of Carthage experienced in the mid-third century.

The Pseudo-Clementine literature from the early third century records a prayer by the community asking for guidance in the selection of one worthy "to sit in the chair of Christ," together with direction for nomination of the candidate by the people or the ordainer, the installation of a bishop by the imposition of hands and prayer, and (something new) the enthronement of the bishop.[24] The idea of a special chair as a symbol of episcopal authority is another example of borrowing from late rabbinic tradition (i.e., the chair of Moses). The election procedure in the Pseudo-Clementines is vague. We can presume that not only the clergy but also the community participated in some way.

The *Didascalia Apostolorum* (third century) does not add information concerning induction into the pastoral office, but it offers extensive commentary on the qualifications of a bishop. He should be no less than fifty years old, and a presbyter should be at least thirty years of age, because that was Jesus' age when he began his ministry. Exceptions can be made. A bishop's wife should be a Christian and chaste, and his children must be God-fearing. A bishop is to be "appointed" in "every congregation," and if he is illiterate he should at least be well versed in the Word. The author provides extensive material on the virtues requisite for ordination, reinforcing the suggestion that ministerial authority rested primarily on personal quality rather than formal rites, though the latter were necessary for one to be recognized by the community as legitimately holding office.[25] Conversely, when one who had been ordained to the ministry was guilty of moral lapse, he was summarily dismissed from office. His ordination, perhaps gifted by the Spirit, did not rescue him.

The literature of this period regularly uses two Greek words for the formalities of induction into office. The Greek *cheirotenein* is used for appointment to office, whether by Roman emperors or the church. It is used in the Septuagint for appointment to the priesthood, and in early Christian literature it is equivalent to ordination. Alongside it we find *cheirothesia* with its parallel *epithesis cheirōn*, which includes the laying on of hands. The former is always used of bishops, presbyters, and deacons, whereas the laying on of hands may include minor offices and the chrism of baptism. Appointment to office does not necessarily include the imposition of hands, and the laying on of hands may be used in rites other than ordination. By the end of the third century clerical ordination usually included the hands as the most significant aspect of the rite, but it is not always mentioned.[26]

We first find the Latin equivalent of "ordination" in Tertullian's apology against the Gnostics ("their ordinations are hasty").[27] *Ordo* has a definite sense in Roman institutions referring to social classes, the highest ordo being the senate. Those not found in any ordo whatever are the plebs. In Tertullian, ordo and plebs are used to distinguish between clergy and laity. After Constantine, bishops inherited the ordo of the higher classes, the senate, and decurions. Gregory the Great addressed letters to the ordo and people of various cities. Within the ordo of clergy there came to be several gradations, those listed after major orders (bishops, presbyter, and deacon) being referred to as minor orders. These are first listed in a letter by Cornelius of Rome to Fabius of Antioch in the year 252, and include doorkeepers, readers, exorcists, and acolytes. Cornelius later added the subdeacon to the list, which became a major order only in the thirteenth century. By introducing this Roman understanding of social and political stratification of society into ecclesiastical life, Tertullian gave direction to the church's understanding of relationship between clergy and people, and to the selection of clergy. Following the Roman secular model of advancement in rank from the lesser to the greater, clergy advanced from the humbler orders to the highest offices of presbyter (priest) and bishop. Vestiges of this system remain in some churches today, and for most Christians the ancient Roman influence remains in terms such as ordination and holy orders. The principal effect of ordination in the third century appears to have been the induction of a candidate into a given order, but it is still too early to speak of a sacramental character of order, which is first fully articulated by Augustine in the fifth century.

By the year 250 we find a monepiscopal bishop in every church, assisted by his presbyters and deacons. He is the administrative and spiritual supervisor of his own congregation. His office derived from the council of presbyters, evolving by force of circumstances to satisfy a need for organization, a sign of unity, and a defense against heresy.[28] While every bishop was a presbyter, not all presbyters were bishops. Irenaeus often speaks of the bishop as presbyter (*Against Heresies*, 3:2:2, 4:26:2) but never vice versa. Presbyters were not thought of as derived from the episcopacy but as part of the same collegium to which the bishop himself belonged. It is highly unlikely that a bishop by himself would have selected the presbyters.[29] A modern authority writes that "the process by which the bishop came to be distinguished from his fellow presbyters and at last to occupy a position of authority over them and the church can no longer be traced."[30] The bishop's right to ordain, as in Hippolytus, was a result of the emergence of the monarchical episcopate, and not a means by which it developed.

Jerome insisted that the episcopacy developed from the presbytery.[31] The role of bishop as one limited to a single congregation is reflected in their large numbers. An early council found 42 bishops in proconsular Asia, an area of about one thousand square miles, and there were 470 episcopal towns in third-century North Africa.

The correspondence of Cyprian reveals developments in the pastoral office in Carthage at mid-third century. In a letter addressed "to the presbyters, deacons, and all the people," he acknowledges the practice of consulting them in all ordinations, including those of minor orders.[32] The occasion for this letter was to justify his action in ordaining a reader without the customary consultation. In the more important election of a bishop he refers to the Old Testament precedent where the vestments of Aaron were placed upon Eleazer before the entire congregation (Num. 20:25, 26). So also the bishop must be selected in the presence of the people so they may be certain the choice has fallen upon one of good character.[33] This does not imply that a formal vote was taken in every case, but it prevented someone from being advanced to office who did not enjoy widespread approval among the people. During a vacancy the neighboring bishops were to meet, and a new bishop was to be "selected" in the presence of the people (*plebe praesente*).

Cyprian became involved with a contested episcopal election in Rome, where he supported the claims of Cornelius, "who was made bishop by the judgment of God and his Christ, by the attestation of almost all the clergy, by the approbation of the people then present, and by the body of older priests and of good men."[34] When the congregations at Legio and Asturica complained about their priest being unfit, Cyprian in effect told them it was their own fault, for they had elected him. Furthermore, the people who elected the bishop or priest share the "contagion of sin," because they had given their consent. "The congregation has the power both to elect worthy priests and to refuse unworthy ones."[35] He reminds them that the priest is chosen in the presence of the people, under the eyes of all, and is approved as worthy and suitable by public judgment and testimony. Then repeating the reference to Num. 20:25, he says that "God commands a priest to be appointed in the presence of the whole assembly." He adds the interesting note, "it was pondered by the vote [election] and judgment of all." In this same letter, Cyprian outlines the process for the ordination of a bishop:

> To carry out ordinations properly, whichever bishops of the same province are nearest, gather with that congregation for which a bishop is to be ordained, and the bishop is chosen in the presence of the people, because they know the lives of the individual candidates quite thoroughly, and have examined each one in the manner of his living. . . . This was done by a vote of the entire brotherhood and by the judgment of the bishops who had convened in your presence.[36]

Cyprian develops new ideas not found before in his identification of the apostles as the first bishops, in which they were succeeded by other bishops having the same authority as the apostles.[37] In his controversy with the church of Rome he more clearly established the authority of the episcopal college as the heir to the apostolic college. In earlier times the connection between apostolic authority and clerical office was present but fluid; under Cyprian the equation is made more firm. Bernard Cooke finds this shift significant in that office via ordination now has the potential for taking precedence over interior qualities and aptitudes of the candidate.[38]

But for the present it remained essential for sacerdotal effectiveness that the presbyter possess sanctity as well as proper order, for Cyprian is convinced that through sinfulness or schism one could lose the Spirit and thereby one's office.[39] Whatever efficacy was gained through ordination could be annulled. His dispute with the Roman church over the rebaptism of those initially baptized by schismatics is instructive for his views on ordination. In his sometimes violent correspondence with Stephen of Rome, he insisted that the only valid baptism was that administered within the catholic church even though the schismatic ordainer had himself been validly ordained. The efficacy of ordination (or consecration in the case of bishops) could be annulled by schism, and certainly by heresy.

This issue will return with Augustine's dispute with the Donatists over a century later, also in the context of baptism, in which the bishop of Hippo will take the opposite point of view. He will recognize the sacred rites performed by one in schism, provided he had initially received valid orders within the catholic church. It has been debated whether Cyprian harbored incipient Donatist views, as he associated the efficacy of sacred rites with the moral and doctrinal probity of the administrator. His position is complicated by statements he made in his dispute with the confessors of Carthage who claimed to possess the right to forgive sins by virtue of their confession. "Let no one deceive himself: only the Lord [and not human beings] can grant mercy."[40] Clergy may only pronounce what God has given, but on their own authority they do not forgive. Origen called it "ridiculous" that any bishop bound in the chains of sin should claim the power to bind and loose only because he was called a bishop.[41] And yet Cyprian is certain that something is conveyed in ordination rites when performed within the orthodox community. "How can a man give that which he does not possess?" A heretic does not have the Holy Spirit; how then can he give the Spirit to another?[42] The invocation of the sacred name cannot be efficacious without the (orthodox) faith that accompanies it.[43]

It was during the third century that the term "priest" came to be applied to presbyters and bishops. The New Testament does not give this title to any leaders in the church but to all the faithful (1 Pet. 2:9). The idea of priesthood is inseparable from the Eucharist understood as a sacrifice. This understanding was associated with a growing tendency to view the Old Testament as the model for the church, a trend that accelerated in the years prior to the Council of Nicea. Already in the *Didache* the sacrament is called a sacrifice, and Clement of Rome speaks of the president "offering the gifts." The text most often associated with the Eucharist was Mal. 1:11, "incense is offered to my name and a pure offering." The first mention of the table as an altar is probably in the apocryphal Acts of John, and the first reference to a cleric as a priest comes from Polycrates of Ephesus (c. 190), who gives the title to John, the Lord's beloved. Tertullian, who was much influenced by Old Testament thought, was the first Latin writer to call clergy priests (*sacerdos*, c. 200). The title was a direct outgrowth of liturgical developments. If the Eucharist was the New Testament counterpart of Old Testament sacrifices, it logically followed that the minister of the sacrament was a priest. The title was used occasionally but sparingly before Nicea, but in the fourth century it came increasingly to be applied to bishops.

Hans von Campenhausen writes that the functions of a priest were completely apart from any sacerdotal character, which at this time did not yet exist, but the priests derived their dignity from the community. "[Tertullian] concludes that the authority which a bishop can exert for his part is not by any means his own authority, but simply *auctoritas ecclesiae*, and the service he performs is not of his order but is the service of the church."[44] For Tertullian this is clear in his insistence that any layman may function as a priest if no church official is available. Despite these egalitarian and admittedly Montanist views, the assumption of the priestly title by the clergy played a significant role in the later development of the pastoral office, its functions and status, and the meaning of ordination.

By the year 300 the monarchical episcopate as we find it under Cyprian in North Africa fifty years earlier has become the norm. Each congregation has its bishop with assisting presbyters and deacons, together with various minor orders. Their relationship was collegial. The presbyters had a voice in the election of their bishop, they were consulted by him in important decisions, they sat with him in deciding judicial cases as well as the restoration of the lapsed, which also required the presence of the people. Presbyters were consulted by the bishop before admitting anyone to orders. But the presbyterial duties were increasingly understood to be by delegation of the bishop, in his name and with his authority.

The next stage in the development of the pastoral office is the emergence of a bishop as supervisor over several churches. This began in the cities, especially in Rome. Fabian, bishop of Rome (236–50), is credited with the assignment to the regions of the city of seven deacons and subdeacons. Under Dionysius (260–69) the city was organized into parishes (called *tituli*) each under its own presbyter. By the end of the century there were no less than forty parishes in Rome.[45] We have the enumeration of Roman clergy under Cornelius (251–53), which in his time included 46 presbyters, 7 deacons, 7 subdeacons, 42 acolytes, 52 exorcists, readers, and doorkeepers, and more than 1,500 widows and distressed persons.[46] The unity of the Roman church was symbolized by sending a portion of the consecrated bread of the bishop's church to be mingled with the wine in each of the presbyterial churches at each Eucharist (the *fermentum*). It is not known when the Eucharist came to be celebrated in its entirety by the presbyters apart from the bishop, but it appears there was considerable presbyterial autonomy in this regard. The right to baptize was still reserved to the bishop in those churches where episcopal governance was developing over parishes.

In Alexandria the presbyters retained their original position as a college longer than at Rome, but by the end of the third century the church there also had but one bishop who delegated his authority to the presbyters serving in parishes. By the time of Dionysius (247–64) a system similar to that of Rome was emerging, but the "charismatic" ministry of teacher was still very much alive in the person of Origen and the catechetical school. He had left Alexandria earlier, but his influence was still alive. He proposed the idea that the spiritually enlightened Christian or gnostic was the true priest and counterpart of Aaron. Origen was called upon to settle theological disputes and to lecture bishops while he was still a layman. He may have been "the last of the Christian charismatic and independent teachers."[47] On the selection of priests/presbyters, Origen informs us that "the presence of the people is necessary, so that all might know and be sure, because that man is chosen for the priesthood who is more outstanding among the whole people, more learned, holier, more eminent in every virture."[48] He says it should be an open decision lest anyone have second thoughts, and he bases this on the fact that "Moses called together the whole assembly." In Alexandria we also find one of the more bizarre cases of laying on of hands where a bishop came to be consecrated by the hand of his deceased predecessor who was suitably robed and propped up in his episcopal throne as a final gesture of legitimation and benediction.[49]

By the time of the end of the persecution and the beginning of the imperial church, which came with the conversion of Constantine (312), we find this situation with respect to the pastoral office. The selection of presbyters and bishops always included the laity, either by direct vote or acclamation. Deacons were selected by the bishop as having a special relationship to him as his direct assistants. The consecration of a bishop was not considered complete until he had received the approval of at least one fellow bishop, and preferably three, through the laying on of hands. In the case of priests, ordination was likewise through a bishop's hands. Of the two actions, selection and ordination, the latter was essential, and it was understood that the candidate received a charism, whether a gift of the Spirit or the Spirit. Criteria for the selection of clergy included outstanding sanctity of life, and the authority of the cleric was as much dependent on his moral example as on his ordination. The Spirit-filled community was the source of the cleric's authority rather than the rite of induction. "In all the first three centuries of the church not a single bishop appealed to his consecration to claim for the clergy a privileged position as a priest over against the laity."[50] Through moral lapse, heresy, or incompetence one could be deposed from office and lose whatever had been given in ordination. The laying on of hands was a visual sign of continuity with the apostolic tradition. It served to accent a succession in office rather than one of consecration, and it was done with reference to a definite community of Christians, who participated in the selection.

A concept of apostolic succession was also in place, whether that of Clement's idea of order or Irenaeus's of apostolic teaching, but presbyters and especially bishops were understood to be in such a succession through the rites of ordination or consecration. T. M. Lindsay is highly critical of this development and refers to it as "a legal fiction required by the legal mind" to connect clerical authority with ancient Christianity.[51] However, there was nothing sinister about the concept in the third century, as it was associated with apostolic teaching and bestowed on those whom the people had elected. Furthermore, the concept was born in the struggle against heresy and disorder to offer some assurances that the church was in continuity with its origins, and it was not intended to divide the clergy from the people or to make of the clergy an elite order.

In earlier times presbyterial authority was not derived from episcopal delegation, as the offices were identical, but by the year 300 such delegation is progressing in the metropolitan centers. Bishops in smaller communities were still the pastors of local congregations, often numbering less than two hundred members. Cyprian, for all his considerable visibility and influence, had no church building but still met his congregation in a private home. The Christian community was a loose federation of churches with only a hint of the future patriarchal organization. Councils of bishops (which included laity when selection of clergy was on the agenda) played a consultive role but had little direct juridical authority over the churches, as witness the councils of North Africa under Cyprian. Councils were increasingly called to deal with the problems raised by heresy or schism, but their authority at best was local and not general. But the decisions of local councils served as a precedent and guide for other localities. For instance, a synod in Antioch (268) deposed Paul of Samosata, and Cyprian convened five synods to deal with the reconciliation of the lapsed. Councils facilitated the cohesion of the larger community and fostered a sense of collegiality and unity among the Christian churches.

The Imperial Church

The triumph of Christianity after the conversion of Constantine found the role of the church and clergy significantly altered from the third century, although in many ways the changes were simply a further development of what was already taking place. The fourth century offers a wealth of material for reflection on the clerical office. But for our purposes only a few examples will be cited to illustrate such changes.

Dramatic changes for the clergy came with the Peace of the Church. They were immune from municipal levies and administration, suggesting that Constantine believed that clergy were generally recruited from the lower classes.[52] These financial exemptions led many city councillors (*curiales*) to apply for clergy status, which was resisted by the emperor. Further privileges were granted to the clergy by placing the public post at their disposal to attend the Council of Arles in the year 314.[53] In the year 318, bishops' jurisdiction was given the same validity as that of magistrates, and the jurisdiction of church courts was extended. Plaintiffs could substitute an episcopal tribunal for a secular, and slaves could be manumitted before the clergy instead of a civil magistrate. All this legislation recognized the clerical order as a civil institution as well as religious, with a corresponding enhancement in status. This naturally affected the type and number of candidates who presented themselves for ordination and the meaning of the rite.

Clerical legislation from the Council of Arles (314) convened by the emperor reveals much about their status and functions. Clergy are to remain fixed in the same places where they are presently serving (can. 2); state officials who are Christians are subject to their bishop in matters of church discipline (can. 7); clergy who lend money at interest are to be excommunicated (can. 13); the ordinations of bishops guilty of surrendering the holy books remain valid (can. 14); deacons may no longer celebrate the Eucharist (can. 16); deacons may not baptize or preach without the presbyter's knowledge (can. 18); bishops may not be ordained by fewer than three other bishops (can. 20); presbyters and deacons cannot be transferred to churches other than where they were ordained (can. 21).[54] Canon 14 is of special interest in that traditor bishops, themselves guilty of a form of apostacy, nevertheless validly conveyed holy orders in their ordinations.

In the same year as Arles, the Council of Ancyra was held. It also legislated for the clergy. If a man who had been consecrated bishop was not so received by his church, he shall revert to the order of presbyter (can. 18). This reveals a practice of consecrating without a congregation's assent, and in the absence of such assent, the consecration (for all practical purposes) is not valid.[55]

The Council of Neocaesarea (c. 315, but before 325) declared that married presbyters should be removed from office (can. 1). Of greater significance, it declared that "ordination blots out other kinds of sins" (i.e., preordination sin; can. 9). Ordination is coming to have a sacramental—that is, baptismal—character.[56]

This brings us to the first ecumenical Council of Nicea (325), convened by the emperor who also paid all its expenses including the travel of the delegates. As such it had greater authority than the previous regional councils, and its canons were entered into imperial as well as ecclesiastical law. Self-made eunuchs were not to be ordained, but those upon whom this had been inflicted against their will could proceed to ordination (can. 1). Novices in the faith were not to be ordained (can. 2), which is evidence that the office was being sought by opportunists and status seekers. Bishops should be consecrated by all the bishops of a province, or at least by three, and the act must be ratified by the metropolitan (can. 4). Here first we find the need of approval by a metropolitan. The occasion seems to be the Meletian schism in Alexandria where Meletius had been consecrating bishops on his own authority. K. J. Hefele comments that Nicea canon 4 "takes away from the people the right previously possessed of voting in the choice of bishops and makes the election depend entirely on the decision of the bishops of the province."[57] Canon 9 states that presbyters are not to be ordained without first having passed an examination, but if ordination has been given without such examination, or if later they are found to be guilty of preordination sin, the ordination is invalid. Apparently the sacramental nature of the rite had not yet reached Nicea. Those who had lapsed may not be ordained (can. 10). "Neither bishop, presbyter, or deacon shall pass from city to city" (can. 15), which refers to the self-aggrandizement of ambitious prelates. Presbyters may not be received who have deserted their own bishop (can. 16). Furthermore, a bishop may not ordain someone who is from another jurisdiction (i.e., reminiscent of Origen). Canon 18 sets the boundaries for the rights of the various clergy.

What shall we make of this decade of conciliar activity? We can say that a hierarchy is firmly established in every church, although the large majority function only locally. Exceptions are Rome, Alexandria, and probably other cities having more than one congregation. Selection of presbyters/bishops remains with the people and other clergy, although episcopal selection of presbyters in not unknown and Nicea opened the way to selection of bishops by other bishops. Candidates for ordination must be males of proven virtue not less than thirty years old, subject to an examination (assumed to include teaching as well as life). Episcopal ordination is by a minimum of three bishops, preferably more, and by the laying on of hands of one of them. Despite Neocaesarea canon 9, no more is said about the remission of sin. Unworthy clergy are still subject to dismissal, though Arles conceded the validity of orders conferred by an apostate bishop. This raises a question, why the rites of an apostate bishop are valid, but an apostate presbyter must be deposed. And for bishops a third step has been added following selection and ordination, that of ratification by the metropolitan.[58]

It was at the Council of Antioch in Encaeniis (341) that the fourth-century church further defined the episcopacy. Although this council is usually classified as semi-Arian, its canons were declared authoritative by Chalcedon. Bishops deposed by a synod, or presbyters and deacons deposed by a bishop, cannot function elsewhere or be restored by another synod (can. 4). (This was against Athanasius whom Rome had restored after he was deposed in Alexandria.) Troublesome priests/deacons may be deposed by a bishop, and if they persist, the civil power may be called in (can. 5). One wonders what "troublesome" may include as criteria for defrocking. An excommunicated cleric may be restored only by his own bishop or by a synod (can. 6). This implies that a synod can reverse a bishop's decision, something Cyprian had stoutly denied. Bishops in every province must acknowledge the superiority of the metropolitan who has precedence in rank (can. 9). Does this canon imply that the novelty of metropolitans was being resisted? No clergy may appeal to the emperor without the metropolitan's approval (can. 11), but deposed clergy may appeal to a synod of bishops (can. 12). No bishop may ordain in another's jurisdiction (can. 13). Canons 14–16 speak of the authority of a synod of bishops over a bishop. Canon 17 declares a bishop excommunicated who refuses to accept his ministry. This is curious, for it implies enforced ordinations, to be considered later. Canons 18–23 state that bishops are elected and ordained by the provincial bishops and the metropolitan. If he is rejected by his people, he should not be forced upon them. These canons suggest that the relationship between bishop and people has been seriously undermined. In the year 380 the Council of Laodicea expressly forbade election by the people.[59] "The election of those who are appointed to the priesthood is not to be committed to the multitude" (can. 13). The various commentators on this canon claim it was ignored, and lay participation to both priesthood and episcopate continued. Mob elections such as that of Ambrose is what was forbidden.[60]

Leaving aside conciliar decrees on this issue, we turn to a few statements by fourth-century theologians. John of Antioch (Chrysostom) was clear about election to office. "The vote of the churches also regulates in no accidental way those who come to spiritual offices. For this reason he who is going to ordain someone calls at that time for the prayers of the faithful, and they themselves vote their approval."[61] In this homily Chrysostom underscores the similarities between priest and people, "for it is not the priest alone who gives thanks [consecrates] but the whole people. When the Seven were selected all the people were consulted." But this homily from Chrysostom is also a lament at the loss of the ideal pattern. "The present state of things is grievous. . . . Whatever seems profitable should be ratified by all."[62] Here is evidence that lay persons are losing their role to "tyrants" in making decisions. He minimizes the distinction between bishop and priest, and writes that the only distinction between them is the bishop's power to ordain. "Only in this do they excel the presbyters."[63]

As to bishops, they are (in his time) selected by the priests in synod (despite Antioch, 341). His account of such an election is sarcastic and humorous. He calls it a public spectacle where most appointments to ecclesiastical office are made. Priests are assailed with as many accusations as there are people present. The presbyters agree neither among themselves nor with their bishop. Each man stands alone. No one concentrates on spiritual worth. Other considerations include the man's wealth, family, or connections. Piety alone is not sufficient, says Chrysostom, for a bishop should also be intelligent, but at episcopal elections intelligence is a hindrance. Neither is age a guarantor of wisdom, or youth of frivolity. He makes the charge that some even campaign for a reprobate priest in the hope that by elevation to the episcopate he may change his ways. All this makes for instability in the church. "Christians damage Christ's cause more than his enemies and foes."[64]

Despite Chrysostom's egalitarian views of clergy vis-à-vis laity, it is certain that priests possess something the laity do not have, the power of consecrating the Eucharistic elements. True, he calls the congregation cocelebrants, but it is the priest who, like Elijah, calls down the Holy Spirit. "What priests do on earth, God ratifies above . . . it is patently mad to despise this great office without which we cannot attain to salvation or God's good promises."[65]

As to the powers of unworthy priests, Chrysostom appears to anticipate or echo Augustine. "Even if their morals are completely discredited—if you take heed to yourself—you will suffer no harm at all in the matters entrusted to them by God." Even if the priests are thoroughly evil, God will effect all that God wills, and will send down the Holy Spirit. What has been entrusted to the priest is God's alone to give; and however far human wisdom reaches, it is inferior to that of grace.[66] As much as this appears to assume a form of *"character indelibilis,"* von Campenhausen insists (below) that this is different from that which developed in the West, as efficacy in the East always assumes a worshiping community and is not the personal possession of the priest.

Basil of Caesarea has no trace of sacerdotal powers imparted in a sacramental way, although he almost forcibly ordained Gregory of Nazianzus. But Gregory of Nyssa is clear:

> The same power of the Word that hallows the simple water of baptism also makes the priest holy (*semnos*) and worthy of honor, when he is set apart by the blessing from the multitude. Just now he was but one of many, one of the people; suddenly he appears as leader, as superior, as teacher of piety, and as director (*mystagogos*) of the hidden mysteries.

By an invisible power and gift (he is) changed in his invisible soul to something better.[67]

The one ordained possessed an actual grace of perfection, which if violated in actual practice was lost. Ordination was also an act of the community, and the priest's ministrations were always within the community and were validated by that association. There was no possibility of a "private" Mass. Given these presuppositions, the question of how the community, if its priest was secretly a sinner, can be certain of the validity of the sacrament was not addressed. One must simply be careful never to ordain an unworthy person. In the East a bishop was selected by all the people (*ab omni populo*) and ordained with the consent of all (*consentientibus omnibus*).[68] His ministry was bound up with the community.

Another side of the question of priestly power is to ask what the minister does. Does he cause grace and forgiveness of sins, or does he proclaim that God has given such gifts? In the West after the thirteenth century the church consistently taught that the sacramental character of the priest was an intrinsic and permanent causative power. Chrysostom insisted that it was the "right hand of Christ, shown by the very words of the one baptizing. He does not say, 'I baptize so-and-so,' but 'so-and-so is baptized,' showing that he is only the minister of grace and merely offers his hand because he has been ordained to this end by the Spirit."[69] The same formula was used in absolution, where the minister announced God's forgiveness rather than to say "I forgive you."

Meanwhile in the West we find Jerome opposed to the growing pretensions of the bishops in his letter to the presbyter, Evangelus. "The Apostle clearly teaches that presbyters are the same as bishops." Who is the bishop to arrogantly exalt himself above "those at whose prayers the body and blood of Christ are confected?" The selection of a bishop in early times, he says, came about as a remedy for schism, "the presbyters always chose one of their number, placed him in the higher rank and named him bishop."[70] But Jerome is fighting a losing cause. By the end of the fourth century the provincially organized episcopate was fully in place, speaking in their corporate capacity as organs of the Holy Spirit. Under imperial patronage the episcopate had received judicial as well as municipal responsibilities and status. Bishops had also become the imperial *defensores civitatis*, ombudsmen to protect the population against official injustice. They were at the pinnacle of the Roman ordo, the *cursus honorum*, serving both as civil and religious officials, and receiving stipends from the government. And yet despite the incursions of the "state" into ecclesiastical affairs, Ambrose writes to the church at Vercelli, "let the man [bishop] be chosen by all." In this letter he urges that the bishop and priest be celibate and preferably a monk.[71]

We have seen the tendency to understand ordination as the rite that conferred the Spirit and divine grace, empowering the recipient validly to perform the sacraments, principally the Eucharist. In this development the practice of enforced ordinations is instructive in that ordination was thought to operate apart from the intention and disposition of the candidate. This develops only late in the fourth century and accelerates into medieval times. Basil was tricked into an unwilling ordination by Chrysostom, who defended his action on the grounds that the end justified the means. "I glorified God that my stratagems had worked out well."[72] One Dracontius swore he would run away if ordained, but Athanasius persuaded him to return and perform his duties, even though onerous to him. Epiphanius ordained Jerome's brother against his will after being roughed up and gagged.[73] Gregory Nazianzen grieved over his ordination and referred to it as an act of tyranny.[74] Sozomon reports that one Nilammon died rather than accept a bishopric; a monk, Ammon, after vainly cutting off his ear to forestall ordination, threatened to cut out his tongue as well to foil his nominators. One Ephraim acted like a madman so his abductors would turn him loose.[75] What these episodes convey to us is the increasing understanding of ordination as an *ex opere operato* event. There was no election or examination or community involved. The true marvel is that the unwilling candidates themselves acknowledged that with ordination they were changed persons, albeit against their will.

For Augustine the idea of ordination is closely allied with his doctrine of baptism. Earlier baptisms were considered valid only when administered within the catholic church. Those administered by heretics were to be "repeated." Cyprian is representative of this view, but the ideas of Cornelius and others gained wider currency. Baptism, if in the name of the Trinity, imparted a specific gift, a concept intensified with infant baptism. As with ordination, infant baptism was efficacious totally apart from the will or inclination of its object.

A corresponding line was taken by Augustine in the ordination of priests, agreeing in this with Tychonius, and always appealing to the analogy of baptism. Ordination conferred a definite and irremovable imprint, a "character" which empowered its recipient to perform valid priestly functions (not necessarily efficacious for salvation). This definition was a result of the African church's struggle against the Donatists. The heart of the issue was pastoral, whether recipients of the sacraments could be certain of receiving grace. Augustine's response was twofold. First, one could find assurance in the fact that the priest possessed *dominis character indelibilis* independent of his personal state or disposition, and this by virtue of ordination.[76] The second reassurance was that all sacraments are gifts of God and are independent of the giver who is the mediator.[77] Augustine did not originate indelible character (some believe this is already what Irenaeus had in mind in the year 200 with his use of *charisma veritatis*), but he gave it a theological rationale and a clear articulation.

As compared with earlier comments about Eastern concepts of ordination always being associated with the community, the Western concept of priestly powers had nothing to do with hierarchical pretensions or the subjugation of the laity, as later polemicists charged. The priestly character was introduced not with a view toward making the priest independent of the community but independent of his own weaknesses, which were not allowed to impair his services. As in the East, the question was approached from the side of the community— that is, the question of certainty of salvation. Ideas of privilege and distinction via ordination appeared later and were foreign to Augustine's conception.[78]

In the early fifth century there was no universal pattern for the selection of bishops and priests. As late as the sixth century Justinian's code insists that "a vote by the persons inhabiting the said city should be taken concerning three persons . . . so that from these the most suitable should be selected for the episcopate."[79] Bernard Cooke believed that "through the fifth century the voice of the local community was truly determinative, though not sufficiently so, in the selection of their bishop."[80] On the powers of the priesthood conveying either the judgment or the mercy of God, this statement is provocative: "There never seems to be as much assurance about excommunication effecting alienation from God as there was about absolution effecting reconciliation."[81]

Pastoral Authority

At the time of Augustine's death (430) the lines of authority within the pastoral office were taking a fixed form, in both the East and West. The hierarchy of bishop, priest, and deacon was well established, with the minor orders still in a state of development. Bishops were increasingly becoming the supervisors of churches within a given geographical territory, which followed the Roman political subdivision, the diocese. The jurisdiction of the bishops of the principal cities extended over larger territories, the province, and they assumed the title of metropolitan. The principal provinces were those of Rome, Alexandria, Antioch, Ephesus, Jerusalem, and (after 381) Constantinople, whose bishops became patriarchs. In this development the church was the heir of the old Roman state religion as it inherited the organization of the Roman imperial cult. One author says that "the pagan organization was everywhere the forerunner of the Christian . . . the conquering church took its hierarchic weapons from the arsenal of the enemy."[82]

After Christianity became the official religion of the empire c. 390 under Theodosius, the Christian hierarchy inherited the social positions and authority that formerly had belonged to the pagan priests and bishops, including titles and even dress. The chasuble, dalmatic, stole, and maniple were borrowed directly from the Roman magistracy, and in every municipality where there had been a *flamen* to superintend the worship of the emperor, there was now a bishop who inherited his privileges. These included an imperial salary, a seat on the city council, the right of direct access to the emperor, and rank second only to the provincial governor. Bishops were now becoming persons of great influence and office, accompanied by a retinue of servants bearing their insignia of office in processions, which instead of the Roman eagle was now the cross. The same development occurred among the priests, who were likewise salaried and became the custodians of the imperial religion in the churches, vested with authority by the state as civil officials. A further development after Constantine was that church councils were convened and supported by the government, and their edicts became part of civil law. This meant that anyone who disagreed with a conciliar decision was not only guilty of heresy or schism, but of treason as well. At the same time, there was a decline in the election of bishops, not because the church wished it so, but because of the intervention of the government. Inasmuch as bishops and priests hàd become civil officials, the government came to play a role in their selection. We need only recall the appointment of Nectarius as bishop of Constantinople in the year 381, in which the emperor made the selection, or of the massive involvement of the Roman government in the Arian controversies of the fourth century, including the five exiles of Athanasius in addition to his five reinstatements to office, all by government decree.

However, it would be a mistake to view paganism's legacy to the church as intrinsic to pastoral authority. Of far greater significance to the development of authority was the use of Old Testament models for the church's ministry, a process already at work in Clement of Rome before the end of the first century. As the distance in time increased between its Jewish cradle and the maturing church, so did the use of Old Testament imagery to describe the clergy. "You also, O bishops, are priests to your people, and the Levites who minister to the tabernacle of God. . . . You are to your people priests and prophets, and princes and leaders and kings, and mediators between God and his faithful. . . . The priests and the Levites now are the presbyters and deacons. The high priest is the bishop."[83] Such analogies can be multiplied many times from the literature of the later centuries, which vests the clergy with the status of the Jewish officials, high priests, priest, Levites, prophets, and kings. Jerome writing in the fifth century says that "apostolic traditions are drawn from the Old Testament. The fact that Aaron and his sons and the Levites were in the temple justifies the presence of bishops and presbyters and deacons in the church."[84]

The authority associated with being in continuity with the priesthood of the Old Testament derived principally from the Eucharist, understood as the new oblation offered by the New Israel. Just as in the former Israel the role of the priests was to sacrifice, so in the church the new priesthood of the clergy was to lead in worship, centered on the Holy Communion. The status and authority of the clergy (presbyters and bishops) were derived from this function, and this was true almost from the beginning, totally apart from any associations with Roman imperial ideas, which emerged only in the fourth century. In addition to the Eucharist, priestly authority derived from serving as the minister of baptism, but by the fourth century this was sometimes reserved to the bishop at the annual Easter Vigil.

Clerical authority was also associated with the right to absolve penitents from their sins (Matt. 16:19). This right was not fully articulated until the third century with the growth of public penance, but from then on it was associated with clerical authority and discretion. The role of the clergy can be seen in the ordination prayer of Hippolytus for bishops. "Grant to thy servant whom thou hast chosen to be bishop to serve as thy high priest . . . to offer the gifts of thy holy church . . . and to have authority to remit sins according to thy commandments . . . according to the authority thou gavest to thy apostles."[85] Hippolytus's rubric for ordaining presbyters states that the same things should be said "as we have prescribed above concerning the bishop." Over two centuries later, Chrysostom speaks of clerical authority when he points to the centrality of Baptism and the Eucharist for the life of every Christian. "Now it is certain that we cannot receive these good things save at the consecrated hands of the priest. It is the priests who bring us to spiritual birth through baptism." It is also the priests who "bring us to life again in his body . . . and remit faults committed after baptism."[86]

It appears, then, that the principal element of clerical authority was in the cultus—that is, in worship and the sacraments. But behind these lay the more compelling concept of apostolic succession. The reason the clergy had the exclusive power to perform the sacred rites was their continuity with apostolic authority, conveyed to them through ordination. In theory priestly authority was derived from the bishop, and it was delegated by him. By the fifth century, however, this view was not uniformly held, and priests often celebrated the Eucharist or absolved sins in their own right. In the West by the year 450 the one sacred rite still the exclusive preserve of the bishop was Confirmation, in addition to that of ordaining priests and deacons. Whether bishop or priest, apostolicity was still the foundation of authority. We have already seen that apostolicity took several forms. With Irenaeus the single basis for episcopal and presbyterial authority is the link with the apostles in faith. For Clement of Rome and Cyprian it was simply a matter of order. With Augustine it becomes associated with a special charism. By the fifth century Augustine's views tend to dominate, not only in the West but also through Gregory of Nyssa in the East. Yet there appears to be a difference. The church in the East continues to associate the authority of the priest to perform sacred rites only as a representative of the community and within the worshiping community (*auctoritas ecclesiae*). His rights can be forfeited through malfeasance of office. In the West the concept is growing that the priest's charism is a personal possession independent of the community he serves. But it is a paradox of this observation that communal participation in the selection of clergy prevailed much longer in the West than in the East. Both in East and West the community (i.e., universal church) was that which conferred authority through the hierarchy, but the Western medieval church tended to lose sight of this theory and placed the transmission of the apostolic succession solely within the hierarchy itself, emanating from the bishop of Rome who represented the people of God.

Associated with the development of pastoral authority in the early church are also the functions of administration, dispensing charity, adjudicating disputes, and serving as a model of the Christian life. In addition to these roles, the priest and bishop were preeminently teachers and preachers, as well as pastoral counselors. These pastoral functions, as well as the role of the pastor as leader in worship, will be explored in greater detail in forthcoming chapters.

2 Pastor and People

The Christian Congregation

The Roman empire, which witnessed the birth of Christianity, was an urban civilization. It was dominated by the city, or *polis*, a political entity that included an urban area and its environs. The earliest Christians, including Paul, depended upon the city for their livelihood. Even though many of the images and metaphors of the Gospels have to do with farming, planting, harvesting, and agriculture, the fact is that the church was planted in the cities. It was there that the largest numbers could be reached in the shortest time. The cities were where power lay, and where change could be effected. "The cities of the Mediterranean world were at the leading edge of the great political and social changes that occurred from Alexander to Constantine."[1] Christian congregations were established in such places as Corinth, Damascus, Edessa, Carthage, Thessalonica, Alexandria, Ephesus, and Antioch. The mission originated in Jerusalem and was carried along the Roman road system to the farthest reaches of the empire, but of greatest significance was the penetration of Rome itself. It was not until the time of Irenaeus (c. 180) that we hear of any attempt to carry the word to "wild and barbarous" people outside the city walls. Even with the triumph of the church in the fourth and fifth centuries, Christianity in the Roman empire remained an urban phenomenon, to the extent that the term for peasant, *paganus*, became synonymous with an unbeliever. By the end of the third century we find the emergence of *chōrepiscopoi*, bishops who were appointed for country areas but subordinate to the urban bishop. With the exception of the monks, who established their houses in the deserts and rural areas, and excepting the mission territories of Phrygia and northern Europe, the countryside remained the last conservative bastion of the Roman gods.

Christianity spread along the main commercial and military arteries of the empire. Jesus had commanded his disciples to preach the gospel everywhere, "beginning from Jerusalem" (Luke 24:47). The Book of Acts describes how the word spread like a series of concentric circles with the chief provincial city at its center, until the gospel reached Rome, with a hint that it reached Spain. The cities where Paul worked "were centers of Roman administration, Greek civilization, of Jewish influence, and of some commercial importance."[2] Given the two centuries of peace following Augustus, the excellent roads, and Greek as the universal language, the times were propitious for evangelism. It was a mobile society. Traveling, whether for business or pleasure, "was contemplated and performed under the Empire with an indifference, confidence, and above all, certainty, which were unknown in after centuries," until two hundred years ago.[3] All these factors facilitated the growth of Christianity, so that shortly after the turn of the first century, Pliny, the governor of Bythinia, complained to Emperor Trajan that Christianity was attracting converts from every class of society. Writing a century later, Tertullian said that "though we are but of yesterday, we have filled all that is yours, cities, islands, fortified towns, country towns, centers of meeting, even camps, tribes, classes of public attendants, the palace, the senate, the forum."[4] He is clearly exaggerating, especially when he continues, "nearly all the citizens you have in nearly all the cities are Christian."

Eusebius, in describing the growth of the church in the mid-third century, writes, "The faith was increasing and our doctrine was boldly proclaimed openly in the ears of all."[5] Although we may fairly suspect some overstatement in these assessments, it is nevertheless a fact that Christian congregations were growing in numbers and extent, which meant that the clergy were expending much time and energy in receiving converts, educating and baptizing them, and in pastoral oversight. And this was taking place long before Constantine's conversion

gave the faith status and prestige. It was said of Gregory the Wonderworker that when he arrived in Neocaesarea, the capital of Pontus,
he found only seventeen Christians, but when he died thirty years
later there were only seventeen pagans in the city.[6] By c. 245 North
Africa had at least ninety bishops, and we have already seen that at
the same time the Roman clergy numbered at least 155 of various
ranks.[7] Robert Grant suggests that these clergy served approximately
seven thousand Christians of a total Roman population of about seven
hundred thousand.[8] By the time of Diocletian (285–305) the advance
of Christianity was such as to cause alarm among the ruling elite and
may have been a cause of the Great Persecution. When Emperor
Maximin entered the capital, Nicomedia, in 311, he found that "nearly
all" the inhabitants were Christian.[9]

Yet we should not conclude from this that congregations were
large—it was simply there were so many of them. If Rome indeed
had seven thousand Christians, they were distributed among some
thirty-five churches, which means each congregation numbered about
two hundred members, small enough to maintain discipline and internal cohesion. The increasing number of bishops points to the growth
of churches, especially of "daughter" churches in the larger cities.
Although pastors were engaged in receiving converts, the house church
was still the norm, which meant that a congregation was only as large
as could be accommodated in a large home or in its courtyard. It is
true that there were some church buildings, as Diocletian had them
destroyed, but they were not on the grand scale of the post-Constan-
tinian era.

With Christian congregations growing in size and number, we may
ask what kind of people were attracted to the new faith, and what was
their social status? This question has been debated by scholars for
many years with varying degrees of consensus. A recent study by
Wayne Meeks brings together contemporary scholarship about the
Pauline churches. He concludes that in Paul's day the churches
represented a fair cross section of urban society. They were upwardly
mobile and had achieved status rather than inherited it; they possessed
drive, ability, and they sought opportunities for social advancement.
At the same time these congregations had a high degree of intimacy,
interraction, and internal cohesion, what today is known as small-
group sociology.[10]

Robert Grant refers to early churches as small clusters of more or less intense groups largely middle-class in origin.[11] It is certain that Christianity was not limited to the proletarian or lower classes, as the tensions in Corinth were between the rich and the poor. When Paul greets those of "Caesar's household" (Phil. 4:22), it is possible he had high-ranking officials in mind. Hippolytus's reminder to remove all jewelry prior to baptism, and Tertullian's diatribes against costly apparel and expensive rings and necklaces, indicate the attraction of Christianity to some people of wealth. According to Eusebius, at the time of Commodus (180–92), "large numbers even of those at Rome, highly distinguished for wealth and birth, were advancing towards their own salvation with all their households and kindred."[12] Tertullian tells us that Gentiles of "every status" were coming to Christianity, including those of the senatorial class.[13] Cyprian (250) was the first bishop to emerge from the Roman status of senator.

Yet we cannot simply dismiss Celsus's statement as prejudiced contempt when he describes converts to the faith. He writes that most Christians were artisans, slaves, women and children in major households, gullible and stupid people who are easily moved by propaganda.[14] That there were many more women in early Christian congregations than men is generally acknowledged by all students of this period, and this is confirmed by Celsus's statement. He does not, however, admit that many of them were also high born, but he finds Christianity contemptible simply because of the large number of women who were converts to the faith. We also know that the practice of almsgiving, which was so prominent in the activity of early Christians, indicates a large number of poor people, although the distribution of alms was not always limited to Christians. The evidence suggests that Christian churches included the extremes of society, with the predominant membership coming from between the extremes. What is striking in the catacombs of Rome is the large number of very simple graves, including a disproportionate number of infants and children testifying to the truth of Celsus's statement that the church had many young persons.

Frend concludes that "it is difficult to build up a convincing overall picture of the social level of the Christian congregation," but it is certain that after the year 250 an increasing number of the upper classes were being won for the faith.[15] However, it is also true that the more conservative aristocrats and senatorial class in general was opposed to the new faith, and it was they who were partly the instigators of the last great persecution under Diocletian. It was only with the conversion of Constantine that this group was eventually won over. This brings us to the conclusion that the social composition of pre-Constantinian churches was mixed, depending upon location and circumstances, but in general Christianity appeared to attract what Meeks referred to as the upwardly mobile middle—artisans, people engaged in business, merchants, and "professionals."

An anonymous second-century Christian apologist writes that Christians were really not much different from anyone else:

> Christians cannot be distinguished from the rest of the human race by country or language or customs. They do not live in cities of their own; they do not use a peculiar form of speech; they do not follow an eccentric manner of life. . . . They follow the customs of their country in clothing and food and other matters of daily living . . . but only as aliens. They marry like everyone else, and beget their children, but do not cast out their offspring. They share their board with each other but not their marriage bed. They obey the established laws, but in their own lives they go far beyond what the law requires. They love all men, and by all men are persecuted. They are poor and yet they make many rich; they are completely destitute, yet they enjoy abundance. [16]

In theory, if not always in practice, the church taught the value of every individual in God's sight, where there was neither bond nor free, male nor female, but all were one in Christ. With the possible exception of some Stoic philosophers, this idea was unique to the world of antiquity. But the fact that Christians still kept slaves indicates a gap between the ideal and the reality.

The age of the martyrs and the persecutions of the early church came to an end in the West with the Edict of Milan (313), which proclaimed toleration in which all were to have "free choice of following whatever form of worship they please." [17] In the East the same toleration came about ten years later with Constantine's victory over Licinius. In actual practice, however, the emperor favored the Christian cause without restricting the Roman religion. As the fourth century advanced, emperors increasingly identified with the faith, to the point where Theodosius forbade the practice of the Roman religions in the cities and announced civil disabilities for those who participated in the old cults (391). Given the absence of persecution and prompted by imperial favor, the church in the fourth century made dramatic gains in membership despite being torn internally by various controversies, notably those of Donatism and Arianism.

As with the ante-Nicene church, it is difficult to offer a statistical analysis of the growth of Christianity during this period with any degree of confidence. In the year 300 there were only five bishops in northern Italy, and by 400 there were about fifty. The same century found an increase of bishops in Gaul from twenty-two to seventy.[18] The first ecumenical Council at Nicea in 325 found approximately 250 bishops gathered (although tradition assigns to it 318); by the fourth ecumenical Council at Chalcedon (451) there were 630 bishops present. Augustine, writing about 400, declared that in Hippo there were houses where no pagans were to be found, but there was no house that was without Christians. But he also complains that among the Christians there is more chaff than wheat, including the clergy. "Do you perhaps believe that weeds do not come creeping right up to the apse?"[19] Fourth-century literature is full of indications that the church is growing dramatically, and that paganism is in decline, but far from dead. The size and number of church buildings increased to accommodate the numbers, variously described as multitudes, throngs, hosts, or crowds. This is especially true in the cities and of congregations addressed by such orators as Augustine, Ambrose, Athanasius, and Chrysostom. The increase in numbers presented challenges to pastoral care, not only in the cathedrals but over all of Christendom, as discipline was strained with the influx of those minimally committed to the faith, social classes competed for status, and heresies emerged that demanded refutation. The growth of Christianity was the occasion for conflicts within the congregations, both before and after the triumph of the church, which engaged the time and energies of pastors and people.

We know there was dissension among the Christians already within the Pauline congregations, primarily in Corinth. "It has been reported to me that there is quarreling among you, my brethren" (1 Cor. 1:11). This factionalism was caused by competing perceptions of leadership, some claiming to follow Paul, others Apollos, Cephas, or Christ. Another source of friction appears to have been caused by social status, with the wealthy despising the poor. Other disciplinary problems were immorality, drunkenness, and litigation in the civil courts. Paul's response is the well-known appeal to the metaphor of a body in which all the members must work in harmony for the well-being of all (1 Corinthians 12).

Not long after Paul's death, there was another schism in Corinth, this time also one involving leadership. The ruling presbyters had been deposed by a faction of younger men. We do not know the cause of the dissension, but Cyril Richardson suggests it was between charismatics and the regular ministry.[20] Clement of Rome sent a letter to Corinth admonishing them for their factiousness, in which he begins by offering an outline of the ideal church, characterized as being respectful to leaders, "rich in peace with an insatiable longing to do good," not jealous of position and bearing no grudges, obeying orders rather than issuing them.[21] Clement appeals to the model of order in the universe and to the metaphor of an army. Not everyone can be an officer or a general. It was in this context that he became the first to appeal to an apostolic succession of clergy from a direct chain of appointments from the apostles to validate their ministry. The malcontents had violated this order. We do not know whether this admonition on the part of the Roman church was successful in resolving the conflict.

The appearance of Gnosticism in the second century was a challenge to pastoral leadership, to the unity of the church, and to one's assessment of the role of philosophy in the development of doctrine. There was a difference of opinion between Greek-speaking Christians who believed, as did Justin, that philosophy was a preparation for the gospel, and others like Tatian, who represented a studied hostility toward everything in Greek culture. Tertullian, who was well versed himself in Stoicism, called philosophy the mother of all heresies and asked the question, "What has Jerusalem to do with Athens, the church with the academy?"[22] On the other hand we have Clement of Alexandria who championed Christian Gnosticism and the use of philosophy in expounding the faith. These were crucial issues in the second century, which caused friction within congregations and between churches. The tensions also appear to have been between Greek-educated Christians and those not educated, or between the upper and lower classes, as well as between the East and the West.

Second-century Rome was not immune from internal problems. Hermas writes that those who had shown themselves "always faithful and good . . . strive among themselves for precedence and honor, for the first seats in the assembly."[23] This applies especially to the leaders of the congregation, who do not listen to each other or who serve themselves rather than the people. "How do you expect to instruct the elect if you yourselves have no training?"; that is, be our example.[24] This seems to be a recurring problem throughout the history of the church.

Before the triumph of the church, a source of conflict within Christian congregations lay in one's reaction to persecution. Not all Christians were steadfast and faithful under torture and stress. More succumbed to apostasy to one degree or another than were witnesses to the faith. Following the time of trials, a major task of the pastor was to reconcile those who had lapsed with those who had suffered, such as the widow whose husband had been martyred being reconciled with the married woman whose husband had denied Christ. The practice of penance developed out of the reconciliation of the lapsed following a persecution. Another cause of internal tension within the Christian community as a result of the persecutions was the role of leadership assumed by the confessors—that is, those who had suffered—and who thereby undermined the office of bishop. Cyprian convened no less than five councils to deal with this problem of authority in the congregations of North Africa. The tensions between confessors and bishop were an extension of the earlier struggle between the charismatic and the institutional ministry, a conflict that continued into the fourth century between monks and officeholders.

Ministering to a congregation in time of persecution required a special gift of courage and fortitude, and more often than not, the bishop was the first to suffer or die, as under Emperor Decius (249–51). In this persecution bishop Fabian of Rome was tried before the emperor himself and executed. Decius is reported to have said he would rather face a usurper to the throne than another bishop of Rome, indicating the respect given to this office and its incumbent.[25] Babylus of Antioch was also killed, and Alexander of Jerusalem died in prison. Cyprian of Carthage went into hiding, as did Gregory the Wonderworker. Dionysius of Alexandria escaped with the help of local peasants, who were not Christian, but they despised Decius even more than they opposed the faith. The beatings suffered by Origen caused his death soon after the persecution was ended. It required unusual heroism to minister under these circumstances, and not all clergy were equal to the challenge. Many were among the lapsed who sought restitution to the church after it was all over.

A vignette of a family under stress during the persecution of North Africa in the year 180 indicates another dimension of pastoral guidance in a fractured situation. Perpetua, a young mother twenty-two years old with an infant at her breast, refused to deny Christ, and she was jailed with her slave, Felicitas, herself eight months pregnant. They were joined by three other Christian captives. Perpetua's account of what transpired was written by herself in prison, including the desperate pleas of her pagan father to do whatever was necessary to be released. "Daughter, pity my white hairs! Pity your father . . . with these hands I have brought you up to your prime of life. Look upon your son who cannot live after you are gone. Lay aside your pride. So spoke my father in his love for me."[26] Perpetua suffered martyrdom, together with her companions. Felicitas gave birth to a daughter before she died, who was brought up by "one of the sisters," and we would like to believe the same was true for Perpetua's son. The account does not say that these martyrs were strengthened in prison by their pastor, but it offers us an example of the types of family conflicts occasioned by the persecutions in which pastoral guidance was required. Equally painful are those situations where a priest could be called upon to encourage a woman to remain steadfast unto death against the pleas of her pagan (or Christian) husband and their tearful children. Whatever the outcome, congregations tended to divide over these issues, and it is a piece of romantic fiction to say that persecutions strengthened the church by winnowing out the chaff. In most cases the times of trial caused division, rancor, uncertainty, and strife.

But if persecution caused internal strife, freedom from external pressures resulted in even greater strife within Christian communities. Here is how Eusebius describes the situation in the last quarter of the third century:

> But when, as the result of greater freedom, a change to pride and sloth came over our affairs, we fell to envy and fierce railing against one another, warring upon ourselves, so to speak, as occasion offered, with weapons and spears formed of words; and rulers [clergy] attacked rulers and laity formed factions against laity, while unspeakable hypocrisy and pretense pursued their evil course to the furthest end.[27]

The pastoral task of reconciling warring factions was made more difficult by the factions among the clergy themselves. As far as we know, the roots of this turmoil lay in disputes over discipline, property rights, transfers of clergy, developing hierarchy, and the growing influx of converts. This is based on the canons of the Council of Nicea (325), which attempted to restore order to the church (see chap. 1). As indicated earlier, this period was also one of surging growth, which so alarmed the government that it resulted in the great persecution under Diocletian. Despite the wrangling among Christians in the last part of the third century, for which period we have the least evidence from the first three centuries, we know that Christianity attracted great numbers. It was a time of relief from persecution, but the pastoral task remained one of reconciling divisive forces in addition to that of receiving converts and attending to the nurture and edification of the congregation.

The recognition of Christianity by Constantine brought freedom to the church, but the Council of Nicea inaugurated a half-century of turmoil with the Arian controversy. Although Nicea established the creed with its anti-Arian statement that Jesus was "of one substance with the Father," large numbers of clergy and laity, especially in the East, remained unconvinced. The issues of this controversy can be reviewed in any history of dogma. It is sufficient for our purpose to recognize that the controversy divided congregations and caused some violence within the Christian community. It was a challenge to pastoral leadership, as we find dramatized in the life of Athanasius, who was exiled five times from his church for supporting the Nicene faith. The doctrinal controversy over the deity of Jesus was not merely an esoteric issue among theologians detached from the world, all of whom were pastors of congregations, but it also gripped the population, much to the annoyance of Gregory of Nyssa who writes about the excitement of the people in Constantinople. "If in this city you ask anyone for change, he will discuss with you whether the Son is begotten or unbegotten. If you ask about the quality of bread, you will receive the answer, that 'the Father is greater, the Son is less.' If you suggest that you require a bath, you will be told that 'there is nothing before the Son was created.' "[28] Theology was of intense interest to the laity in these contentious times, and there were few clergy who could avoid addressing the issue or establishing their position.

Another witness to the conflicts among early Christians is from the abortive administration of Julian the Apostate (361–63) who belatedly tried to return the empire to the Roman gods. He was a nephew of

Constantine, orphaned by palace intrigues, and made a ward of Bishop Eusebius of Nicomedia. He grew up among the Arian controversies following the Council of Nicea, became disenchanted with the machinations of the Christian bishops, and developed a fascination for the old Roman religion. When he became emperor at age thirty, he had developed a hatred for Christianity and was determined to overthrow it. He ascended the throne at the height of the Arian controversies, when many clergymen, including Athanasius, had been exiled for supporting the Nicene faith. Julian decreed that all exiled clergy should return to their churches. He shrewdly believed, on the basis of his experience, that when the exiles returned, there would be dissension in the churches between the incumbents and the exiles, which would weaken the church. The fourth-century Roman historian Ammianus Marcellinus describes Julian's motives. "On this he took a firm stand, to the end that, as this freedom increased their dissension, he might afterwards have no fear of a united populace, knowing as he did from experience that no wild beasts are such enemies to mankind as are most Christians in their deadly hatred of one another."[29] Such were the impressions of a well-placed inside observer of the fourth-century church.

Naturally one would expect a system of litigation to develop within contentious communities, and so we find the emergence of church courts. St. Paul warned the Corinthians not to take their cases to pagan courts but to develop their own judges and officers. By the third century we find ecclesiastical courts a fixture in Christian communities, with the bishops serving as the judge. After Constantine, civil cases could be heard in either imperial or ecclesiastical courts, and with the growth of more litigation we find the development of church (canon) law, by which Christians judged both their faith and life. Such law began with conciliar decrees, but during the Middle Ages it included a host of material from other sources. It was not until the twelfth century that this mass of contradictory and often confusing law was codified and given some coherence by Gratian.

This is the context of ministry in the early church. We cannot simply speak of preaching, counseling, or the care of souls without being aware of the kaleidoscopic political, social, and cultural ferment in which it was done. In the first three centuries it was in an environment of a church under persecution, followed by the imperial church with all its promise and failings. But it would be a serious distortion of reality if we were to dwell on internal conflicts alone within the Christian congregations. The image of a community torn by factions is not one to attract large numbers of converts beginning already before the mid-second century. On the positive side was the fact that the Christian message answered a need that the Roman religions did not satisfy; Christian hospitality and almsgiving served to alleviate the distress of the poor. The ideal of individual worth despite social status attracted those who shared this vision. Indeed, it was the very promise and strengths of Christianity that occasioned tension. Behind the Arian controversies, with whatever personal, economic, and imperial motivations may have been present, lay a serious commitment to the faith by clergy and laity. Almsgiving had the potential for strife in both receiving and distributing the church's resources, and the task of realizing the ideal of social equity in a class-conscious society clearly was formidable, and has not been achieved to this day.

Pastoral leadership in the early Christian congregation had to meet the challenges of growth and the assimilation of converts, of integrating various social levels, and of dealing with conflict. With the absorption of numerous pagan converts, who were either marginally instructed or not at all, we find a growing presence of ideas and practices brought into the church from the old Roman religions. This includes magic, demons, and the power of words and signs. The church was relatively free of these influences before the fourth century but starting with the increase of converts after Constantine there was also greater evidence of superstition. Many Christians, it seems, continued their old habits after baptism. A member of Augustine's congregation informed him, "To be sure, I visit the idols, I consult magicians and soothsayers, but I do not forsake the church of God. I am a Catholic Christian."[30] Leo I (440–61) preached a sermon against members who first worshiped the sun before entering St. Peter's cathedral, and he mentioned a bishop of Troy who continued to worship the sun while bishop.[31] Tertullian speaks of clergy who are also makers of idols, and the Council of Elvira (306) excommunicates Christians who kill people through the use of magic.

Ramsay MacMullen recalls examples of syncretism in Christian tombs. In Pannonia a grave was ornamented with a relief of the gods, Orpheus in the center, Sol and Luna in the corners, but with the Christian Chi-Rho as well. Other graves include Peter and Paul with the gods.[32] Borrowing from pagan motifs abounded in early Christian art; Cybele, the mother goddess who holds up her son for adoration, becomes the model for Mary and the infant Jesus; Orpheus, the shepherd god, has become the Good Shepherd; Apollo has become Christ by the addition of a cross and halo as he guides the sun across the sky. It is difficult sometimes to draw a clear line between pagan and Christian.

Of more significance than these borrowings are deeply rooted superstitions, such as the intrinsic power of words, especially the name of Jesus. In Athanasius's *Life of Antony*, where there are many demons, a huge one was shriveled up by the name of Jesus, while another one was scorched.[33] Tertullian, who specializes in demons, confessed that "all the authority and power we have over them is from naming the name of Christ."[34] Origen said that "such power, indeed, does the name of Jesus possess over evil spirits, that there have been instances where it was effectual when it was pronounced even by bad men." He points out that such practices were especially prominent among uneducated Christians, which to Origen's way of thinking showed how powerful the name was.[35] The trinitarian formula in baptism was especially potent. Cyril of Jerusalem says that "the font acquires sanctifying power when it receives the invocation of the Holy Spirit, of Christ, and of the Father."[36] The controversy over the necessity of repeating baptism given by heretics hinged on the question of using the sacred words alone. The Council of Arles made the use of the trinitarian formula the sole criterion of validity.[37]

The words of Jesus in the eucharistic rite were said to effect a change in the elements. Gregory of Nyssa believed that the bread "is at once changed into the Body by means of the word [of Jesus]. The bread again is, up to a certain point of time, common bread, but when the sacramental action consecrates it, it is called and becomes the body of Christ." Ambrose insists that "the very words of the Lord and Savior operate" to change the elements in the Eucharist.[38] Another gesture considered efficacious was making the sign of the cross, which was effective to ward off evil. Hippolytus urges his hearers that when they are tempted to evil, the sign of the cross will be effective against the devil, and Lactantius in the fourth century suggests that the sign of the cross will make one safe from demons, who will flee from one's body.[39] "Exactly like pagan magicians, the Christians used the sign and symbol of the cross as a device to assure divine protection for themselves, and they claimed that the cross was more powerful than pagan magic symbols, and it was thus able to confound the demons and bring pagan magic to nought."[40] The great persecution under Diocletian was said to have been inaugurated after a Christian who was present at a pagan sacrifice was seen to be making the sign of the cross and so negated the efficacy of the sacrifice. These were practices that entered the worship life and piety of pastors and people alike, with parallel antecedents in pagan religions. It was also in this context that we have seen the development of the meaning of ordination, the laying on of hands, and the conferral of indelible character to those being ordained.

But the church strenuously opposed other pagan influences that entered the congregation. One was the continuation of the practice of holding vigils at the altars of the old idols, but now they were held at the graves of martyrs. There was usually an excess of drinking and other abuses. The Council of Elvira in the year 305 warned against women attending them, and Augustine called for a reform in the practice. Another abuse that came from the Roman religions was the collection of the relics of the martyrs, accompanied with superstition and fraud. For example, in the fourth century the emperor Theodosius forbade cutting up the bodies of martyrs for sale. The Council of Laodicea in the mid-fourth century warned against Christians worshiping angels or keeping idols in their homes. It also warned priests against serving as magicians or soothsayers, and to put away their magic amulets, "which are chains for their own souls. Those who wear such we command to be cast out of the church."[41]

When the Christian congregations accepted converts for baptism, and in the early church these were mostly adults, it was unrealistic to expect them immediately to forget their old worship practices and habits after following them all their lives. The best that could be done was to substitute Christian rites and festivals (e.g., Christmas) for pagan celebrations, and to curb the excesses associated with former idol worship. This was the pastor's task as he lived with his congregation.

Worship

Pastoral life in the early church derived its existence and reason for being from the Christian community, and the community was gathered primarily to worship Jesus Christ as Lord. When the early Christians met together in small congregations for worship and mutual encouragement, they appeared to be not much different from many other organizations around them gathered for similar purposes, who were often led by *episkopoi* or overseers. Wayne Meeks has offered four models for congregational life that influenced the early Christian congregation: the household, the voluntary association, the synagogue, and the philosophical school.[42]

Typical of New Testament gatherings for worship was the house church, especially in Pauline congregations. Paul baptized the household of Stephanas (1 Cor. 1:16), and elsewhere we read of the conversions of households, such as that of Lydia (Acts 16:15), the Philippi jailor (Acts 16:31), Crispus (Acts 18:8), and others. The household in antiquity consisted of a network of relationships that included, in addition to an extended family, slaves, servants, hired workers, freedmen, and fellow tradesmen. The internal structure was hierarchical, with the *paterfamilias* at the head. The household was a fixture of social life, and it usually included the observance of some religious practices. When we read in Acts that a household was baptized, it reminds us of the communal nature of religion in the Roman world. "Not everyone who went along with the new practices would do so with the same understanding or inner participation."[43] The house churches in early Christianity did not have the modern equivalent of a prayer group in someone's living room. The household was a defined social community with its own symbols and beliefs. The development of several congregations in one city may be due not only to the subdivision of a growing mother church but also to the presence of a number of households of Christians.

The early Roman empire witnessed the growth of large numbers of voluntary private associations gathered around some special interest. The Roman government was careful to maintain control over them, for there was always the potential for such groups to foster unrest or revolution, especially when they met in secret or engaged in illegal practices. These collegia, which included burial rites for the members, usually observed some religious practices in their assemblies. The groups were small, membership was voluntary, and they often were subsidized by a wealthy patron in whose home they would meet. Such clubs may have served as a model for Christian congregations, or the government may have perceived the churches in this light, but there were some notable differences. The church was exclusive in the sense that only those baptized in the name of Jesus could join, and it was more inclusive than the collegia in admitting persons of every social status. On the other hand, both types of organizations engaged in charitable activity, and to some extent their internal organization was similar. When Christians gathered for worship, it is not unlikely that those outside the church viewed them as being another social club, harmless, perhaps, but because of their exclusiveness and secret rites, easily suspected of being dangerous to the welfare of society.

The Jewish synagogue was the most natural model for the Christian churches to follow and it was from the Septuagint that the term *ecclesia* was derived. The early church's worship grew out of the synagogue pattern, and Christianity itself developed out of Judaism. Unlike the Greek and Roman households and social clubs, the synagogue was part of a much larger ethnic community, just as the local churches were part of the church universal. The synagogue also had its own court system to adjudicate disputes, something Paul encouraged the Corinthians to emulate, and the Jews enjoyed the status of *religio licita* that the Christians were continually struggling to gain for themselves. Although the parallels between the church and the synagogue are many, there are also differences. The terminology and functions of the leaders of the church differ from that of the synagogue, and the role of women in Christianity is one of greater freedom and responsibility. Furthermore, church membership was based on acknowledgment of Jesus as Lord, and it welcomed Gentiles as well as Jews, while the synagogue was based upon ethnicity. The struggle to eliminate circumcision as a Christian requirement indicates the determination of Paul to separate the church from the synagogue.

A fourth model to which the early Christian churches have been compared is that of the philosophical school. This applies more to the leaders and their associates than to the congregation as a whole. The schools of antiquity followed an ideology that maintained unity among the devotees—Pythagoreans, Epicureans, Stoics, Platonists. Paul and his fellow workers did carry on teaching, and Justin in the second century refers to Christianity as a new philosophy. Among the schools there were initiatory rites after a period of probation, and cultic rituals in the regular assemblies. Those who veered away from the accepted teachings were labeled heretics and were expelled from the group.

All these four models offer analogies for the early Christian congregation, but none of them captures the totality of the Christian life. The household is the basic structure of the Pauline churches, with further parallels in the voluntary associations, synagogue, and schools. Whatever resemblances there may have been between these institutions and the church, the Christian congregation was itself a unique creation, which in the course of the first three centuries developed into a "state" within the state. The Roman empire was forced either to eradicate it or succumb to it.

It was within this new creation that pastor and people gathered to worship. The early Christians appear to have had three distinct types of meetings—that for prayer, for the Eucharist, and for business. Christians gathered for prayer, and in this they followed the Jewish antecedents for the service of the Word. We know of no prescribed leader of worship in the Pauline churches, but by Justin's time (160) a "president" (bishop or presbyter) is the leader. The emphasis is on the reading of the sacred writings and an explanation of them, or the homily. The psalms are either spoken or sung, and in some places (i.e., Alexandria) we find the beginning of Christian hymnody. Intercessory prayer is offered for those who are in need, together with prayers for the government. The Pauline congregations appear to have included prophesying or speaking in tongues, but he cautions against the latter unless someone present can interpret what has been said. This is in brief an outline of the more formal communal worship of the first century, which was held every Sunday and was then followed by the Eucharist. The service was conducted in the home of one of the wealthier members (patron); following the Jewish practice, the men and women were separated. Justin's description of the Sunday prayer service is familiar to many. "There is an assembly of all who live in the towns or the country; and the memoirs of the apostles or the writings of the prophets are read, as much as time permits. When the reader has finished, the president gives a discourse, admonishing us and exhorting us to imitate these excellent examples. Then we all rise together and offer prayers."[44]

In addition to the weekly worship, Christians said table prayers, and following the custom of Daniel (Dan. 6:10), prayers were said at home three times daily, upon arising, at noon, and in the evening. *The Teaching of the Twelve* suggests that the Lord's Prayer be said at these hours. Hippolytus and Tertullian also suggest prayers at midnight, because that was when the cry rang out announcing the bridegroom's arrival. The practice of prayer seven times each day, made popular in later monasticism, derived from Jewish practice based on Psalm 119:164, "Seven times a day I praise thee." Most Christians today are familiar with two of these hours, Matins and Vespers, but the daytime hours (Terce, Sext, and None) were already observed by Jesus' disciples who were found at prayer at 9 A.M., 12 noon, and 3 P.M. (Acts 2:15; 10:9; 3:1).

The Eucharist was celebrated every Sunday, following the prayer service or service of the Word. Whereas assisting ministers served as readers, and all members contributed to the intercessions, the pastor (bishop or presbyter) was solely responsible for presiding at the Communion. In *The Teaching of the Twelve* this is still in the context of an agape meal, which was simply a weekly potluck dinner. The service in Justin began with the kiss of peace, followed by the presentation of bread and wine mixed with water to the presider, who "gives thanks at length for our being granted these gifts." This is the eucharistic prayer, which Justin said each presider offered "to the best of his ability," indicating that there was no set formula of "consecration" at this time. The people gave their assent by saying "Amen," and all present who were baptized received the bread and wine. Deacons then took the elements to those who were absent, the assumption being that the only reason for absence was illness. Justin explains that "we do not receive these gifts as ordinary food or ordinary drink . . . but as the flesh and blood of Jesus who was made flesh," and he suggested that the transformation occurred "through the word of prayer which we have from him."[45] The service concludes by receiving the offerings of all those who are able, and these were used "to aid the orphans and widows and all who are in want through sickness or any other cause." It was part of the pastor's responsibility to supervise the distribution of alms to the needy.

A half-century after Justin we have a description of a service in Rome from Hippolytus's *Apostolic Tradition*. The service is early on a Sunday morning, and it is in the home of a wealthy member. A doorkeeper greets the worshipers, numbering perhaps a hundred, so everyone is known. The men stand on one side and the women on the other. There is a table and behind it a few chairs for the bishop and his assistants. The people stand during the service, and this practice will continue for the next thousand years and beyond. The clergy are dressed in ordinary street clothes. When all have gathered, the door is shut, and the pastor begins with a prayer. Someone from the congregation reads a lesson from the Old Testament, which is followed by a psalm. A presbyter reads from a New Testament epistle, and then a deacon reads from the Gospels. The bishop, seated in his chair, explains the lessons that have been read. This is followed by the intercessions for the emperor, the church, the sick, and all others in need of God's help. All present exchange the kiss of peace, men with men and women with women. Then everyone comes forward with an offering, which was primarily intended for the needy. It included clothing and food, such as bread, wine, cheese, olives, oil, and milk. But Hippolytus cautioned against bringing onions or garlic, for reasons which are best known to him. This offertory procession by the people, depositing their gifts on or near the table, remained part of the Christian Sunday service for several centuries, until the large numbers made it impractical and the gift of money replaced food. Following the offerings, the bishop proceeded with the preface, which is still common to most Christian churches today:

Pastor: The Lord be with you.
People: And with your spirit.
Pastor: Lift up your hearts.
People: We lift them up to the Lord.
Pastor: Let us give thanks (i.e., *eucharistōmen*) to the Lord.
People: It is proper and right to do so.

The eucharistic prayer follows and the distribution of the bread and wine to those present, beginning with the bishop and his assistants, with the understanding that by receiving the elements first they provide an example to the faithful. The service ends with prayer after which all go to their regular employment, for Sunday did not become a holiday until the fourth century. The bishop distributes the alms to the needy while the assistants take the Communion to those who are absent. As in the Eucharist of Justin, there is yet no fixed formula for the consecration of the elements, but each presider improvises as he is able. It was not until the fourth century that special significance was attached to the words spoken or to the precise moment of "change" in the eucharistic consecration. At the time of Hippolytus the people actively participated in the prayers, the responses, the kiss of peace, the offertory, and the receiving of the sacrament, gathered closely around the table and the bishop.

Each congregation was self-governing unit, which necessitated some means for arriving at communal decisions. In the New Testament churches this was done in a business meeting where all the members apparently had the right of appearing and taking part in the discussion and voting, women as well as men. The agenda of these business sessions would include problems of discipline, communicating with other churches (1 Cor. 7:1), or gathering money for the relief of a sister church (1 Cor. 16:1-2). Decisions could include the expulsion of unworthy members (1 Cor. 5:1-8), and the adjudication of disputes within the congregation. One of the most important actions taken by a congregation was the election of its bishop, and it was on these occasions, with bishops of sister churches present, that questions of heresy were discussed together with matters of discipline. Each church was autonomous and governed its own affairs, yet was conscious of being part of the greater church and aware of the need for unity among the churches in teaching, the practice of Christian virtue, and the mutual consolation and edification of the entire church.

Baptism in the early church was usually administered on the night before Easter, although the vigils of Pentecost or Epiphany were also favored times for the sacrament. Here again Hippolytus is a primary source of information, and he informs us that those to be baptized were instructed for a period of three years, though the time was not rigidly prescribed. The period of the catechumenate was one of the principal institutions for the formation of Christian virtues; as such it served as an important forum for pastoral contact and counsel with the people. Baptism of adults was the usual practice in the missionary church, but infants were not excluded. When we consider the conversion of households as one of the ways in which the church grew, it is not surprising that infants were included in the sacrament.

The third-century rite was full of dramatic symbolism. It was administered at midnight by a lake or river, with the candidates facing West and renouncing Satan and all his pomp and empty promises. Then they turned to the East and confessed faith in Christ in words that became the Apostles' Creed. They removed all their clothing, which signified putting off the old nature, as well as being a type of the naked Christ on the cross, whose death they were imitating in baptism. Nudity also was a sign of new birth symbolizing the new life and innocence of the newborn. Baptism was by immersion at the hands of the bishop, although in some cases deaconesses were used for the women. After the baptism they were clothed in white garments as a sign of putting on Christ, and the bishop either poured oil (i.e., the chrism) on them or signed their foreheads with it as a sign of conferring the Holy Spirit. In the West this anointing became Confirmation during the fifth century. Then the baptismal group walked to the church where the rest of the congregation waited for them to begin the Easter Eucharist at dawn. Baptism was an event filled with rich symbolism, which left a deep impression upon those who had experienced it.

The worship life of the pastor and people included various devotional practices in addition to public worship and private daily prayer. Tertullian, in his treatise *On Prayer*, suggests several ways in which personal piety can be fostered. One need not wash one's hands before praying for they are already clean through baptism. Against the prevailing custom of praying out loud, or at least in a whisper, he says that prayer can be silent. Women should cover their heads or wear a veil even when praying at home, and all should kneel, except on Sundays or during the Easter season. He advocated frequent use of the sign of the cross, even before taking a bath. The sign was not made as it is today, marking a cross by touching one's forehead, breast, and then from shoulder to shoulder, but in ancient times it was simply made on one's forehead. A fourth-century writer said that every Christian should "retain in memory the Apostles' Creed and say it daily before going to sleep and on rising. So too with the Lord's Prayer and the sign of the cross with which he arms himself against the devil."[46] We learn from Tertullian and Cyprian that in the third century it was common for husband and wife to receive Communion every morning in their bedroom upon rising. They brought home part of the consecrated bread from the Sunday Eucharist and kept it in a small container (*arca*). At the end of the persecutions Communion was available daily in the churches, but the practice of house Communion was still prevalent in Augustine's time in Alexandria and Rome. Evidently the clergy permitted bread to be taken away from the church. In the course of time people associated the consecrated bread with magic, and they carried it about with them on journeys to ward off evil. The church stopped the practice by placing the bread directly on the tongue of the recipient to be reasonably certain it was all consumed at the time of the Eucharist in the church.

Martyrs were given special veneration almost from the beginning of the church. The earliest such commemoration was that of Bishop Polycarp of Smyrna, who was killed in the year 156. We read in the account of his martyrdom that his followers gathered his bones "like precious pearls," and buried them. "There the Lord will permit us to meet in gladness and joy to celebrate the birthday of his martyrdom both in memory of those who fought the fight and for the training and preparation of those who will fight."[47] Such a commemoration usually was observed with the Eucharist at the grave of the martyr. In time, especially after the persecutions ended, elaborate tombstones were erected at the site, or a chapel, and finally large churches such as St. Peter's in Rome and many others. We have already seen how the practice of holding a meal, the *refrigerium*, at the grave site led to abuses of food, drink, and immorality, which prompted calls for reform from councils and theologians.

The anniversaries of martyrs became fixed in the church year as saint days. The veneration of relics was another practice associated with the martyrs, and by the sixth century there was a heavy trade in relics. As larger churches were built, elaborate reliquaries were fashioned to display the martyrs' remains. Honoring the memories of heroic Christians was a natural impulse and served as an encouragement to the same kind of fidelity among the living. But with the large number of nominal or political converts under the imperial church, this laudable practice became associated with non-Christian elements. Following the end of the persecutions the practice of pilgrimage became popular, which usually was a journey to the shrine of a popular martyr or a site associated with Jesus' ministry. Although the practice had its roots in popular piety, it was also subject to abuse, for people were liberated from the moral restraints of home and occasionally fell into sin along the way. The pilgrimage could also cover with a veneer of religion someone fleeing from debt or the husband from family responsibility. This brought the censure of the church on the practice, although during the Middle Ages a pilgrimage could be undertaken as a form of penance.

Congregational life was regulated by the church calendar. Both in Judaism and in Roman culture, the year was marked with religious festivals. For Christians the primary celebration was Easter, and the church year took its date as the center from which other dates were reckoned. Early Christians were never agreed on this date, however; even though the Council of Nicea tried to bring uniformity to its calculation, as late as the year 700 Easter was still celebrated on as many as five different Sundays in the same year. With Easter as the starting point, the period of Lent was established, a time for intense preparation for candidates to be baptized at the Easter vigil. Advent likewise took on a baptismal significance as the time of preparation for those to receive the sacrament at Epiphany (January 6). The second major festival, Pentecost, commemorated the birth of the church, and it fell fifty days after the Jewish Passover, which Christians now called Maundy Thursday. Easter and Pentecost come directly from the New Testament, but Christmas did not appear until the fourth century. The earliest date we have for its observance is the year 366 in Rome, with December 25 possibly selected by Constantine. It was intended to counteract the gnostic denials of Christ's true humanity, and so the feast of the incarnation was a theological response to heresy, and it may have been intended to substitute a Christian festival for the Roman Saturnalia. In any case, from its inception Christian preachers denounced the pagan overtones that remained in the festival. Chrysostom complained that Christmas was too much surrounded with unseemly feasting, drinking, and "commercialization." In addition to the three major festivals, a large number of minor days began to be observed, which commemorated events in Christ's life or those of the apostles and martyrs. Some of the more popular included The Name of Jesus (January 1), The Presentation of Our Lord (February 2), The Annunciation (March 25), St. John the Baptist (June 24), St. Michael (September 29), and All Saints (November 1). Some of these dates were selected not because of their historical accuracy but in order to counteract pagan festivals on those days.

Where did the early Christians worship? We know that in the first two centuries Christians worshiped in homes. They did not build churches, primarily because they were an illegal sect (organizations outside the law were not given building permits); what funds they had, and what money they collected, went for charity. Before Justin's martyrdom he was interrogated by the Roman officials: "Tell me where do you meet, or in what place do you gather your disciples?" Justin said, "I lodge above in the house of Martin, near the baths of Timothy, and during all this time I have known no other place of meeting but this house."[48] As the church grew in numbers during the third century, it also began to own property, despite the intermittent opposition of the Roman government. The earliest evidence of the church in possession of property is under Bishop Zephyrinus of Rome (199–217) when the church owned a catacomb, and toward the end of the century church buildings were being constructed in the larger cities. In the great persecution of Diocletian (c. 301) it was decreed that Christian church buildings should be destroyed.

We have some idea of the nature of these buildings from the ruins of the Christian meeting house discovered at Dura-Europos dating from c. 230. It followed the general plan of a house church, but it was larger. The bishop and his assistants sat in chairs on a raised platform in front of the assembly, separated from the congregation by a low railing. At Dura-Europos the meeting room was only 17 by 43 feet, accommodating a congregation of no more than sixty people. There is a small baptistry with a tub. We also have the police records of a Christian church in North Africa, impounded c. 303, in which we find listed a number of chalices and lamps, and in a storeroom they discovered a large amount of clothing, presumably for distribution to the poor. It is interesting that most of the clothes were women's apparel, which may indicate both a large number of women believers or needy. There is another room that served as a library, with bookcases and chests. Adjoining the church was a living area, probably that of the clergy.[49] Churches built before Constantine seem to have been constructed along the same pattern as a private dwelling. Their resemblance to ordinary houses would have made them indistinguishable in their environment. There was nothing about their architecture that would have identified them as a Christian church.

The fourth century brought dramatic changes in Christian worship and in houses of worship. Much larger meeting rooms were required. The church could not borrow architectural patterns from paganism, because in the old religion houses were built only for the gods and not for people—for example, the Parthenon of Athens. Christian worship was communal, and it required a space to accommodate large numbers. The building type that recommended itself was the basilica, a long, rectangular building with a long nave, two or more aisles, illuminated by the windows of the clerestory above. The basilica was borrowed for Christian use from the Roman law courts and places for commercial exchange. The term "basilica" applies more to function than design, and basically it served as a covered extension of the

Roman town marketplace where friends met to exchange business or gossip. Christians adapted the former magistrate's throne in the apse for the bishop's chair, and a freestanding altar stood on the same raised dais where the bishop sat behind it, facing the people. Sometimes a small chapel was constructed under the altar to house the relics of a martyr after whom the church was named. The building was often "oriented"—that is, so constructed with the altar toward the East that one entered the church through a courtyard and an entrance porch (narthex) from the West. A large baptismal font may have stood near the entrance, or in some cases the baptistry was a separate octagonally shaped building situated near the entrance.

Constantine had seven churches built in Rome, the largest being the church of St. John on the Lateran, the cathedral church of the bishop of Rome. St. Peter's on the Vatican, the predecessor of today's grand basilica, was constructed over a shrine said to contain the relics of the apostle. In addition to encouraging endowments for church buildings, Constantine was instrumental, with his mother, Helena, in building large churches in Tyre and Antioch, as well as the Church of the Holy Sepulcher and Church of the Ascension in Jerusalem and the Church of the Nativity in Bethlehem. But the emperor's plans for the new faith went far beyond church building. In order to escape from the constrictive pagan atmosphere of Rome, he built a new city (he called it Neapolis), later named Constantinople, intending it to be a Christian city. There he built two large churches, that of the Twelve Apostles in which he was buried, and the Church of Holy Peace (Irene), which was named to commemorate the peace he had brought to the empire.

The larger buildings and numbers changed the style of worship from the intimacy of the house church to the grandeur of ceremonial appropriate to a basilica. Clergy marched in procession, preceded by incense, candles, and a crucifer. Their vestments did not change much from earlier times, but that of the rest of the population did, which made clerical garb unique. The fifth century mosaics in the churches of Ravenna show striking similarities between Roman civil garb and that adopted by the clergy, in part because the clergy had themselves become civil officials. The liturgy itself became more elaborate with the addition of ceremonial—that is, the washing of hands by the presider at the Eucharist, the Lord's Prayer after the consecration, the *Agnus Dei,* the Gospel procession, the *Gloria in*

Excelsis, and a choir to sing the responses. Under the circumstances, the elaboration of ceremony was not only a natural development but also necessary, and there was theological rationale for every new addition to the liturgy, so that worshipers who understood the symbols were undoubtedly edified by the experience. The Creed was added to the service by Cyril of Jerusalem (c. 350) as an anti-Arian polemic. Public worship appealed not only to the senses, but in the sermon it sought to edify the mind as well (see chap. 3).

Early Christian attitudes toward music were at first ambivalent. Clement of Alexandria was opposed to the use of instruments, though Basil of Caesarea believed music had an educational value, "that through the softness of the sound we might unawares receive what is useful in the words." Jerome speaks of the office of a cantor who was to lead in song. Augustine was opposed to melodic singing, and insisted that it should resemble speech "with little wavering of the voice." But he also writes, "What better thing can the people do than sing? I know of nothing better than that." Ambrose wrote hymns to popularize the Trinitarian doctrine, including "O Splendor of God's Glory Bright," and "O Trinity Most Blessed Light." The inclusion of Ambrosian hymns in the Benedictine rule (526) was the first time hymns officially became a part of prescribed liturgical practice. The fourth century saw the beginning of the four great Western liturgies, the Mozarabic in Spain, the Gallican in France, the Ambrosian in northern Italy, and the Roman. Roman bishops from 400 onward were engaged in the development of plainsong chant, but it was under Gregory I (c. 540–604) that liturgical chant took its definite and typical form, which has become known as Gregorian.

Pastoral leadership developed primarily out of the worship life of the congregation. Although other administrative and judicial responsibilities became associated with the office, it was chiefly as presider at the Eucharist and as the principal homilist that the role of the pastor as shepherd and guide emerged. As congregations grew from house church to basilicas, so also did the number of clergy assigned to a congregation. By the fifth century team ministries were common in many churches with a distribution of the various responsibilities among acolytes, doorkeepers, lectors, deacons, deaconesses, catechists, and gravediggers, but the chief responsibility for the worship and welfare of the church remained with the pastor (bishop/presbyter) who alone was permitted to preside at the Holy Communion, or if he wished, delegate the task to assisting presbyters.

Called to Be Holy

After being baptized into Christ's death and resurrection, the Christian was expected to "walk in newness of life" (Rom. 6:4). From the beginning the church saw itself as a community separate from the rest of society. Peter wrote that "as he who has called you is holy, yourselves be holy in all your conduct since it is written, 'You shall be holy for I am holy' " (1 Pet. 1:15). The New Testament does not offer any specific code of behavior other than the new commandment of love toward God and neighbor. The specific ramifications of this demanding ethic were to be determined by each believer, following general guidelines of the Ten Commandments (Rom. 13:8-10) even to the point of mental obedience to them (Matt. 5:28) together with Christ's example and the Sermon on the Mount. By the second century this elastic but demanding view of Christian behavior had become more narrow and systematic to the point of rigidity and legalism. A considerable amount of pastoral time and energy was devoted to maintaining the discipline of holiness within the congregation.

The Teaching of the Twelve (c. 130) offers a lengthy "way of life" and "way of death," which outlines in great detail the dos and don'ts of the Christian life. In so doing, it is the first to enumerate the cardinal sins, at one time offering seven and elsewhere twelve, which led to expulsion from the community. Throughout early Christian literature we find repeated descriptions of Christian morality contrasted with that of the pagan world. Justin's portrayal is typical of many others: "We who formerly delighted in fornication," he says, "now embrace purity alone; we who formerly used magic arts now dedicate ourselves to the good and unbegotten God; we who loved the path to wealth and possession above all, now bring what we have into the common stock, and give to any in need." He continues by describing the social equality among Christians who formerly would not even "sit at the same fire" with people of different customs; now Christians love their enemies rather than hate them; and in general the believers "live in accordance with the fair precepts of Christ."[50]

The new morality embraced all facets of life. Roman entertainment, especially the arena, gladiatorial combats, circus, and theater were to be avoided. The theater was usually immoral, and the gladiatorial combats were nothing more than ritualized murder. Athenagoras said "We see little difference between watching a man being put to death and killing him. We have given up such spectacles."[51] Home entertainment was likewise brought under supervision with warnings against excessive eating or drinking. Tertullian writes, "We begin even before we sit down by praying to God. We eat only an amount necessary to satisfy our hunger, and we drink only what is necessary and modest."[52] He continues by saying that the table talk is as though the Lord himself were present.

Tertullian represents an extreme in puritanical rectitude, although it is certain he speaks for a large number of believers. One of the five essays he wrote for women is entitled *On the Apparel of Women*, where he suggests that women should try to appear as plain as possible, avoiding cosmetics and jewelry. Any enhancement of nature's's endowments was a criticism of the Creator, implying somehow negligence, and a woman who tried to make herself attractive was leading men into temptation. He was also critical of men who dyed their graying hair. "The more old age tries to conceal itself, the more it will be detected."[53] In this treatise *On Idolatry*, Tertullian finds idolatrous any behavior that ignores God or gives any credence to paganism, such as swearing "By Hercules" or "By Jupiter," which was still common among converts. Robes with broad borders or stripes are not to be worn, for they come from pagan practices. Concerning military service, he writes that no Christian may join the army, not only because of the potential for breaking the commandment not to kill but also because of the many pagan oaths required in the daily life of a soldier. "Our Lord, when he took away Peter's sword, took away the sword of every soldier."[54] But not all moralists were as rigid as Tertullian. Clement of Alexandria approved of jewelry, although it should be Christian symbolism, such as a dove, fish, or cross. Hippolytus (215) said jewelry should be removed before baptism, and we assume the aristocratic women and men who entered the church before and especially after Constantine continued to wear jewelry.

Holiness also involved one's occupation, and a number of vocations were forbidden to Christians. Hippolytus in the *Apostolic Tradition* offers a list of such, including sculptors, painters, makers of idols, teachers of young children (perhaps because of the requirement of teaching pagan legends), charioteers, actors and actresses, military commander, or a civil magistrate (because of the role of pagan oaths in their daily lives).[55] In business life the church was against lending money at interest, and any cleric who was detected in this practice was dismissed from office. But when it came to legitimate occupations, Christian apologists were quick to remind Roman authorities that believers were good citizens who gave an honest day's labor, were just and upright, and did not cheat the government or their neighbors.

We find an early development of the legislation of holiness in some of the conciliar decisions. The Council of Elvira (306) dismissed clergy engaged in taking interest on loans, forbids Christian women to marry pagans or heretics, insists on rigorous fasting every Saturday, forbids all pictures within a church (in fear of their being worshiped), calls for the excommunication of any cleric who eats with a Jew, opposes giving the priest a gift at a baptism, excludes from communion any who play dice for money, and warns women against associating with hairdressers or men with long hair.[56] A reflection of the times is also this canon, "A woman may not write to other lay Christians without her husband's consent. A woman may not receive letters of friendship addressed to her only and not to her husband as well."[57] Also we find the stipulation that anyone who fails to attend the Sunday service for three consecutive weeks is to be expelled for a short time and endure public reproach. But we also find some remarkably lenient legislation. A woman who beats her servant thereby causing the servant's death will undergo seven years of penance if it was intentional and five years if it was accidental. And in the absence of a bishop or presbyter, any deacon may validly baptize, with the bishop conferring the imposition of hands at a later time.[58]

Other councils offer a similar variety of legislation intended to insure the holiness of the church. That of Ancyra (314) speaks of the problem of those who lapsed under persecution, prohibits the sale of church goods, speaks of virgins who disregard their profession, and of the degrees of homicide. The Council of Gangra (c. 345) opposes false asceticism, permits the marriage of the clergy, questions some motivations toward celibacy, forbids private assemblies outside the church, is against women wearing men's clothing or cutting their hair short, and concludes with an essay on the true nature of asceticism.

The one area that appears to receive the most attention in the early attempts to regulate the Christian life is that of sexual ethics. Early councils appear to contain more decrees on this subject than any other, unless perhaps there may be more regulating the life of the clergy. It may be this is due to an inordinate preoccupation with sex in the minds of puritanical rigorists, but it may also be caused by the fact that Christianity was born within a Roman society in which family stability and moral discipline had given way to flagrant decadence. Some Christian writers have exaggerated the moral decline of ancient Rome in order to provide a favorable contrast with the radical ethical demands of the church. Notwithstanding, there is strong evidence that Roman family values were in serious trouble. In the first century after Christ, Caesar Augustus attempted to stem the declining birth rate through legislation that gave bonuses for families having children and severe penalties for immorality, with no success. One problem was the decline of available men, due to casualties in war. In the year 9 over eighteen thousand Roman men were killed in battle, and other men were disinclined to marry, partly because of the repeated economic dislocations of the times. A Roman orator, Quintillian, commented on the situation as he found it in the first century. He spoke of parents corrupting their children through the examples of wicked lives, teaching them to despise the gods and decency. "They see our mistresses, our male objects of affection; every dining room rings with impure songs; things shameful to be told are objects of sight." He continues by saying that the unfortunate children learn vices before they know they are vices.[59] Seneca, a famous Roman philosopher at the time of Christ, said, "No woman need blush about breaking her marriage, since the most prominent ladies have learned to reckon the years by the names of their husbands."[60] We have already spoken of the decadence of the theater and the arena, spectacles provided by the Roman government.

There can be little wonder that Christian sexual standards appeared to be radical, given this environment. Monogamy was the Christian rule, and infidelity was a grave offense both for husband or wife, just as fornication by a single person was cause for excommunication and severe penance. Divorce was forbidden, and even infidelity was not an automatic cause for separation of spouses. Even second marriages, when a spouse had died, were frowned upon, although the church never officially condemned such marriages. Justin Martyr wrote, "Those who make second marriages according to human law are sinners in the sight of our Teacher."[61] The Council of Laodicea (365) states, "Communion should be given to those who have freely and lawfully joined in second marriages after a short time, which is to be spent by them in prayer and fasting."[62] But the ideal was that one whose spouse had died should remain unwed. Given the shorter life expectancy of males, this resulted in a large number of widows within the church. Conjugal intercourse was considered permissible only if there was an express purpose of producing children. All other coitus was in the category of fornication, even though it was with one's spouse. This attitude resulted in the prohibition of all forms of contraception. Despite these strictures, the early church gave marriage a high status, and eventually it became a sacrament. Tertullian, the unreconstructed puritan, writes, "How can we describe the happiness of this marriage which the church approves, which the sacrifice confirms, which the blessing seals, which the angels recognize, which the Father ratifies?"[63] Augustine wrote a book, *The Good in Marriage,* which he found to be threefold—children, fidelity, and sacramental union. Both Tertullian and Augustine indicate that the marriage ceremony took place in the context of the eucharistic service.

The church confronted a problem in mixed marriages with a pagan spouse. A larger number of women than men was attracted to the faith, so Callistus, bishop of Rome (217–33), permitted aristocratic women to marry Christian men of lower status, which was contrary to imperial law. The church was opposed to unions of Christian with non-Christian because of the difficulties involved. The ideal Christian couple was to "pray together, fast together, instruct, support, and exhort each other. They share each other's tribulations, persecutions, and revival. They delight to visit the sick, help the needy, and give alms freely."[64] The same Tertullian who wrote these lines scorns a mixed marriage. "How," he asks, "can a Christian woman arise to pray at midnight when a slave of the devil lies at your side?"[65] In the fourth century Constantine made Christian–Jewish marriages illegal, and in 338 under Constantine's sons a Roman law declared that those who contracted a marriage with a non-Christian were living in adultery.

Despite these ideals expressed for marriage, it was still considered to be inferior to celibacy. At best, marriage was a safety valve for the less heroic ones who were not gifted with continence. Origen wrote, "God has allowed us to marry wives, because not everyone is capable of the superior condition, which is to be absolutely pure."[66] His attitude, with some exceptions, prevailed in the church for many centuries. For Augustine sexual continence and the renunciation of all personal property made the truly spiritual person. But the most extreme panegyrist in antiquity for virginity was Jerome, who combined his aversion to marriage and his contempt for sex with a low opinion of women in general, despite his admiration for the aristocratic women who constantly surrounded him. His longest polemical treatise was *Against Jovinian*, a proponent of marriage who accused the church of lapsing into the Manichean heresy with its low estimation of sex. Jerome insisted that Adam and Eve became married only after they had sinned, and so it was a result of the Fall. Marriage may replenish the earth, but virginity replenishes paradise. He explained away the marriages and even polygamy of the partriarchs, and said that Solomon bitterly repented of his thousand wives by writing the book of Ecclesiastes. Intercourse in marriage was an obstacle to prayer and the reception of the Eucharist. "I praise marriage, praise wedlock," he said, "but I do so because they produce virgins."[67] His statement about the Eucharist refers to the common belief that the blessings of Holy Communion were invalidated for those who had engaged in intercourse during a period of time before receiving the sacrament. The same prohibition applied to those presiding—conjugal relationships of a priest and his wife made for an invalid sacrament for the entire congregation.

It was in this social environment of concern for purity in every aspect of life that early Christian clergy undertook their tasks. From the mid-third century and the time of Cyprian the church had developed a system of penance related to excommunication whereby those who had been guilty of offenses in ethics or morality could make amends and be restored to full communion. Although the councils attempted to offer guidelines for the severity and the duration of the penance commensurate with the lapse, it was impossible to legislate for every conceivable offense, which left considerable latitude for the judgment of the pastor. From the second century on it had been the practice of the church to require a public confession of sin for the most serious postbaptismal infractions of morality, to be followed by exclusion from communion for a period of time, which could extend to one's deathbed. During this time the penitent was required to stand with other penitents at the Sunday services, but they could not receive Communion. Excommunication did not mean expulsion from the congregation. Penitents were still in the church, attended its services, and performed whatever duties or austerities their penance required.

When the pastor judged that their penance had been discharged, they were readmitted to the fellowship of the sacrament. This was done in a public absolution, in later years often on Maundy Thursday. Such a penance was permitted only once following baptism, based on an interpretation of Heb. 6:4, "It is impossible to restore again to repentance those who have once been enlightened, who have tasted the heavenly gift." Although this text infers that no forgiveness is possible after "enlightenment" (i.e., baptism), the church, since the Shepherd of Hermas, permitted one and only one opportunity for absolution from serious sins committed after baptism. Lesser sins, which all Christians regularly committed, were to be forgiven through almsgiving (see chap. 4). Given the nature of public penance, it is easy to see why many Christians postponed their baptism until late in life, or even when at death's door.

It was not until the sixth century that the more evangelical practice of private confession and absolution was gaining in popularity. The earliest evidence for private confession as a sacrament is from the Council of Toledo in the year 589, although we also know that troubled sinners sought the counsel of their clergy in private long before then, which was a form of private confession. Public confession was often required only where there had been public offense. Augustine took the view that sins that had remained secret did not require public penance: "The evil must die where it has taken place"—that is, in secret (chap. 4).[68] The theory behind the practice of a penitential discipline was commendable, that of showing true repentance for sin and a determination to amend one's life. Where relationships had been broken, they had to be mended, and where people had been defrauded, restoration must be made. But by reserving absolution until the discipline had been undergone, people began to view the discipline itself as "payment" for sin. Part of the rationale underlying the theology of penance was a theology of sin, which viewed sin as inhering in the deed rather than in the person. That is, the performance of sinful deeds is what made one a sinner, and if one could diminish the number of sins, one could become more holy. This was the thinking of Pelagius in the late fourth century. He believed that in theory every person could become holy by sinning less. The opposite view was that sin was a human condition, of which individual deeds were symptoms. One could not eradicate the underlying disease by treating only the symptoms. Augustine said, "We are not sinners because we sin, but we sin because we are sinners." Before the fifth century these ideas were not fully articulated in the theology of the church. Ordinary Christians who were troubled by their sins and sinfulness found release by beating their breasts at the "forgive us our sins" of the Lord's Prayer, through prayer, giving alms, doing works of charity, and fasting.

Considering the infinite potential for pastoral care in the context of the church's expectations of holiness, it is not surprising that we do not find uniformity in pastoral practice. An early conflict developed between rigorists, such as Tertullian and Hippolytus, who refused to allow the presence of the impure in the church, "the spotless bride of Christ," and those such as Callistus of Rome who viewed the church as a mixed body, containing worthy as well as unworthy members. Callistus is said to have remarked, "Let the tares grow together with the wheat," while others pointed out that the church as Noah's ark should contain all types of people.[69] The North African view of the church as a gathering of saints continued in the Donatist movement of the fourth century, but the Roman idea of the church as a mixed community that included sinners was more widespread. Pastoral practice regarding the restoration of lapsed sinners therefore was affected by ecclesiology, or one's understanding of the nature of the church.

The various images of the church that emerged had a direct bearing on the role of the pastor and on clerical identity. If the church was understood as a sanctuary of saints, the pastor served as judge and disciplinarian to insure its purity. St. Paul uses the military metaphor (1 Thess. 5:8), which Basil of Caesarea also finds useful. It follows that Christians as soldiers of Christ require a captain, and the relationship of pastor to people becomes that of a military leader. The church is also seen as the spotless bride of Christ, which influenced the interpretation of the Song of Songs well into the Middle Ages. More popular was the metaphor of a flock of sheep, which finds antecedents throughout Scripture, but most directly from the words of Christ (John 10). Basil and many other early theologians utilize this imagery, and the role of a shepherd was given to the bishop, complete with staff and (later) woolen pallium.[70] Already in the third century the ordination prayer of Hippolytus gives the primary task of the bishop to "feed the holy flock." Jesus' acts of healing in the Gospels commended to the clergy the role of physician, which in turn implied that the church was a gathering of sick people. The political model especially became popular, viewing the church as an organization similar to the state. "When ecclesiastical problems, such as the baptism of heretics, forced the bishops of Africa to meet for discussion, their gatherings gradually came to resemble the meetings of the Roman senate."[71] Church councils followed Roman political procedures, much as modern churches follow *Robert's Rules of Order.* Thus the Roman governor served as a role model for the clergy. Augustine's *City of God* reinforced the metaphor of the church as city, with the pastor as ruler. Indeed, the term "ruler" is frequently employed by Gregory the Great for the pastor. The use of Old Testament imagery in seeing the church as the New Israel led directly to the new priesthood, the Eucharist as sacrifice, and a clerical hierarchy. Therefore when considering the life and practice of the clergy in any age, a prior question must be asked of the nature of the church. In modern times the church has adopted the model of a democratic political state in a pluralistic society where religion is a matter of free choice. In such a situation the pastor becomes a team player, enabler, or facilitator. In the early church his role was far more autocratic and patriarchal, which does not exclude the attributes of compassion, nurture, and love.

Hospitality and Charity

Works of charity distinguished the Christian church from the very beginning. We read in Acts of sharing goods, and St. Paul spent considerable energy in collecting money to relieve the suffering in Jerusalem. "There was not a needy person among them, for as many as were possessors of lands or houses sold them and brought the proceeds . . . and distribution was made to each as they had need" (Acts 4:32-35). Justin informed the emperor that "we who once took pleasure in the means of increasing our wealth and property now bring what we have into a common fund and share with everyone in need."[72] Although I have earlier commented upon the middle-class nature of the church, it did not lack for the poor and sick. Periodic persecutions alone could quickly change one's status, and the number of widows was large. The ultimate responsibility for such distributions lay with the pastor or bishop, who may have delegated the actual task to deacons, from which the office of deacon emerged.

Christians practiced charity not only among themselves but to those outside the faith as well. Dionysius gives an account of such charity by Christians during a plague in Alexandria. He writes: "Most of our brethren . . . visited the sick without thought as to the danger. . . . Most gladly departed this life along with them, being infected with the disease from others." He continues by describing how they took up the bodies of the dead, closing their eyes, shutting their mouth, bathing them, and giving them burial. He contrasts the Christian behavior with that of the "heathen," who deserted their dying friends or treated their corpses as vile.[73] This kind of self-sacrificing conduct did not go unnoticed by the Romans. The satirist Lucian, who enjoyed ridiculing the new faith, offered this grudging compliment: "It is incredible to see the ardor with which the people of that religion help each other in their wants. They spare nothing. Their first legislator has put it into their hearts that they are all brothers."[74]

The work of relieving the needy was integrally associated with the Eucharist, for at the offertory the people came forward with their gifts for the poor, which in early times was usually in kind rather than in money. We have seen that in Rome such gifts included not only clothing but various kinds of food as well, mostly perishable, which meant they were distributed immediately following the service. In modern days the churches are also engaged in works of charity, but that is usually done through budgets and the writing of checks. In the early church assistance was direct and immediate. No one could leave home for the service without bringing some gift for the needy, and in this way the Eucharistic celebration bore a direct relationship to the world. But money was also collected and deposited with the bishop for charitable purposes. Tertullian informs us where the money was spent. He emphasizes the voluntary nature of the collection: "Each member may bring a monthly donation, if they desire, as a voluntary offering." The funds are never used for banquets or drinking parties, but to feed the poor and to bury the dead, to help boys and girls with no parents, for the elderly and shipwrecked. They also relieve the suffering of workers in the mines or those imprisoned because of their faith. He continues by referring to the indifference of Christians to social status, and ends by criticizing the Romans for their selfishness, neglect of the poor, and their general profligacy.[75]

Cyprian offered a theology of almsgiving in his treatise *On Works and Almsgiving*, in which he associated it with the purging of sin.

"By almsgiving and faith sins are purged . . . the flame of sin is smothered by almsgiving and works of justice" (chap. 2). Although baptism grants a full remission of sins, he says that through the works of charity that flow from the baptized person the mercy of God continues to be manifested toward others. Almsgiving serves to wash away one's postbaptismal sins. "The only way to appease God is through almsgiving and works of mercy" (chap. 4). Cyprian includes works of justice as efficacious for the remission of sins. This means helping those who are oppressed, who are in trouble, or who are alone. In addition to forgiveness of sins, "our prayers become more efficacious through almsgiving and such acts of mercy protect us from dangers and rescue our souls from death" (chap. 5). He turns his attention to some of the wealthy who evidently were neglecting their obligations, "whose minds are barren and confused. . . . What excuse is left for the lazy? What defense for those whose lives bear no good fruit?" He appeals to Christ's statement that acts of mercy done to others are done to Christ himself, and to the rewards that await the merciful in the hereafter.[76] Cyprian's chiding of the wealthy who refused to give alms is a healthy dose of realism and a caution not to idealize the early church beyond the facts. But the facts appear to support the assessment offered by the church's enemies, that the Christians excelled in charity and works of mercy.

Besides Lucian, another writer hostile to Christianity offers his testimony to Christian generosity. When Julian "the Apostate" became emperor in 361, he was determined to stamp out the new faith, but to do this he found it necessary to encourage his pagan supporters to imitate the Christians in their zeal for charity. He wrote this to a pagan high priest in Galatia: "The Hellenic religion does not prosper as I desire. Why do we not observe that it is the Christians' benevolence to strangers, their care for the graves of the dead, and the pretended holiness of their lives that has done the most to increase atheism [i.e., Christianity]?"[77] The Christians must be overtrumped. "For from Zeus come all strangers and beggars. And a gift, though small, is precious. Then let us not, by allowing [the Christians] to outdo us in good works, disgrace [ourselves] or abandon the reverence which is due to the gods." This was the same Julian whom, as we have seen, also observed how the Christians fought among themselves, and he shrewdly recalled exiled bishops to their homes, hoping to incite divisions in the church. So we have conflicting images of the early church from the same author—Christians excelled in showing love and charity, and they were a quarrelsome lot. Both images appear to have been true.

With the growth of the church following the Edict of Milan, there was a corresponding growth in the number of needy, so that institutions of mercy developed to assist orphans, the sick, and travelers. Basil of Caesarea, after Pachomius the founder of Eastern monasticism, was one of the earliest to establish a center for charity. The story goes that while he was visiting the hermits in Egypt and Syria, he read in the lesson for Maundy Thursday that after Jesus had washed his disciples' feet he said to them, "I have given you an example that you should also do as I have done to you" (John 13:14). It occurred to him that if one lives alone, apart from a community, "whose feet will you wash?" He returned to his home in Asia Minor and there founded a monastery with its vocation being that of service to the needy. He built a hospice for the poor, a home for the elderly, a hospital, schools for children, and a daily ration for the hungry. Gregory of Nazianzen, who lived with Basil for a time, described his foundation as a new city. "Go forth a little way from the city, and behold, the new city, a storehouse of piety, where disease is regarded in a religious light, and sympathy is put to the test."[78] Modern excavations have revealed that, while the old Caesarea declined in importance, the new town centered on Basil's new buildings grew to considerable proportions. At first it was called New Town, but then Basileiad, after Basil.[79] Basil's monasticism was a way of Christian life in which the monk was dedicated to the service of his fellows. "It came as near as any movement within the early church to a Christianity that aimed at changing society and transforming organized religion into a social as well as an individual creed."[80]

Basil's example was followed by other Christians. The Code of Justinian reflects a situation of well developed ecclesiastical organization of charity. It presumes the existence of a hostel, along with hospital, almshouse, orphanage, and nursery as common elements in the property to be administered by a bishop.[81] Together with the alleviation of poverty and sickness, there developed in many areas the practice of providing hostels for travelers. Whereas in earlier days, security and comfort while traveling had been the privilege of the wealthy, "these domestic advantages were now extended to the whole household of faith, who are accepted on trust, though complete strangers."[82] As the number of Christians increased, the practice also developed of carrying letters of recommendation from one's bishop in order to become accepted in a new community, or to be received at a hostel for travelers. In the West the care of the poor and hospitality for travelers was a basic principle in the Benedictine *Rule*.[83] During the early medieval period the care of the needy and hospitality for travelers, as well as the instruction of the young, was virtually the sole province of monks.

We can see that the range of activity supervised by the bishops and other clergy continued to grow. The care of the needy became a regular responsibility of the clerical life, made more urgent in the West with the disruptions in society caused by the barbarian invasions and the complete dislocation of political stability. By the time of Gregory the Great (600) it was decreed that 25 percent of church revenues should be expended for charity. Just as earlier we noted the relationship between the Eucharist and charity, there was also a baptismal dimension. When Hippolytus interrogated the candidates for baptism and their sponsors, he did not inquire into their doctrinal beliefs, other than the recitation of the creed, but he asked, among other things, whether those who sought the sacrament had "honored widows, whether they had visited the sick, whether they have been active in well-doing."[84] At the risk of moralizing with history or romanticizing the past, one cannot help but wonder how many churches today would venture to make works of charity a condition for membership.

Chrysostom reminds us that not all was ideal, just as Tertullian earlier had chided some of his wealthy hearers for refusing to contribute to charity. But by the fourth and fifth century almsgiving for some had become an obligation removed from the liturgy and had simply become an onerous duty. Chrysostom exhorts his congregation, "You are not able to become propertyless? Give me your possessions. You cannot bear that burden? Divide your possessions with Christ. You do not want to surrender everything to him? Hand over half a share, even a third."[85] Some Christians responded that the poor were being cared for by the church's general treasury, or through their taxes, so why should they continue to give? Besides, they argued, many of the poor were so because of their laziness, and they were not sufficiently grateful for the gifts they received. In order to elicit sympathy and possibly guilt from his congregation, Chrysostom would have beggars sitting in a row in front of the church. "They sit here that they may also make you compassionate, that you may be inclined to pity."[86]

In the end it was a losing battle, as the bishop of Antioch lamented in concluding a homily: "I am ashamed to speak about alms, for though I have often discussed this subject, I have achieved no results worthy of the exhortation. A little more has come in but not as much as I wanted."[87]

Evidence from the early church indicates that Christians placed hospitality and care for the needy high in their priorities, and their enthusiasm for this work elicited admiration from those outside the faith. The office of bishop was entrusted with this work, and episcopal authority was in part based upon the collection and distribution of funds used for charity. Under the imperial church the care of the needy expanded and became institutionalized as the church became progressively coterminus with the state, and we find resistance to the quest for alms, just as there was dissatisfaction among recipients.[88] Regardless of the success or failures of the endeavor, the works of charity constituted a major element of the life of pastor and people.

Pastoral Life

"A bishop must be above reproach" (1 Tim. 3:2). Before all else, the pastor was to be a model of the Christian life, an imitator of the Christ one professed. Christian perfection may have been the obligation of every believer, but the pastor was held to the highest standards of sanctity. Ignatius used the criterion of behavior as one way to discern the false prophet from the true. "It is better for a man to be silent and be a Christian, than to speak and not be one. It is good to teach, if he who speaks also acts."[89] This theme of pastoral holiness runs throughout early Christian literature. Gregory's *Pastoral Rule* devotes twenty-five pages to it in a modern English translation. He should be pure in thought, exemplary in conduct, discreet in keeping silence, profitable in speech, a sympathetic neighbor to everyone, exalted above all others in contemplation, a companion of those who lead good lives, zealous for righteousness against the vices of sinners.[90] A pastor whose life does not embody his teaching cannot expect any parishioner to take his advice seriously.

The *Didascalia Apostolorum* (c. 200–225) devotes considerable space to the pastor's life. He is to be no less than fifty years old to ensure his immunity from the lusts of the flesh, although a younger man who is trustworthy may also be chosen. The pastor's wife must be a believer and beyond reproach, and his children should be well disciplined. He should be frugal in his food and drink, not a lover of riches, not quarrelsome or eager for advancement. He should be a friend of all, but preferring the company of the faithful to that of the heathen. He should be diligent in reading the Scriptures, and in his exposition he should be careful to distinguish between the law and the second legislation (gospel). In short, "As you have Christ for a pattern, so you also be a pattern to the people under your charge."[91] Origen, writing at the same time in the early third century, insists on the presence of the people at an ordination, "so that all might know and be sure, because that man is chosen for the priesthood who is more outstanding among the whole people, more learned, holier, more eminent in every virtue."[92]

But such an ideal could not be uniformly maintained among human clergy, and we read of many who fell short of these expectations. We can read between the lines of Jerome's satirical letter to Nepotian. He speaks of clerical businessmen who, after ordination, have used their office for personal gain. He warns against having woman live in the same house as a priest. "Always remember that it was a woman who ejected [Adam] from paradise" (chap. 4). It is dangerous to pay frequent attention to a woman's face, or to sit alone with one without a witness. He is especially scornful of pastors who seek to be popular or well liked. (We know from Jerome's life and writings that this was not one of his failings.) "A pastor who is often invited to dinner and does not refuse is easily despised" (chap. 15). He also castigates anti-intellectual clergy who pride themselves on their holy ignorance, but if one must make a choice, "a holy peasant is much better than a sinful scholar" (chap. 9). Jerome complains about the lack of care in choosing pastors, permitting some to be ordained who are so given to wine that they do not "give" the kiss of peace, they "pour" it (chap. 11). Finally, he speaks of sins of the tongue, being too ready to listen to gossip and to share it. "One household should not learn from you what is happening in another" (chap. 15). He concludes his letter on the qualifications of a pastor by warning that any who criticize him should first admit that they fit his description of an unworthy priest.[93]

We are not surprised that some priests did not live up to the expectations of their calling. But Chrysostom defends the clergy against unwarranted accusations made against them and the slander

of the people. The office of pastor is a demanding one, and he runs
the risk of offending people no matter how circumspect or saintly he
may be. In a *Homily on Acts* the bishop of Antioch elaborates on his
theme. The people easily pardon someone who gets angry, but the
pastor is not pardoned. "He is exposed to everyone's tongue and
everyone's judgment, both the wise and the stupid." Whereas a layman
will hesitate to spread rumors about someone in power or a wealthy
man, the pastor is an easy target, because he has no acceptable means
of defense. "No one is afraid of accusing and slandering him." If he
is tired from overwork, no one will give him consideration. If he
appears friendly, he is accused of fawning; if he appears reserved,
he is said to be coldhearted. The pastor has many burdens to bear—
the welfare of each soul under his care, the finances of the church,
the sins of the impenitent, and fidelity to sound teaching. It is in this
context that Chrysostom writes, "I do not think that there are many
among the priests who are saved; many more are perishing." The
reason they are perishing is because the demands of the office cause
them to neglect their own souls. Whereas others sin publicly and
privately, the pastor as a saint dare not even sin in private. To add
to his burden, some people will constantly bring to mind the virtues
of a former pastor. They do this not to praise him but to embarrass
the incumbent. He concludes by warning aspirants to the priesthood
to be realistic about the office. He says they are like civilians who
glorify war, but after experiencing the battle they understand its true
nature.[94]

We have seen that the church maintained ideals for the personal
qualifications of a pastor, however these may have failed in realization.
What, then, was the work of a pastor as he went about his daily tasks,
or burdens as Chrysostom called them? His first task was not to
function in any special activity as such, but simply to be an example.
The pastoral vocation included the ontological dimension—that is,
he was called to *be* someone as well as to *do* some things. He was to
represent Christ to the people, and as Christ's representative, he was
to exemplify Christlike virtues. The pastor's first and primary task
was simply to live in the community of the faithful; in modern terminology we would say as a role-model. In Gregory's advice to clergy,
he warned against excessive time spent in overt action and practice
to the neglect of inner discipline and spiritual formation. He was
critical of the activism that "delights in being hustled by worldly

tumults" and yet "remains ignorant of the things that are within."[95] The pastor's primary task was that of spiritual discipline. He was the principal "witness" for the congregation, and in times of persecution, it was often the clergy who were taken first, in the hope that a leaderless flock would scatter or apostacize.

Associated with his personal sanctity went leadership in worship. The bishop's role and authority derived primarily from the Eucharist and his presidency of the liturgy. However his office was understood in relation to the apostles, the pastor/bishop/presbyter alone was authorized to preside at the "sacred mysteries." This was true at least from the second century and possibly earlier, long before Augustine introduced the concept of indelible character into the theology of ordination. During the fourth century the Eucharist was celebrated daily, but this was also common in the second and third century. In later years the Eucharist and Vespers were expressly referred to as the "daily acts of worship" by Augustine.[96] The large collection of sermons we have from Chrysostom is partly due to the fact that he preached almost every day. In addition to the Eucharist and Vespers, services were also held early in the morning. Augustine found it necessary to encourage some men who attended the daily morning services, because when they arrived at their job they were ridiculed by their fellow workers for their piety: "You have been up to heaven like Elijah," or "You have your legs hanging out of the sky."[97] The men in question returned such mockery by denying they had been worshiping, and this was the occasion for Augustine's encouragement. The *Apostolic Constitutions* instruct the bishop to "command them to come constantly to church, morning and evening, every day, and by no means forsake it on any account."[98] Attendance at the daily services was not equal to that of the Sunday Eucharist, but it still required the presence of the pastor and often a sermon.

After conducting the morning worship, the pastor turned his attention to administrative tasks, which included the distribution of alms to the needy. This was a task delegated to deacons, but the pastor was ultimately responsible. We have seen that Augustine did not relish this task, for it was difficult to determine who were the truly needy, and there was sometimes dissatisfaction among recipients. Even in the third century the churches themselves had become charitable institutions with buildings and estates to maintain, under the direction of the clergy. On the anniversary of a bishop's ordination he was expected to give a dinner for the poor who were on the church roll. Caring for orphans cannot have been an easy task, especially when their wards turned out to be turbulent teenage girls.[99] Orphans would be taken into the bishop's household (we think of Athanasius who lived in the bishop's house from his youth) and the special care for waifs and strays is often mentioned in the epitaphs of bishops.

In addition to the supervision of charity, there was the administration of property, especially after the triumph of the church. Augustine disliked administration: "I call God as my witness and declare to you that I only carry on with the administration of church property against my will and look upon it as a hideous burden. If I could get rid of this task, I would do so."[100] After Constantine it was legally possible for the church to inherit property, which sometimes found bishops spending time in courts defending the church's rights. By the year 400 it was common practice in Syria for the devout to bequeath one-third of their estates to the church, while in the West it was customary to offer the equivalent of a child's share of the inheritance.[101] Augustine rebuked those who give to the church to the neglect of their own children.

After the care of the needy and the administration of church property, the bishop's time was devoted to serving as a judge. Arbitration became a major preoccupation of the clergy by the third century, as we find well documented in the *Didascalia*. In third-century Syria it was the rule to set aside every Monday for cases to be heard, giving the parties the rest of the week to be reconciled before the Eucharist of the following Sunday. Christians were not to take their grievances before a civil magistrate, nor were they permitted to admit pagan testimony against a Christian. The bishop is assisted by the presbyters and deacons, who are urged to keep both parties in friendship toward each other, and the bishop is cautioned to judge fairly, for he will ultimately be judged by Christ. Judgment should be tempered with mercy, the object being to save the person rather than destroy. The instructions go into great detail on methods of eliciting evidence, motivations, previous history, and mitigating circumstances. The overriding concern of the episcopal court was the reconciliation of the parties rather than "justice," which was secondary.[102] Constantine permitted civil cases to be transferred to ecclesiastical courts at the request of either party, but there was no appeal from a bishop's decision. Augustine found his duties as arbiter onerous and tiresome, and he observed that most litigants were at best only marginal members of his congregation and were contentious and quarrelsome people.[103] Furthermore, many cases involved the rich against the poor, in which a bishop would invite criticism no matter which way his judgment went.

Associated with the bishop's role as judge was the practice of the church as a haven for fugitives—that is, the right of asylum. This was sought not only by bandits on the run, but by debtors and runaway slaves. Asylum itself was a legacy from paganism, where the altars of pagan gods gave temporary protection to fugitives. We find parallels also in the Old Testament. Although the practice was subject to abuse and was not always respected, Augustine and Chrysostom defended it. Justinian finally decreed that asylum could be sought by all oppressed persons excepting criminals. Bishops in the fourth century were also, by virtue of their office, the *defensores civitatis* in each province, which meant they were to protect the populace, Christian as well as non-Christian, against unfair practices by imperial officials. "The role of the bishop as protector of the poor made him the natural leader of a large proportion of the urban population, and therefore a figure of political consequence. . . . In general the bishop was a figure that people wanted to like, and of whom they hoped that their expectations would be realized."[104] After Constantine bishops were normally given signs of public respect, such as the title "God-beloved," or rising when he entered a room.

We have seen that early Christians held celibacy in high regard, considering the gift of continence of greater value than marriage. This attitude also affected the life of the pastor, and the question of clerical celibacy was frequently debated in the early church. One of the roots of this teaching is found in St. Paul's statement that "the unmarried man cares for the Lord's business . . . but the married man cares for worldly things" (1 Cor. 7:32-33). Against this we have Timothy's description of a bishop as the husband of one wife (1 Tim. 3:2). A factor that may have contributed to the avoidance of marriage in the early years was a sense of Christ's imminent return, and to hold oneself in readiness for that event. The first Christian advocate of clerical celibacy was Tertullian, who wrote that "chastity has obtained the honor of ecclesiastical order," for those who have become wedded to God.[105] Charles Franzee believes the change that came around the year 200 in the West was caused by the growing demands on the cleric's time plus the association of liturgical effectiveness with moral chastity.[106] In the East, however, the older tradition of married clergy persisted in Ephesus and Alexandria. We have noted that the Syrian *Didascalia* assumed a married clergy, only insisting that the priest's wife must also be a Christian.

Mention has been made of the dominant influence exerted on the development of the pastoral office through the use of Old Testament models and precedent. "By contagion and imputation the eucharistic president himself became looked upon as at least analogous to the high priest of the Old Covenant and the spokesman of the entire royal priesthood, which is the church."[107] The association between sexual intercourse and impurity is ancient and can be found among Semitic peoples as well as in Hellenistic and Roman religions. In the Jewish tradition, priests who had intercourse were not only unclean for the whole day but were not permitted to eat any of the food offered for sacrifice.[108] The principal effect of such uncleanness was to prohibit the individual from performing any act of worship, and a ritual bath was required for the restoration to purity. Although priests such as Zechariah were married, during their time of duty in the temple they lived apart from their wives in order to assure the efficacy of their sacrifice. One of the most striking examples of the relationship between sexual abstinence and a valid Eucharist comes from Tertullian, who discouraged laymen from second marriages, because they may be called upon in an emergency to preside. "The simple solution is: do not remarry and, when a genuine necessity arises, you will have no problem. God wishes all of us to be ready at all times to administer the sacraments."[109]

At the local Council of Elvira in Spain (306) clergy were required to keep themselves from their wives and have no children. But the first general Council at Nicea (325) stopped short of this prohibition, insisting only that following ordination priests may not marry, nor should unmarried priests permit a woman to live with them in the same house. This was probably to halt the strange ascetic practice in which a priest and woman contracted a "spiritual marriage," sometimes even sharing the same bed, all the while insisting that their discipline was so heroic that they were above reproach.

Asceticism reached its flowering with the rise of monasticism during the fourth century, which was in part a reaction to the institutional church, which had become wealthy and had seemingly lost its spiritual direction. Monasticism was also a lay movement, somewhat in op-position to the clergy who now enjoyed status in the imperial church. Monks were the principal critics of the clergy, epitomized in Cassian's advice to "flee from women and bishops."[110] The hostility was recip-rocated by the clergy. Augustine had sharp words for the failings of the monks. In his essay *On the Work of Monks* he finds them unstable, beggars, eccentric, quarrelsome, shabby, and always in need of a haircut. But it was not long before the monastic ideal also influenced the clergy—that is, we find the monasticization of the clerical life. During the fourth and fifth centuries almost all the noteworthy bishop-theologians of the church had either been monks or had a strong affinity for the monastic life. This tendency reinforced the ideal of celibacy for the priesthood and made of monks and priests a spiritual elite. A further result was the practice of clergy living together in community, first attempted by Eusebius of Vercelli (d. 371) and made popular by Augustine, who lived in community with his clergy.

Clerical celibacy was the dominant ideal by the fifth century, yet the practice was not universally observed. Gregory of Nyssa, one of the great Cappadocian fathers, was married (although he later regretted it), and the father of Basil of Caesarea was a bishop. One of the priests in Augustine's church at Hippo had children, and Siricius, bishop of Rome (384–99), writes "we have learned that very many priests of Christ, and deacons, after a long period of dedication, have begotten offspring, both from their own wives and out of sinful unions."[111] Siricius was not especially pleased by this discovery, but it indicates that "very many priests" were married. In this same letter the pope permits the ordination of married men provided they henceforth live in continence. In 349 Emperor Constantius exempted all clergy and their children from all fiscal obligations in regard to their cities, and the Council of Seleucia (486) took a negative stand against the in-troduction of clerical celibacy. Basil, the father of Eastern monasti-cism, insisted on celibacy for his monks, but he permitted the bishops, presbyters, and deacons to keep their wives.[112] I have mentioned Jovinian's strong opposition to Jerome's deprecation of marriage, and the Council of Gangra (c. 345) aligned itself against the acceleration of asceticism. It anathematized those who refused the ministry of married priests and questioned the motives of many who espoused celibacy.

Despite these voices, celibacy became the ideal for the clergy in the West. In the East, clergy could marry prior to ordination but not thereafter, and bishops were required to be celibate. The ideal was not always realized, and throughout the medieval period in the West we read of married clergy, to the extent that in the sixth century a special blessing was included within the liturgy for the wives of married priests on the day of their husband's ordination. These wives were called presbyteresses and were entitled to wear special dress.[113] It was not until the eleventh century that Pope Gregory VII attempted to enforce the prohibition against married priests throughout the Western church.[114] One of the best descriptions of the pastor and his life comes to us in the eulogy that Gregory of Nazianzus delivered at the death of his father, also named Gregory, who had been bishop of Nazianzus. He was one hundred years old when he died, "with all his excellence, and all the skills of pastoral organization which he had gathered in a long time, full of days and wisdom." He came from humble origins and from a pagan family, but from his youth he displayed such superior virtue that "even before he was of our fold, he was one of us." The oration devotes considerable space to the equal virtues of Nonna, Gregory's wife and the orator's mother, who was present at its delivery. It was she who by her words and example turned the future bishop toward Christianity. She was his "teacher and leader in virtue," was thrifty and pious, constant in prayer, and kept herself aloof from all contacts with paganism. When Gregory finally consented to be baptized, divine epiphanies attended the rite to indicate God's approval. After a time he was ordained to the priesthood and assigned to "the woodland and rustic church" at Nazianzus in Cappadocia. His congregation apparently had reverted to un-Christian ways during the vacancy following the death of his predecessor, and by "words of pastoral knowledge and by his own example" he won the people away from their barbarism. Although he had become a Christian late in life, he was so assiduous in the study of Scripture that he soon was the equal or superior to those who had spent a lifetime in study. He lived during the height of the Arian controversies, but he never wavered from the orthodox faith. In his discourse he was not a polished speaker but plain and simple—"taking second place as an orator by surpassing all in piety." He helped to reduce the tensions caused by theological controversy through his evenhanded conciliatory approach, especially toward the "overzealous part of the church [i.e., monks]," who were causing tumults everywhere.

Gregory devoted much time to the work of charity, dispensing not only the church's funds but his personal resources as well, "for he thought it much better to be generous even to the undeserving for the sake of the deserving," rather than run the risk of denying the truly needy. Nonna was given the responsibility for overseeing the couple's own finances, which she did with wisdom and skill. The bishop and his wife displayed humility in their way of life, wearing plain clothing and being frugal in their diet. He was void of malice and bore no grudges; stern with sinners, but even then he displayed no anger, and he reproved with kindness. When Julian the Apostate demanded the surrender of the church building, Gregory successfully resisted the police who had been sent to take over their possession. He cared diligently for the sick, although he himself "was at no time free from the anguish of pain." The oration concludes with the admonition that these words are not intended for the wise and the proud, but only for those who "know they are mortals, following mortals to the grave."[115]

The pastoral life encompassed the requirements of holiness, together with the duties of worship, arbitration, the care of the needy, and supervision of the properties of the church. In addition to these tasks, he was the teacher of the flock through sermons and instruction, and he engaged in the care of souls through visitation of the sick, comforting the bereaved, admonishing sinners, and counseling those troubled in heart. It is to these aspects of pastoral life and practice we next turn our attention.

3 Pastor and Proclamation

From the beginning of the church the gospel message was proclaimed by the faithful wherever they lived or traveled. In his treatise against Celsus, Origen writes that "Christians do all in their power to spread the faith all over the world. Some of them make it the business of their life to wander not only from city to city but from township to township and village to village, in order to gain fresh converts for the Lord."[1] The spread of Christianity was accomplished not only by preaching as we understand it today, but through the testimony of countless unknown witnesses to the faith. The example of the martyrs and the lives of the Christians was compelling testimony that attracted a growing number of converts to the faith. But within the community it was necessary to nurture the faithful, to exhort, rebuke, discipline, and encourage. Pastoral teaching and preaching was crucial to the life of the church. Such proclamation included outreach to non-Christians, defending the faith against its critics, and the preservation of orthodox apostolicity against the threat of heresy, but the primary pastoral focus was teaching and preaching to the faithful, and it is to this aspect of pastoral life we turn our attention.

The Ministry of Teaching

Jesus, by word and example, gave his disciples the dual mandate to "preach the kingdom of God" (Luke 9:60), and to make disciples of all people by "teaching them to observe all things that I have commanded you" (Matt. 28:9). Jesus was first known by the title of rabbi, or teacher (John 3:2). *Kerygma* and *didache* were the key elements in proclamation, but it is not always clear that a formal distinction can be drawn between these two activities, or that they are limited to oral discourse. The pastor's life was to be as powerful a witness as his words, and the sacraments were visible testimonies—that is, proclaiming the Lord's death until he returns (1 Cor. 11:26). And yet the gospel had a content that went beyond mere ethics, which included the apostolic traditions as set forth in the apostolic writings and the Old Testament. Already within the writings of St. Paul we find early creeds intended to capsulize the content for purposes of instruction and worship. Converts to the faith, in addition to adopting the Christian way of life, were required to learn the rudiments of Christian teaching, and for this purpose the office of teacher emerged in the first two centuries. Such teaching was largely done during the period of the catechumenate that preceded baptism, and despite the presence of teachers designated for this task, by the year 200 the bishop/pastor was considered the primary teacher for his congregation. We have seen that the bishop's role as teacher was one of the factors in the emergence of the monepiscopate, and the pastor's chair in the apse of the church was a symbol of the teaching office. Chrysostom placed great emphasis on the pastor's role as teacher, insisting that simple piety was not enough for a leader of the church, for virtue was expected of all Christians. "Example is one thing and instruction is another."[2] One who was unskilled in teaching should not be ordained, for being "apt to teach" was a biblical requirement for the office.

The nature of the catechumenate varied in time and place, but its general outline can be reconstructed from the literature of the third and fourth centuries. Instruction was given daily, and it was open to all who chose to attend. The catechesis in Alexandria was attended by Jews and pagans as well as Christians, and so it also served the purpose of evangelism. The *Apostolic Constitutions* state that after the instruction has been given, all unbelievers must leave.[3] Cyril of Jerusalem composed his *Catechetical Lectures* bearing in mind the fact that not all those present were Christians. According to Hippolytus, the catechumenate lasted for three years, although this period could be shortened, "if a man be earnest and persevere well, because it is not the time that is judged but the conduct."[4] The Council of Elvira (c. 306) referred to a two-year catechumenate, and Justin's Code fixed it at this.[5] By the late fourth century it was reduced to eight months, and in some places to the forty days of Lent. On the other hand, under the imperial church some people remained catechumens most of their lives, preferring to postpone baptism until late in life because of the practice of treating postbaptismal sin with greater severity and the rigors of penance. The observance of Lent developed from the catechumenate as a period of intense instruction in the faith prior to baptism. The Lenten focus on Christ's passion developed much later.

The Apostles' or Nicene creeds, or their approximations, formed the basis of catechetical instruction. Augustine introduces his series of lectures by saying that "we have the catholic faith in the creed, known to the faithful and committed to memory, contained in a form of expression as concise as possible, that individuals who are but beginners and sucklings . . . should be furnished with a summary expressed in a few words."[6] The centrality of the creed in early Christian pedagogy is well attested. Theodore of Mopsuestia expounded the Nicene Creed in the first ten of his catechetical sermons, and Cyril of Jerusalem devoted thirteen of his lectures to it, insisting that every Christian must commit it to memory. Inasmuch as the catechumen was required to confess the creed at baptism, it was necessary to do so with intelligence and conviction.

In addition to the creed, catechesis included instruction in salvation history. Augustine wrote a handbook for clergy, *On Catechizing the Uninstructed*, in which he offers suggestions for the curriculum. "The narration must begin with the fact that God made all things very good, and must be carried down to the present times of the church in such a form as to assign to the several events the causes leading to the end of love."[7] This should include an account of the fall, the flood, Abraham, the exodus, the Babylonian captivity, David, Pentecost, and the work of St. Paul. Gregory of Nyssa in his *Great Catechism* includes these events but adds instruction on Baptism and the Eucharist. Most of the catecheses of the fathers include anecdotal material from the Scriptures to illustrate points of doctrine, so that biblical material became both content and method of instruction.

Instruction in the Lord's Prayer also formed part of the daily catechetical discourses. Origen used the prayer as the basis for his treatise *On Prayer*, and Theodore of Mopsuestia's catechetical homilies on the prayer emphasized the idea that prayer is not only petitions but includes one's entire life of virtue as an offering to God. Inasmuch as the catechumens were preparing for Baptism and for the reception of the Eucharist immediately thereafter, catechetical instruction included these sacraments. Ambrose's *De Mysteriis* and *De Sacramentis* are treatises on the sacraments given to those who were about to be initiated in baptism. Cyril of Jerusalem reserved his five lectures on the sacraments to the week after Easter, believing that such privileged information could not be entrusted to the unbaptized. Such was the content of pastoral instruction to the catechumens, consisting of expositions on the creed, biblical history, the Lord's Prayer, Baptism, and the Eucharist. Throughout these instructions we find a recurring emphasis on relating doctrine to life. It was the pastor's responsibility to offer classes on Christian teaching throughout the year, and with the influx of large numbers of converts in the fourth century, a considerable amount of time was devoted to teaching by the clergy.

The methodology of early Christian instruction is best illustrated by Augustine's handbook, Cyril's *Catechetical Orations*, and Chrysostom's *Address on the Right Way for Parents to Bring up Their Children*. Cyril prefaces his lectures with an outline of the course, adding, "You have entered into a contest, toil on through the race, attend closely to the lectures, and though we should prolong our discourse, let not your mind become weary."[8] He also warns his hearers that he will be "observing each man's earnestness and each woman's reverence," so that the stubbornness of unbelief be hammered out. Chrysostom also prepares his hearers for what is to follow. "He who is about to approach these holy and dread mysteries must be awake and alert, must be clean from all cares of this life . . . and banish from his mind every thought foreign to these mysteries."[9] Gregory of Nyssa proposed that instruction should proceed from the known to the unknown. In the case of a Hellenist, one should begin with the student's assumptions of deity and ideas of goodness. The instructor must diligently seek out points of contact between the teachings of the church and ideas already acceptable by the hearer. Instruction must vary with the needs of the learner. "We cannot use the same arguments in each case. A man of the Jewish faith has certain pre-suppositions; a man reared in Hellenism others. . . . You will not heal the polytheism of the Greek in the same way as the Jew's disbelief about the only-begotten God. We must have in view men's precon-ceptions and address ourselves to the error in which each is in-volved."[10] Augustine also insisted that instruction must be student-oriented: "With those who are slower of understanding we must pro-ceed by way of more words and illustrations."[11]

Augustine's guide to teaching contains many suggestions. A good teacher should stay close to the subject and not allow digressions. "You must keep on the beaten track," especially when instructing neophytes. With advanced students one may indulge in speculation, but the teacher's own doubts or peculiarities should be muted. Fre-quent summaries are encouraged, especially when the material is difficult or voluminous. Instruction should be concise and to the point.[12] One should make concessions to human frailties. "It is often the case that one who at the outset was listening gladly, wearied by listening or standing, opens his lips no longer in praise but in yawning." As soon as this happens, one should inject humor into the discourse, or offer him a seat. Augustine continues by saying that he had heard of churches "overseas" where the students sat during the instruction, and he thought it a good idea.[13] The catechist should also elicit a response. "We must discover by questioning him whether he understands, and must give him confidence to lay freely before us any objection that occurs to him." The teacher should then either explain more simply or refute the objections without using malice or sarcasm.[14]

Early Christian teachers were fond of illustrations. Chrysostom in very short order referred to wrestling, painting, marriage, the army, and the theater to illustrate the Christian's growth in knowledge.[15] Rufinus used the sun to clarify the doctrine of the godhead, a drowning man to speak of God's rescue in Christ, the phoenix to illustrate the virgin birth, and numerous references to classical mythology as points of contact for Christian truths.[16] But he cautions that "when examples or illustrations are used, the resemblance cannot hold in every par-ticular, but only in the one point for which the illustration is em-ployed."[17] Augustine recognized that discouragement is common to all teachers when students fail to grasp the message. He maintained that basic to all instruction is love for the student. "Let not the thought of the hen quit your heart, who covers her tender chicks with trailing feathers."[18]

Catechetical instruction was designed primarily for adults, but Chrysostom offered an *Address on Vainglory and the Right Way for Parents to Bring up Their Children,* which involved the clergy as well. He suggests that the primary goal of all education is not knowledge but the virtuous life. Such education is the primary responsibility of the father (parent) and not the church.[19] The child's soul is like a city or kingdom over which the parents draw up rules and establish disciplines. As to corporal punishment, "have not recourse to blows, and accustom him not to be trained by the rod." Good habits should be formed, as it takes only two months for bad habits to form. He encourages storytelling, for these excite the imagination and strengthen the bond between parent and child. When telling a story, preferably a Bible story, the child should be asked to repeat it to make sure it has been understood. The father should also "go and lead him by the hand into the church. You will see the child rejoice because he knows what the other children do not know," when he hears a familiar Bible story.

An interesting digression leads Chrysostom to expressing his opinions on naming children. They should not be named after their parents, for this is an implicit desire to perpetuate one's name, and hence a denial of the resurrection. Rather, name them "after the righteous— martyrs, bishops, apostles." In this way the child will have an ideal to follow. He places great value on the child's relationship to the pastor. "Let him often see the head of his church, and let him hear words of praise from the pastor's lips." Chrysostom concludes this delightful essay with a warning against mixing the sexes in education. Young men should be separated from young women, and the story of Joseph's temptation should be told frequently. As a boy grows to puberty, he warns that he will become interested in girls. "The medical guild tells us that this desire attacks with violence after the fifteenth year. How shall we tie down this wild beast? What shall we contrive? How shall we place a bridle on it? I know of none, save the threat of hell fire." Chrysostom's essay was part of his teaching ministry, an attempt to help parents in the spiritual nurture of their children.

Although the content of early catechetical instruction appears to have been highly doctrinal, the goal was education for a virtuous and sacrificial life. This can be seen in the prebaptismal questions put to the candidates, "whether they lived piously as catechumens, whether they honored the widows, whether they visited the sick, whether they fulfilled every good work."[20] Cyril reminded his hearers that baptism conferred newness of life, and the faithful Christian was one who constantly waged war against sin.[21] He said that "doctrines are not acceptable to God apart from good works."[22] Clement of Alexandria insisted that the goal of Christian education was "practical, not theoretical. Its aim is to improve the soul, not to teach, and to train it up to a virtuous, not to an intellectual, life."[23]

In addition to teaching converts to the faith, the pastor/bishop in the ante-Nicene church held daily sessions with his associates. Hippolytus informs us that the deacons and presbyters assembled each day to receive instruction by the pastor, "and after they have prayed, each should go to his proper work."[24] We do not know the content of such dialogues among the clergy, but only that they took place under the guidance of the pastor, whose responsibility it was to offer daily instruction in creed and doctrine, with the goal of nurturing the Christian life and the exposition of Christian theology.

The Christian Sermon

The Christian sermon was a direct development from Jewish synagogue worship, in which a text was read and then expounded. The Christian prototype was Jesus' inaugural sermon at the synagogue in Nazareth (Luke 4:16-21), where he read from Isaiah 61, "and he closed the book, and gave it back to the attendant, and sat down; and the eyes of all in the synagogue were fixed on him. And he began to say to them, 'Today this scripture has been fulfilled in your hearing.' " The synagogue itself was a development from the time of the Babylonian exile, where sacred writings were read and commented on, including the Torah (law or instructions) and the prophets. It was an instructive exposition, out of which grew a rich depository of literature known as the Targum, Midrash, and Haggadah. The early Christian missionaries used the synagogue setting to expound the message that the prophecies of the Hebrew Scriptures had now been fulfilled, and the Messiah had come.

But long before the Babylonian exile we find discourses of the prophets to God's chosen people based on revelation or, more frequently, calling to mind God's faithfulness in the past. "Not infrequently, as in Joshua's farewell address, the starting point appears to have been a recital of God's dealings with his people in times past, as well as a recollection of the covenant which made Israel the chosen people."[25] These reminders became the basis for an exhortation that encouraged the people to reform or to undertake their present responsibilities. These exhortations were "prophetic" in the sense that prophecy simply means to "speak for God"; the prophets' messages were prefaced with "thus says the Lord." Prophetic preaching was usually in the context of a moral or political crisis in Israel, and the people were called to repentance and to return to the Lord.

The Christian sermon was deeply influenced by such prophetic preaching. The early Christian prophets saw themselves as being in continuity with the prophets of the Hebrew tradition, and when the prophetic office coalesced with that of bishop/pastor, the tradition of prophetic exhortation was continued in the sermon. In addition to prophetic preaching as a legacy from Judaism, the Christian sermon was also liturgical. The Jewish homily was delivered in the synagogue as part of a service of worship. It was an ingredient in the cultus or pattern of offering praise to God. Unlike the later Christian sermon, which became the sole province of the bishop/pastor, the Jewish homily could be offered by anyone who may have been invited to do so, as Jesus was in Nazareth, or Paul and Barnabus on their journeys. It was this Jewish practice that prompted the author of the *Didache* to insist that when a Christian prophet was present, he should be permitted to give the sermon, although his message should be tested for its orthodoxy.

The sermon was prophetic and liturgical. It was also exegetical. Jesus spoke from a text. The starting point for every Christian sermon was to be a commentary on the lessons that had just been read prior to the address. As Justin writes (c. 160), "the memoirs of the apostles or the writings of the prophets are read, as long as time permits. When the reader has finished, the president [pastor] in a discourse urges and invites us to the imitation of these noble things."[26] Although such edifying discourses had their source in a text of Scripture, there was no guarantee that the preacher would be faithful to the spirit of the lessons that had been read. Expositors had a tendency to use the text for a topic the speaker already had in mind. But throughout the early church, the sermon was formally an explanation of the lessons that had been read in the service, with an application to the lives of the hearers. The Christian sermon inherited the legacy of Judaism in being prophetic, liturgical, and exegetical.

The Jewish-Christian homily was unique in the history of ancient religions. The classical Greco-Roman religions, devoted to the myths of the gods who resided on Mt. Olympus, were centered on ritual and various attempts to foretell the future, such as the oracle at Delphi. Responsibility for carrying out the rituals was given to the priests or priestesses, who meticulously observed the prescribed formulas for gaining the favor of the gods. Ancient religions were not a gathering of the people, but were focused on the god, as can be seen from the various remaining temples such as the Parthenon in Athens, which housed the god but were not intended for a gathering of people. Indeed, in many religions, entrance to the temple was forbidden to all except a few privileged priests, as we also find in the Jewish temple in Jerusalem. The mystery cults, such as that of Mithra, Isis, or Attis and Cybele, centered on the offering of sacrifices for the purpose of securing the god's favor. The official Roman religion was controlled by the state under the office of the Pontifex Maximus and was primarily intended to secure divine favor for the state. In none of these religions was there a gathering of the people for the purpose of hearing a message or reading from sacred writings. Indeed, the writings themselves were often held in such reverence that only the privileged few were permitted access to them. It was with the synagogue and the church that we first encounter religious buildings intended for all the people in order to hear a message.

This is not to deny the considerable influence of classical rhetoric on the Christian sermon. Plato in the *Phaedrus* and Aristotle in his *Rhetoric*, as well as Cicero and Quintillian, had developed the arts of persuasion, which found their fruition in the sermons of the fourth and fifth centuries. This can be seen, for instance, in the funeral orations, which closely followed pre-Christian patterns: "The Christian funeral oration is one of the most elaborate of Christian literary forms. It represents an attempt to adapt to Christian use a pagan Greek form with many hundreds of years of tradition behind it."[27] The Greek form followed a pattern of four ingredients: the epitaph, which recalled the life of the deceased, the encomium or words of praise, the lament, and the consolation. In his sermon at the death of his brother, Gregory Nazianzus followed this pattern, as did Chrysostom and Ambrose in their funeral orations. The only difference in the Christian funeral rhetoric from that of the pre-Christian orators was reference to Christ's resurrection from the dead, which was the focus of the consolation. This, admittedly, is a significant difference, for all the pagans could offer was reminder that time healed all wounds, and the mourners should take comfort in their fond memories of the deceased. But even when discussing the resurrection, Christian orators did not hesitate to use pagan models. Both Clement of Rome and Lactantius used the popular myth of phoenix rising from her ashes to offer evidence for the possibility of a resurrection.[28]

Classical rhetoric was also a model for the Christian homily in terms of style, arrangement, and delivery. Thomas K. Carroll suggests that the sermon of Melito of Sardis (c. 190) "is the first clear example of the use of rhetoric in preaching the Christian mystery," but unlike the Greek orators, rhetoric was at the service of the gospel and never an end in itself.[29] An example of such rhetoric from Melito's *On the Pasch* shows how he effectively uses repetition and symmetry to proclaim his message: "You have despised him who glorified you. You have denied him who confessed you. You have rejected him who proclaimed you. You have killed him who gave life to you."[30] By the fourth century some Christian preachers, notably Chrysostom, had developed the art of oratorical rhetoric to such a degree that the delivery of a sermon became an event for public entertainment. On one occasion Chrysostom scolded his congregation for their frequent applause, but his admonition was delivered with such flowery eloquence that they applauded his admonition. Chrysostom had studied rhetoric under Libanius, the leading pagan orator of the fourth century and the last non-Christian representative of the classical Greek style, which had originated with Demosthenes in the fourth century before Christ.

The Latin sermon found its most significant exponent in Augustine, who closely followed the style of Cicero. Although he did not discount eloquence, he followed the advice of Cicero, "an eloquent man should speak in such a way that he teaches, pleases, and persuades or speaks to the intellect, feeling, and will."[31] This means to explain, edify, and convert. Augustine suggests that preaching should not follow the same pattern but should be adapted to the occasion, the congregation, and the church. Generally the Latin sermon was less florid and ornate than the Greek, and more given to explanation than to a display of oratorical skill. Although the Jewish-Christian homily was unique in the history of ancient religions, the style and method of the Christian sermon was strongly influenced by Greek and Latin oratorical traditions.

The sermon was based upon a reading from the Scriptures, either that of the Hebrew Bible or the developing apostolic tradition, which by the time of Irenaeus (200) was known as the New Testament. From Judaism the church inherited the concept of the inspiration of the Scriptures, and that they were God's Word. "All scripture is given by inspiration of God and is useful for teaching, reproof, and correction" (1 Tim. 3:16). There is abundant testimony from the church fathers that the two testaments were not only considered to be exempt from error, but they contained nothing that was superfluous. Origen believed that there was "not one jot or tittle written in the Bible which does not accomplish its special work for those capable of using it."[32] This attitude of reverence for the Scriptures as God's Word in every part was basic to Christian preaching, as the task of the homilist was to offer a message with nothing less than divine authority based upon God's own revelation in the written word. The assumption of every sermon was that it was prophetic and that the preacher was delivering a message in harmony with God's will, based upon God's word. The exposition of the Scriptures and the application of its message to the lives of the people called for a method of interpretation, or of exegesis. An assessment of early Christian preaching necessarily includes a review of early Christian exegesis.

The earliest Christian sermons follow the example of Jesus' homily in the synagogue at Nazareth when he said "today this scripture has been fulfilled in your hearing." The prophecies of the Hebrew Scriptures were believed to have been fulfilled with the coming of Jesus. His virginal conception fulfilled Isaiah 7:14 (according to the Greek version); his birth in Bethlehem referred to Micah 5:1; Hosea foretold his return from Egypt (Hos. 11:1; Matt. 2:15). The Christian revelation was "according to the Scriptures," or "that the Scriptures might be fulfilled." The story of the two disciples on the road to Emmaus is instructive, for it indicates the church's conviction that the events of Christ's career were the fulfillment of what had been written "in the law of Moses, and in the prophets, and in the psalms" (Luke 24:25-48). Early Christian preaching began with the assumption that the Old Testament was "Christian" literature and could be understood only christologically. This conviction was reinforced in the struggle against Marcion, who refused to recognize the authority of the Hebrew Bible, because he rejected the authenticity of prophecy.

But the Old Testament contained much more than prophecy. It included the history of God's people and the unfolding of God's covenant with them. Early Christian sermons followed a method known as typology—that is, Old Testament events and people (antetypes) pointed to New Testament fulfillments or realization (types). Augustine said that "in the Old Testament the New is concealed; in the New the Old is revealed."[33] Examples of such interpretation include Adam and Moses as antetypes of Christ; the flood pointed to baptism, as did the crossing of the Red Sea; Old Testament sacrifices, especially that of Isaac, pointed to Calvary; the eating of manna in the wilderness foreshadowed the Eucharist; the raising of the bronze serpent was a type of crucifixion. The list is almost endless. One of the distinguishing features of typology was its insistence on the historicity of the original event—that is, accepting the literal truth of the Old Testament stories. Typological exegesis was especially characteristic of the church in Antioch, but it was also influential among the Latin preachers in the West.

Alongside typology, we find allegorical exegesis and preaching, with its center in the church of Alexandria. It proceeded from the assumption that the Bible was inspired in every word, but since some parts of the Old Testament appeared unsavory or even repugnant, there must be hidden meanings behind the words. Origen suggested that behind every word or event there were three interpretations: the literal or historical, which corresponded to the body; the moral sense, which offered a lesson for one's life and corresponded to the soul; and the spiritual sense, which spoke of the mysteries of the faith and the future life, corresponding to the spirit.[34] Origen was the master of allegorical exegesis. When the Psalmist cries, "Thou, O Lord, art my support, my glory, and the lifter up of my head" (Ps. 3:3), he explains that in the literal sense it is David who is speaking, in the second sense it is Christ, who knew that in his passion God would vindicate him, and thirdly, it refers to every righteous soul who by union with Christ would find one's glory with God.[35]

Such interpretations may have been edifying, but allegory tended toward condescension of the literal meaning and looked upon the text merely as a symbol for supporting preconceived notions. In fact, Origen was opposed to the literal sense. "Whoever should interpret the Scriptures literally had better class himself with the Jews rather than with the Christians."[36] To support his idea of the Fall as having taken place before the world was created, which resulted in Adam and Eve becoming enfleshed, Origen used the fig leaves of paradise. After they fell into sin, they were dressed in fig leaves (Gen. 3:7), which were the symbol of flesh. A popular allegorical treatment of the Good Samaritan in the early church which has been repeated in many pulpits into the twentieth century is that we are the man who fell among thieves, the thieves are sin and Satan, the Good Samaritan is Christ, and the inn represents the church. Christ's offer to pay all expenses suggests justification by grace. The literal meaning of the parable, of course, was to answer the simple question: "Who is my neighbor?"

Thomas K. Carroll suggests that through Origen "exegesis and preaching were so united that for long afterwards they remained one and the same. As preacher and exegete he was the foremost homilist of history's Christian mystery."[37] The use of allegory in early Christian preaching was widespread, both in East and West, including such notable Latin fathers as Ambrose and Jerome, though in his later years Jerome was sharply critical of its excesses. On the other hand, the earlier Latins were distrustful of allegorical interpretation. When Tertullian writes that "bad exegesis is no less worse than bad conduct," he had in mind the use of allegory.[38] The Antiochenes, led by Chrysostom, rejected allegorical preaching, for it denied the significance of history. Diodore of Tarsus warned that "we must be on our guard against letting the [interpretation] do away with the historical basis, for the result would then not be [legitimate interpretation] but allegory."[39] But elements of allegory prevailed in the West, and many medieval sermons quickly leave the scriptural text to indulge in flights of fantasy in no way related to the lessons. As with the influence of rhetoric on the Christian sermon, so also the use of allegory was borrowed from pre-Christian practices, notably the interpretation of the stories of Homer by moralists and rhetoricians. The exegesis of Alexandria was also under the considerable influence of the great Jewish scholar Philo (20 B.C.–A.D. 50).

The goals of early Christian sermons, as has always been the case, varied with the occasion. Basic to all homilies was the preacher's theology of the human condition, or malady, and the manner in which Christ's life, death, and resurrection brought salvation. Clement of

Alexandria believed that humans were basically ignorant of God, and the sermon was intended to provide illumination. Thus Christ served as the teacher of *Paedagogus*, the title of a book by Clement. For others who held to a similarly optimistic view of humankind, Christ was portrayed as the moral example after which one's life should be patterned. Where God was understood to be a judge and lawgiver, the homily offered a stern warning against sin and outlined a code of moral behavior. Early Latin theologians tended to view the human condition in terms of a debt owed to God, for which Christ had made satisfaction. Theologians in the West were generally more pessimistic about human nature, which they believed led people into sin and guilt, so their homilies spoke of forgiveness offered by Christ. Eastern theology understood the human condition more in terms of mortality, and salvation was defined in terms of the gradual divinization of humans (*theosis*) whereby the image of God was restored. Gregory I of Rome spoke often of God as the physician who came to heal human sickness.

One should be cautious not to draw the lines too sharply between East and West or among preachers, but it is not surprising that the preacher's theology of human malady and divine salvation would be reflected in his sermons, and there were several such anthropologies and soteriologies present in the life of the early church. After the catechumenate, the sermon was the primary medium for doctrinal instruction, as well as offering exhortation, encouragement, rebuke, praise, and consolation.

One difficulty we encounter in the study of early sermons is our entire dependence upon the printed word. We cannot experience the living word as it was preached. We can only imagine the situation of the hearers, the physical surroundings, the time of day, the dynamics of delivery, or the reception of the message by the hearers. In reading ancient sermons (or sermons of any age), such an imagination is necessary in order to capture the spirit of the occasion.

Preaching in the Ante-Nicene Church

The period before Nicea (325) is the time of persecution and of growth. Church buildings were not yet in existence, with a few exceptions we have noted, and congregations were relatively small and met in homes. The intimate surroundings suggest that the sermon was conversational and related more directly to the lives of the hearers than after Nicea, when large churches were crowded with many hundreds of worshipers. These surroundings lent themselves to displays of oratorical skill and polished eloquence. Unlike the Jewish synagogue, it was the pastor alone who was permitted to preach, which he did while seated behind the altar, facing the people, surrounded on either side by his assisting clergy. The chair was symbolic of the teaching office, which in later times became the bishop's throne. Both before and after Nicea, the people stood for the entire service, including the homily.

During the century following the death of Peter and Paul (70–170), we find very few examples of preaching. This may be due to its intimate and conversational style, which few considered to be worthy of preserving for posterity. The earliest postcanonical sermon we have is by an anonymous preacher commonly referred to as 2 Clement, who lived in Alexandria sometime before 150. His writing was included in the *Codex Alexandrinus* as having apostolic authority. Its purpose is to call the congregation to repentance, to urge them to steadfastness under persecution, and to challenge some gnostic ideas. "While we are on earth let us repent . . . by doing the Father's will and by keeping the flesh pure and by abiding by the Lord's commands, we shall obtain eternal life."[40] He encourages his hearers to be steadfast under persecution, and if not all are crowned (i.e., martyred), at least the rest should "come close to it." The homily contains strong statements on the reality of Christ's flesh. "If Christ the Lord who saved us was made flesh though he was at first spirit, in the same way we too in this very flesh will receive our reward."[41] The sermon contains the first clear reference to a "New" Testament on the level with the Old when the writer cites Matthew, Mark, and Luke as "Scripture." The *Homily of Clement* also asks the congregation to listen attentively to the sermon and not to forget its admonitions when the service is over.

Melito of Sardis also wrote in the mid-second century, and as we have seen his is the earliest example of flowery rhetoric in a Christian address. In his sermon *On the Pasch* he elaborates on the exodus as an antetype of Christ's resurrection. He describes the misery of the Egyptians:

By one blow the firstborn of the Egyptians fell—the first sown, the first begotten, the long desired—on the ground, not only the men but also the brute beasts. And in the plains of the earth was heard the bellowing of beasts mourning their young, the cow her sucking calf, the mare her colt, and the other beasts who had brought forth, groaning and bitterly bewailing their firstborn. And among men there was lamentation and beating of the breast at the disaster because of the death of the firstborn. The whole of Egypt stank of the odor of unburied corpses. It was a dreadful sight, Egyptian mothers with dishevelled hair, fathers distracted in spirit, wailing woefully in Egypt.[42]

We have no examples of Latin or Western preaching from the second or third centuries. Despite his exceptional contributions to theology as an apologist and theologian, Tertullian has left us no sermons, although he is credited with being the one who first gave the Latin word *sermo* to the Christian liturgical address. It has been doubted whether he was a presbyter (although Jerome said he was), which would account for this lack. Neither do we have sermons from Cyprian, who was bishop of Carthage (248–58), but who contributed numerous treatises in theology and discipline relating to various controversies. Clement of Alexandria (200) wrote several significant theological treatises and is called "the first Christian scholar" by Berthold Altaner,[43] but only one sermon has survived. This is his well-known address, *Who Is the Rich Man Who Can Be Saved?* It indicates that a growing number of wealthy persons were being attracted to the faith, and they were disturbed by the warnings against riches in Christian literature. Clement answered that wealth in itself was neutral; one's attitude toward wealth was what mattered:

For he who holds possessions and houses as the gifts of God; and ministers from them to the God who gives them for the salvation of men; and knows that he possesses them more for the sake of the brethren than his own; and is superior to the possession of them, not the slave of the things he possesses; and does not carry them about in his soul, nor bind and circumscribe his life with them, but is ever laboring at some good and divine work, should he be necessarily some time or other deprived of them, is able with cheerful mind to bear removal equally with their abundance. This is he who is blessed by the Lord, and called poor in spirit.[44]

With Origen (d. 254) we have an abundance of homilies by one of the most gifted teachers in the early church. Johannes Quasten says of him, "the outstanding preacher and teacher of the early church, a man of spotless character, encyclopaedic learning, and one of the most original thinkers the world has ever known."[45] About two hundred of his homilies are extant, most of them based on the Old Testament, excepting thirty-nine sermons on Luke, some on Hebrews, and his earliest homilies on John. It was Origen who gave the Greek term *homily* to the Christian liturgical address. The church historian Socrates says he preached every Wednesday and Friday, but Pamphilus, his biographer, claims "he preached nearly every day in the church."[46] Origen appears to be an exception in that he preached before he was ordained as presbyter or at least there was no careful distinction between preaching and teaching. His friends in Palestine attempted to regularize his preaching by ordaining him a presbyter, which alienated him from his own bishop in Alexandria, as the ordination took place outside the bishop's jurisdiction and without his permission. Eusebius records that Origen refused to permit stenographers to take down his addresses until he was over sixty years old, which means that most of his recorded sermons are from his Caesarean period (231–54).

Origen's sermons were often a running commentary on the text, where he would preach on an entire book of the Bible, verse by verse, over a period of time. As such, his sermons can also be categorized as biblical commentaries, so that in modern editions the same writing is sometimes referred to as a commentary or a homily. The word *homily* meant conversation or a mutual search for truth. Origen's homilies often began with a prayer that the Spirit would lead all present into the truth. It was not considered a unilateral pronouncement from the preacher, but a mutual endeavor with the people. He requested the prayers of the people, that "in answer to your prayers the Lord grant me understanding that we are worthy to receive the Lord's meaning."[47] Because the true meaning of the text was hidden under the literal sense, it was necessary to receive a special grace of insight. "Unless Christ himself opens our eyes, how shall we be able to behold the great mysteries that are fulfilled in the patriarchs and are figured by the nights, births, and taking of wives."[48] Although Origen was a man of profound faith and spiritual insight, he was also a Christian intellectual without peer, and at times he may have chafed under the accusation of asking too many questions and raising too many problems, by those who found superior virtue in a simple, unquestioning faith. In a sermon on Psalm 36 he addressed this issue:

> Watch this only, brethren, that no one of you be found not only not speaking or meditating wisdom, but even hating and opposing those who pursue the study of wisdom. The ignorant, among other faults, have this worst fault of all, that of regarding those who have devoted themselves to the word and teaching as vain and useless; they prefer their own ignorance to the study and toil of the learned, and by changing titles they call the exercises of the teacher verbiage, but they call their own unteachableness or ignorance, simplicity.[49]

The sermon actually re-presents Jesus in the midst of the congregation. When the hearers contemplate the message in the service, "your eyes can behold the Lord. For when you direct your loftiest thoughts to contemplate Wisdom and Truth, which are the Only Son of the Father, your eyes see Jesus."[50] The application of biblical teaching to the Christian life was by means of allegory. This is a segment of Origen's treatment of the raising of Lazarus:

> We recognize that there are some Lazaruses today, people who after intimacy with Jesus have lost strength and become dead and remained in the tomb of the dead. Afterwards they have been restored to life by the prayer of Jesus, and are summoned by Him with a loud voice from the tomb to the outer world. He who obeys Him comes forth, with the bands that betoken death and result from past sin bound about him, his eyes still bandaged.[51]

Origen continues to explain the text by describing the process of loosing Lazarus from his burial clothes as the process of penance, until the one who had spiritually died is restored to the life of the Spirit.

In another example of exegesis, Origen suggests that allusions to anthropomorphisms, such as God's anger, are not to be understood literally. "If you hear of God's anger and wrath, do not think of wrath and anger as emotions experienced by God." God is simply accommodating human language to serve the purpose of correcting human faults, as a human father corrects a child. "We too put on a severe face for correcting children, not because that is our true feeling but because we are accommodating ourselves to their level. If we let our kindly feelings show in our face . . . we spoil the child." But God is not really wrathful or angry, yet we experience the effects of wrath when we find ourselves in trouble on account of our wickedness, which is the discipline of the "so-called wrath of God."[52]

Ancient preachers did not hesitate to scold their congregations. At the end of almost a half-century that saw no persecutions, Origen delivered these words: "Nowadays we are not real believers at all. The days of real faith were the days when there were many martyrs, the days when we used to take the martyrs' bodies to the cemetery and come straight back and hold our assembly. . . . There were few believers then but they were real ones."[53] Shortly following this reminiscence of the halcyon days of persecution, Emperor Decius launched the first universal persecution of the church, in which Origen died as a result of torture. Lest we romanticize these early days of the church, Origen also scolds his congregation for its lack of zeal: "The church sighs and grieves when you do not come to the assembly to hear the Word of God. You go to church hardly ever on feast days, and even then not so much out of a desire to hear the word as to take part in a public function." He continues by saying that the greater part of their time, "nearly all of it in fact," is spent on mundane things. "But why complain about those who are not here? Even those of you who are, are paying no attention."[54]

In another sermon, Origen complains about people who leave following the reading of the lessons and do not wait for the homily: "Others do not know that the lessons are being read but stand in the most distant corners of the Lord's house and talk about secular things."[55] Later in the same sermon he faults hearers for not really getting into the spirit of worship, "while women think about their children, their needlework, and their household duties." He has words for the young, whom he has urged to apply themselves to the study of Sacred Scripture, "but as far as I can see, I am only wasting my time."[56] Origen understood the Fall into sin as having occurred by souls in a prebirth condition, with the enfleshment of souls at birth serving as a remedial punishment. Therefore it was improper to celebrate a birthday with rejoicing. "You will never find any of the saints celebrating his birthday, or holding a birthday party; nor keeping his son's or daughter's birthday as an occasion of rejoicing. Only sinners celebrate birthdays with rejoicing."[57] It may be that this way of thinking was one of the reasons for the long delay in observing Christ's birthday, which was not observed until well into the fourth century, and then as an anti-Docetic polemic called the feast of the incarnation.

Origen flourished in the first half of the third century, long before the controversy in the West between Pelagius and Augustine. His sermon on Romans, therefore, is interesting for it contains material that would be used by both sides in the debate over the role of good works in salvation. He sounds Pelagian when he comments on the natural man, "having the works of the law in his heart" (Rom. 2:10):

> If he [the non-Christian] keep justice or preserve chastity, or maintain prudence, temperance, and modesty; although he be alien from eternal life, because he does not believe in Christ, and cannot enter the kingdom of heaven, because he has not been born again of water and of the Spirit, still it seems, according to the Apostle's words, that the glory and honor and peace of his good works cannot perish utterly.[58]

Yet later in the same sermon he says:

> I can scarcely persuade myself that there is any work which can claim remuneration from God as a debt, since even the very ability to do, or think, or speak, comes to us from the generous gift of God. How then can he be in debt to us, who has first put us in his debt?[59]

For Origen, the exposition of Scripture called for illumination, a charism of grace, and the presence of Christ associated with the community at worship, including the homily. The sermon was the preacher's sacrifice. His style was devoid of rhetoric or elaborate eloquence; rather, he spoke in a conversational style as one would speak privately to a friend. This was unlike his younger contemporary, Paul of Samosata (c. 260), who had constructed a lofty throne from which to preach, and who scolded those who did not applaud his sermons, "or wave their handkerchiefs as in the theatre. He slaps his thigh and stamps on the dais."[60] This display of homiletical fervor was not normal for ante-Nicene preaching, and this description is part of a set of charges calling for his removal from office, which occurred in 268, accompanied with more serious accusations of heresy. The preaching of the first two centuries was primarily to awaken and renew faith, to expound the Scriptures, to encourage steadfastness under persecution, and to foster God-pleasing life.

Preaching in the Fourth and Fifth Centuries

The end of the persecutions following the conversion of Constantine witnessed a large number of converts to the faith, with the corresponding need to build more spacious churches. The large number of converts called for greater attention to the prebaptismal instructions and a more extensive catechumenate, as we have seen. The numerical growth of congregations occasioned more elaborate ceremonial, and the sermons became less conversational and more oratorical. The triumph of the church also found the clergy more involved with problems of society, with politics, and with the need to educate the masses of new converts. These concerns are reflected in the sermons of the post-Nicene period. It was also a time of great theological ferment, with debates over Christology, the Trinity, and the meaning of salvation. These controversies are also mirrored in fourth-century homilies. It seems doubtful that many Christians of this period would consider the sermon irrelevant to their daily concerns. We have such testimony from a source hostile to Christianity, Edward Gibbon, in *The Decline and Fall of the Roman Empire*. He writes: "The custom of preaching, which seems to constitute a considerable part of Christian devotion, was not a part of Roman temple worship," but now it was found everywhere. "The pulpits of the empire were now filled with sacred orators who possessed the advantage of not being questioned without danger of interruption or reply." But Gibbon grudgingly admits that preachers recommended the practice of social duties, exhortations to feed the poor, and living a life worthy of the God they worshiped. But it was not all focused on ethics and virtue. Sermons also dealt with "puerile rites, metaphysical subtleties, and the superstitions of their religion," so that congregations were inflamed by passion to oppose heresy and schism.[61] Whatever the prejudice of this critic, it appears there was a response to Christian sermons.

Because early Christianity flourished primarily among Greek-speaking peoples, we have few witnesses to the Latin sermon until later in the fourth century, although Tertullian and Cyprian produced Latin literature in the previous century. Among the oldest examples of Latin preaching are the ninety-three *Tractates* of Zeno of Verona (died c. 375). He does not offer specific texts for his sermons, and the Bible is used superficially. Among his sermons we find the most complete description we have concerning the art of baking bread in antiquity as an exposition of Jesus as the bread of life. He followed a form of typology in expounding the Old Testament, as seen in his treatment of Job: "As Job was tempted by the devil three times, so too Christ was tempted three times. The Lord set aside his riches out of love for us and chose poverty so that we might become rich."[62] Job became disfigured, as did Christ. As Job sat on a dunghill, so all the evil of the world is a dunghill, which was the Lord's dwelling place. And Job's restoration to health and prosperity foreshadowed Christ's resurrection.[63]

In Ambrose we have the most influential Christian personality in Italy of the fourth century. We have testimony to the power of his preaching from Augustine, who heard the bishop of Milan every Sunday, at first to study his use of rhetoric, but in time the message itself brought Augustine to baptism at the Easter Vigil in 387. Although we have ample testimony to the power of Ambrose's preaching, ninety-nine sermons attributed to him have been shown to be contemporary but not by him. Yet those that are considered genuine, such as his homilies on the six days of creation, show his use of allegory, and it was through this means that Augustine, who was sensitive to the linguistic beauty of classical literature and was repulsed by the Old Testament, was won over to the faith.

Ambrose as bishop was deeply involved in the political turmoil of his times, especially in his relationship with the emperor, Theodosius, whom he excommunicated for the massacre of seven thousand innocent citizens of Thessalonica. The emperor did public penance for his crime and was restored to Communion. In his funeral sermon for Theodosius, the bishop referred to the emperor's penance:

I have loved this man who esteemed one who admonishes more than one who flatters. He threw on the ground all the royal attire he was wearing; he wept publicly in the church, for his sin which had stolen upon him by the deceit of others; he prayed for pardon with groans and with tears. . . . What of the fact that when he had gained an illustrious victory, still because the enemy had fallen in battle he abstained from a participation in the sacraments, until he experienced the grace of

God. I have loved the man who in his dying hour kept asking for me with his last breath.[64]

This funeral sermon of Ambrose indicates the extent to which times had changed for Christian preachers. At least in the influential urban centers, they were persons to be reckoned with. Unfortunately, there are no extant sermons from the pastors who were serving the less distinguished parishes scattered in growing number throughout the empire, but the large number of aspirants to the Christian ministry in the fourth century indicates the attractiveness of the office, and its most visible manifestation was in preaching.

On one occasion, a synagogue at Kallinikum on the Euphrates had been set on fire by Christians, and the emperor ordered punishment of the guilty and compensation. Ambrose sent a letter to Theodosius asking him to pardon the incendiaries and cancel the compensation, as it was wrong for the church to give monies to the synagogue. At the next Sunday service, in the presence of the emperor, the bishop preached on the necessity of forgiveness and the perversity of the synagogue. After the sermon, Theodosius approached Ambrose with the words, "You preached about us today." Ambrose refused to continue with the Eucharist until the emperor canceled his orders, which he agreed to do.[65] Such was the respect of the emperor for the authority of the church and the power of the preacher of Milan.

We have already referred to Ambrose's sermons to the catechumens. In these addresses he introduced the idea into the West that in the Eucharist the bread and wine are changed into Christ's body and blood through the power of the words of institution: "The Lord Jesus himself proclaims, 'This is my body.' Before the blessing of the heavenly words another nature is spoken of, after the consecration the body is signified. He himself speaks of his blood. Before the consecration it has another name, and after it is called blood."[66] The conversion is as certain and complete as was the change of Moses's staff into a serpent.

Jerome (d. 420) is best known for his many commentaries on the Scriptures, his letters, his translation of the Bible into Latin (Vulgate), his staunch defense of celibacy, and his testy personality. His fame and legacy is as an exegete and not as a preacher, although we have ninety-six of his sermons, including fifty-nine homilies on the Psalms. In his homilies, Jerome follows the style of Origen by explaining the text, verse by verse, and making his application. In a Christmas sermon he explains that the manger reminds us of prophecy, and the lack of room in the inn means the world's sinfulness left no place for the Christ to be born. "He is born on a dunghill [i.e., stable] in order to lift up those who come from it; 'from the dunghill he lifts up the poor' (Ps. 112:7). He is born on a dunghill where Job, too, sat and afterwards was crowned." The shepherd keeping watch is an exhortation to vigilance, for it is only those who remain alert who will find faith, as well as be on guard against the wolves of sin. So they went with haste, "the ardent longing of their souls gave wings to their feet." The fact that they found Mary and Joseph with the child is proof of the virgin birth, because, says Jerome, had they been married, ancient writers would have said Joseph and his wife. "Let us continue our adoration of him today. Let us pick him up in our arms and adore him as the Son of God." Jesus became human to save humans. "Whatever of man's nature he did not assume, he could not save." Thank God for this festival of Christ's true humanity.[67]

This is a straightforward exposition, accepting the text as it stands, explaining what it meant literally and then offering an application for the hearer. The interpretation, edifying though it may be, reflects imagination tinged with allegory. On Psalm 1, the hearer asks, How can one meditate day and night? When does one sleep? Jerome replies:

> Meditation on the law does not consist in reading, but in doing. Even if I merely stretch forth my hand in almsgiving, I am meditating on the law of God; if I visit the sick, my feet are meditating on the law of God; if I do what is prescribed, I am praying with my whole body what others are praying with their lips.[68]

Jerome preached all of his homilies to the monks in Bethlehem and not to a large congregation, which may account for their appealing conversational style; they were delivered in a small, intimate group.

In a letter to Nepotian, Jerome offers some advice on preaching, which apparently he also followed: "Let the presbyter's preaching be based on his reading of the Scriptures. I do not want you to be a declaimer, or argumentative, or long-winded. To pour out words and to arouse admiration among the inexperienced crowd by the swiftness of one's speech is typical of unschooled men." He continues by saying that too many preachers shamelessly explain what they do not know, and in the end convinced themselves that their foolishness is truth. He found fault with Gregory of Nazianzus for privately admitting that the applause of the congregation convinced him that what he was saying must be true. Jerome cautions that "nothing is easier than deceiving a simple congregation or an uneducated assembly with a fluent tongue; whatever they do not understand they admire all the more."[69] The Latin homilies of the post-Nicene period were generally more textual and less flowery than those in the East.

Our review of the Greek homily in the fourth century should logically begin with Athanasius. Prolific as he was in writing treatises, letters, and works of dogma, we have none of his sermons. This seems strange, for he was bishop of Alexandria for forty-five years, and despite five exiles, he was the weekly preacher in his home church for extended periods of time. From his other writings we know he had a passion for salvation; soteriology is at the heart of everything he wrote, especially in his controversy with the Arians. His theology has been summed up in his own famous words, "the Son of God became man in order that we might become as god [or deified]."[70]

Gregory of Nazianzus (d. 389) was an orator without peer, well versed in the classic art of rhetoric, and was called by the Byzantines "the Christian Demosthenes." We have only one textual homily from him; the rest are the forty-five theological orations in addition to the panegyrical orations, sermons for feasts and funeral addresses or encomiums. In the latter, Gregory follows a style that was centuries old, going back at least as far as Pericles' funeral oration in (450 B.C.). We have already considered the oration he delivered at the death of his father (chap. 2). His oration at the death of his friend Basil of Caesarea extends for over seventy pages in a modern translation, and one cannot help but marvel at the stamina of both speaker and hearer on such an occasion.

He begins with a detailed account of Basil's life, his parents, his youth, education, and ministry. Then beginning with Abraham, he compares him with biblical heroes, including Jacob, Joseph, Moses, Aaron, Joshua, Samuel, and many more. Here is what he says about Jacob's ladder:

> I praise the ladder of Jacob and the pillar which he anointed in honor of God, and his wrestling with Him—whatever its nature was. It was, I believe, the contrast and opposition of man's lowly condition in relation

to the sublimity of God, and from that struggle he bears also the marks of the defeat of his race. I praise also Jacob's skill and success with his flocks and the twelve patriarchs born of him.

Having drawn this portrait of Jacob, Gregory makes the application:

But I praise also the ladder of Basil, which he mounted by his gradual ascents in virtue, and the pillar which he did not anoint but erected to God, branding the teachings of the impious. I praise the contest [wrestling] which he undertook, not against God but in behalf of God, to overthrow the heretics. I praise his pastoral skill by which he enriched himself, gaining a greater number of the marked than the unmarked sheep. I praise his glorious fruitfulness in children begotten according to God [i.e., as Jacob's twelve sons] and the blessing he was to many.[71]

As with many encomiums, the address is to Basil: "This is my tribute to you, Basil, from a tongue that was once most sweet to you. . . . May you look down upon us from on high, O divine and sacred soul . . . inspire us with courage." In this oration Gregory utilized the classical form of consolation through the eulogy, praise of the deceased, comparing him with the heroes of faith, and concluding with a direct address to Basil.

In his encomium on the death of his own brother Caesarius, Gregory offers this consolation:

Let us not then bewail Caesarius, knowing from what evils he has had his release. . . . Caesarius will not rule? No, but neither will he be ruled by others. . . . He will not gather wealth? No, but neither will he suffer loss to his soul by always seeking to acquire [wealth]. . . . He will make no display of the doctrines of Plato or Aristotle . . . but neither will he be worried about solving their specious arguments.[72]

Gregory's theological orations addressed the burning issues of the day, questions of Christology and Trinity. He was one of the principal architects and defenders of the procession of the Holy Spirit from the Father. A group called the Pneumatomachians (fighters against the Spirit) argued that if the Spirit were begotten of the Father, then there are two sons; but if the Spirit were begotten of the Son, then he is the Father's grandson. To which Gregory responded:

He [the Spirit] is not a creature, in that he proceeds from such a source; he is not a son, in that he is not begotten: he is God in that his status is between unbegotten and begotten. What then is "procession"? If you will explain the Father's ingeneracy, I will give you a scientific account of the generation of the Son and the procession of the Spirit, and let us both go crazy for peering into the mysteries of God. Who are we to pry into such matters? We cannot understand what is in front of our noses; the sands of the seashore, the drops of rain, the days of endless time. Still less can we penetrate the depths of God. [73]

Next to Chrysostom, Gregory was the early church's greatest orator. He resigned from his position as bishop of Constantinople during the second ecumenical council in 381, and vowed never again to attend a church convention, which reminded him of the cackling of geese and cranes. "The truth is, my inclination is to avoid all assemblies of bishops, because I have never seen any council come to a good end." Rather than solve problems, councils increase them. They are full of contention, pious irrelevance, and political posturing. [74]

A vision reported by Gregory, describing a celestial service, may be a reflection of his own earthly experiences as pastor and preacher. It is evening, and the congregation has assembled in his church of Anastasia in Constantinople, which is brilliantly lighted. He is seated on the bishop's throne, with the elders and other dignitaries ranged below him. The deacons and other assistants are wearing white robes, while the people, like a swarm of bees, struggle to get close to the front. The virgins and noble women listen with deep attention from the gallery. With a powerful voice and fiery soul, he preached about the doctrine of the Trinity, while some stormed, some fretted, and some openly opposed, and some were sunk in deep meditation, so the congregation resembled a tumultuous sea, until his words began to work on them, and as he called across the tumult, there was a deep calm. [75]

Basil of Caesarea (d. 379) was a close friend of Gregory of Nazianzus, as we have seen, and with Gregory he was one of the three great Cappadocian fathers. He is better known for his active role in monasticism and charity than as a preacher. Nevertheless, we have nine long *Homilies on the Hexaemeron*, the first chapter of Genesis, which are concerned with the literal sense of Scripture, thirteen devotional homilies on Psalms, and twenty-three assorted orations, sermons, and panegyrics on the martyrs. We are not surprised to find that one who gave himself to the care of the needy, and who taught simplicity of life, would preach these words:

> I am filled with amazement at the invention of superfluities. The vehicles are countless, some for conveying goods, others for carrying their owners; all covered with brass and silver. There is a vast number of horses whose pedigrees are kept like men's, and their descent from noble sires recorded. . . . Of household servants the number is endless, who satisfy all the desires of men's extravagance; agents, stewards, gardeners, craftsmen, skilled in every art; cooks, confectioners, butlers, huntsmen, sculptors, painters, creators of pleasure of every kind.
>
> You who dress your walls and let your fellow creatures go bare, what will you answer your Judge? You who harness your horses in splendor, and despise your brother if he is ill-dressed; who let your wheat rot and will not feed the hungry?
>
> If you have a wealth-loving wife, the plague is twice as bad. She keeps your luxury ablaze, she goads your superfluous appetites. No fortune is vast enough to satisfy a woman's wants.[76]

In his sermons on creation, Basil strictly follows the text, verse by verse, but his applications are often creative: "In the beginning" implies "that the world was not devised at random or to no purpose, but contributes to some useful end." Beginning is not yet the finished product, but has within it potential for growth, just as the foundation of a house is not yet the house. Basil takes this occasion to attack the Manichees, who taught that God and the cosmos existed side by side from eternity. The general theme of this first sermon, as it is with the entire series, is to extol the glory of God as Creator, and to speak of the rationality and order that underlie the world and its governance.[77]

When Basil speaks of the creation of birds, he shows his knowledge of the habits of the swallow, and combines it with his concern for the poor:

> Let no one bewail his poverty; let no one who possesses little at home despair of his life, when he looks at the inventiveness of the swallow. When building her nest, she carries the dry twigs in her beak, and not being able to raise the mud in her claws, she moistens the tips of her wings with water, then rolling in the very fine dust, she thus contrives to secure the mud. After gradually fastening the twigs of wood to each

other with mud as with some glue, she raises her young in this nest. . . .
Let this warn you not to turn to evil-doing because of poverty, nor in
the harshest suffering to cast aside all hope and remain idle and inactive,
but to flee to God; for, if he bestows such things upon the swallow, how
much more will he give to those who call upon him with their whole
heart?[78]

Throughout this section of the *Hexaemeron*, Basil uses the various
habits of God's creatures to teach a moral. The turtledove is faithful
to its spouse, but the eagle is irresponsible toward its young, and all
birds with crooked talons are cruel. The crow is a good example of
love for one's offspring.[79] It is no wonder that Basil's sermons have
been an important source for our knowledge of ancient science.

We have seen that Basil accepts the text as it stands, and he finds
his interpretation in the historical or literal understanding of the text.
He was critical of allegory: "Those who do not admit the common
meaning of the Scriptures say that water is not water, but some other
nature. . . . When I hear 'grass' I think of grass, and in the same
manner I understand everything as it is said."[80] Not only did he avoid
allegory, but his sermons are straightforward, without the rhetorical
flourishes or oratorical finesse of a Gregory or a Chrysostom.

Gregory of Nyssa (d. 394), the third great Cappadocian theologian,
was the younger brother of Basil and a friend of Gregory Nazianzen.
He served as bishop in Nyssa and Sebaste, and was held in great
esteem at the imperial court, where he delivered the funeral orations
at the death of the empress and her daughter. Together with his fellow
Cappadocians, Gregory was deeply involved in the christological and
trinitarian controversies of the fourth century. In addition to his numerous treatises, of which the best known is his Great Catechism
(*Oratio Catechetica Magna*), we have eight homilies on Ecclesiastes,
eight homilies on the Beatitudes, five on the Lord's Prayer, and fifteen
on the Song of Songs, in addition to panegyrics on the martyrs and
saints, and funeral orations. He occupies a more important place in
the history of dogma than in the history of preaching, but above all
he is a pioneer in the history of Christian mysticism. His preaching
is often occupied with doctrinal issues, and there is some question
whether the sermons were all actually given to a congregation. In his
style he is more florid than Basil, and reflects more the eloquence of
his namesake in Nazianzus.

We see Gregory's pastoral concern reflected in his introduction to the Lord's Prayer:

> The present congregation needs instruction not so much on how to pray as on the necessity of praying at all, a necessity that has not yet been grasped by most people. In fact, the majority of men grievously neglect in their life this sacred and divine work which is prayer. . . . Men give their attention to everything else, but no one devotes his zeal to the good work of prayer.[81]

Gregory's exuberant use of symbols is reflected in his description of the priest who leads in prayer, who must be adorned with the virtues (clothing) of the Old Testament priests. This is included in his explanation of "thy kingdom come":

> He who has prepared himself so that he may boldly call God his Father is precisely he who is clad in such a robe as described in this sermon. He rings with bells and is adorned with pomegranates; his breast shines with the rays of the commandments, and he bears on this shoulders the patriarchs and prophets themselves instead of only their names; for he has made their virtues his adornment. He has placed on his head the crown of justice and soaked his hair with heavenly adornment; he dwells in the super-celestial "hiddenness" which is hidden to all profane thought and truly inaccessible.[82]

Gregory follows his brother, Basil, in exposing the pretensions of the proud. In a sermon on the Beatitudes he suggests that the Sermon on the Mount was a symbol of Christ's vantage point in being far above humans, so that he is able to discern our real nature. Then he continues on pride:

> You pride yourself on your youth, you look at the prime of your age and are pleased with your handsome appearance, because your hands can move freely and your feet are nimble, because your curls are blown about by the breeze. You are proud because your clothes are dyed in brilliant purple and you have silk robe embroidered with scenes from war or hunting or history. Perhaps you also look at your carefully blackened sandals delightfully adorned with elaborate needlework patterns. At these things you look—but at yourself you will not look. Let me show you as in a mirror who and what sort of person you are.[83]

He then takes a verbal tour of a cemetery, and asks where the glory and pride has gone. "Where in these bones are all these things about which you are now so greatly puffed up?" He concludes by suggesting that his hearers are living in the shadows, they have no sense of the reality of things, and their lives are being lived as in a dream, exchanging "hallucinations" for the truth.

John Chrysostom

John of Antioch (d. 407) is without peer as the preacher of antiquity. He was educated under the great pagan orator Libanius, at Antioch. For about eight years he was a hermit, and from 381 to 398 served as presbyter in Antioch, from where he was called to become the bishop of Constantinople during a time of great political and ecclesiastical turmoil. Because of his outspoken criticism of the imperial house, he died during exile, while on a forced march calculated to hasten his death. After his death he was given the title of golden-tongue (Chrysostom). Hans von Campenhausen writes of him, "The homilies of Chrysostom are probably the only ones from the whole of Greek antiquity which at least in part are still readable today as Christian sermons. They reflect something of the authentic life of the New Testament, just because they are so ethical, so simple, and so clear-headed."[84] He preached every Sunday and saint days in addition to several weekday services for sixteen years in Antioch, which accounts for the eight hundred homilies extant. English readers can find his sermons collected in fourteen volumes of the *Nicene and Post-Nicene Fathers*. Many Christians today often repeat Chrysostom's invocation:

> Almighty God, unto whom all hearts are open, all desires known, and from whom no secrets are hid; cleanse the thoughts of our hearts by the inspiration of your Holy Spirit, that we may perfectly love you, and worthily magnify your holy name, through Christ, our Lord.[85]

Chrysostom represented the flowering of Antiochene exegesis with its emphasis on the text of Scripture, characterized by sobriety and restraint, but delivered with all the oratorical skill of the Greek tradition, which he had learned from Libanius. The power of his sermons was attributable in part to his zeal for souls and love for his congregation. Already before his ordination as a priest he wrote a book, *On the Priesthood*, in which he devotes two of the six chapters to the art of preaching. His observations are as fresh and timely today as when they were first written in the fourth century.

He cautions would-be preachers of "the great toil which is expended upon sermons delivered publicly to the congregation" (5:1), for which the congregation may give them scant credit, "assuming the role of spectators sitting in judgment." The people, he says, often come not to be instructed but to be entertained. "Most people usually listen to a preacher for pleasure, not profit, as though it were a play or a concert." Indeed, despite his love for the people, his expectations are low. "It generally happens that the greater part of the church consists of ignorant people. . . . Scarcely one or two present have acquired real discrimination" (5:6). The preacher must develop a contempt of praise, but also strive for eloquence (5:2). "I do not know when anyone has ever succeeded in not enjoying praise" (5:4), but it is the beginning of the pastor's downfall when he actually believes the compliments people shower on him. The art of eloquence is not given by birth, but the preacher must "cultivate its force by constant application and exercise" (5:4). And if he often succeeds, "he is not allowed sometimes not to succeed—the common experience of the rest of humanity," but not of the preacher. He cautions against the envy of fellow clergy when one does succeed, and the jealousies among the clergy of one who is a gifted preacher. "It requires no ordinary character but one of steel for a man who holds a superior position to be excelled by his inferiors and bear it with dignity" (5:8). He says that a "passion for oratory has recently infatuated Christians" (5:8):

> How, then, can anyone endure the deep disgrace of having his sermon received with blank silence and feelings of boredom, and his listeners waiting for the end of the sermon as if it were a relief after fatigue; whereas they listen to someone else's sermon, however long, with eagerness, and are annoyed when he is about to finish and quite exasperated when he decides to say no more?[86]

Chrysostom apparently did not have this problem, as his sermons were sometimes two hours long, and the people still called for more. He gained strength from his preaching:

> Preaching improves me. When I begin to speak, weariness disappears; when I begin to teach, fatigue too disappears. Thus neither sickness

itself nor indeed any other obstacle is able to separate me from your love. . . . For just as you are hungry to listen to me, so too I am hungry to preach to you. My congregation is my only glory, and every one of you means much more to me than anyone of the city outside.[87]

Perhaps the best known of Chrysostom's sermons was the series of twenty-one homilies he preached after some imperial statues had been torn down during a riot in Antioch. While the bishop, Flavian, was in Constantinople begging mercy for the city, the people were living in fear of reprisals. For two months the people flocked to hear Chrysostom's words of censure and of hope. On Easter Day, 387, Flavian returned with a full pardon:

> Blessed be God, through whose goodness we celebrate this holy feast with such gladness and rejoicing; he has restored the head to the body [i.e., Bishop Flavian], the shepherd to the sheep, the master to his disciples, the high priest to the clergy. Blessed be God who has done for us far more than we asked or hoped for. . . . Let us thank God for our present safety and for the danger he allowed, since we know that he ordered all things for our good.[88]

When reference was made to thank God for the danger, Chrysostom was no doubt referring to the agonizing soul-searching and repentance that resulted from the crisis, and the multitudes who flocked to the church.

His homilies on repentance reveal his understanding of the gospel:

> Have you sinned? Go into church and wipe out your sin. As often as you fall down in the marketplace, you pick yourself up again. So too, as often as you sin, repent of your sin. Do not despair. Even if you sin a second time, repent a second. Do not by indifference lose hope entirely of the good things prepared. Even if you are in extreme old age and have sinned, go in, repent! For here there is a physician's office, not a courtroom. [The church] is not a place where punishment of sin is exacted, but where the forgiveness of sin is granted. Tell your sin to God alone: Before you alone have I sinned, and I have done what is evil in your sight. And your sin will be forgiven you.[89]

Much of Chrysostom's preaching was directed toward the worldliness of society and the sins of his hearers, preaching that today is sometimes called prophetic. But, as in the previous selection, he encouraged his congregation to take heart:

> My reproach of you today is severe but I beg you to pardon it. It is just that my soul is wounded. I do not speak in this way out of enmity but out of care for you. Therefore I will now strike a gentler tone. . . . I know that your intentions are good, and that you realize your mistakes. The realization of the greatness of one's sin is the first step on the way to virtue. . . . You must offer assurance that you will not fall into the same sins again.[90]

Chrysostom preached eighty-eight homilies on the Gospel of John, which are shorter than others, each taking less than a half-hour to deliver. In the following excerpt he indicates his desire that people prepare themselves for the sermon:

> I want to ask a favor of all of you before I turn to the Gospel. Do not refuse my request, for I ask nothing difficult or burdensome of you. . . . What then do I ask of you? That each of you take in hand that part of the Gospels which is to be read in your presence on the first day of the week. Sit down at home and read it through; consider often and carefully its content, and examine all its parts well, noting what is clear and what is confusing. From such zeal there will be no small benefit to you and to me.[91]

This not only suggests that his listeners were literate, but also that they possessed their own copies of the Gospels.

Shortly after his series on John, Chrysostom preached thirty-two sermons on Romans, which were later used by Augustine to demonstrate that Chrysostom could not be accused of sympathy for the Pelagians. He may have had this excerpt in mind:

> What is it that has saved you? Your hope in God alone, and your having faith in him in regard to what he promised and gave. Beyond this there is nothing that you have contributed. If, therefore, it was this [hope and faith] that saved you, hold fast to it even now. . . . Since it found you dead and ruined and a prisoner and an enemy, and made you a friend and a son and a freedman and righteous and a joint heir, how after such liberal generosity and establishment of friendship, could it disappoint you in the future? What is hope? Confidence in the things to come.[92]

As we have seen, Chrysostom was tireless in preaching about social responsibility. To the rich he said, "You say you have not sinned yourselves. But are you sure you are not benefiting from the previous crimes and thefts of others?"[93] In the same sermon he says, "When your body is laid in the ground the memory of your ambition will not be buried with you, for each passerby as he looks at your great house will say, 'What tears went into the building of that house! How many orphans were left naked by it, how many widows wronged, how many workmen cheated out of their wages.' Your accusers will pursue you even after you are dead."[94] On another occasion he said, "I am going to say something terrible, but I must say it. Treat God as you do your slaves. You give them freedom in your will: then free Christ from hunger, want, prison, nakedness."[95] On Chrysostom's social concerns, his principal modern biographer, Chrysostomus Bauer, comments, "In the 90 sermons on the Gospel of Matthew, Chrysostom spoke 40 times on almsgiving alone; he spoke some 13 times on poverty, more than 30 times on avarice, and about 20 times against wrongly acquired and wrongly used wealth; all in all, about 90 or 100 sermons on the social themes of poverty and wealth."[96]

An example of such indignant invective against pretentious wealth is from his sermons on Matthew:

> Oh! The sheer horror of money which drives many of our brethren from the fold! For it is nothing but that grievous disease, that never quenched furnace, which drives them hence; this mistress more ferocious than any wild barbarian or beast, fiercer than the very demons, taking her slaves with her, is not conducting them round the Forum, inflicting upon them her oppressive commands, nor suffers them to take a little breath from their destructive labors.[97]

Chrysostom had his critics, both ancient and modern. The historian Socrates, writing in the next generation and who was sympathetic to him, said that he had "too great a latitude of speech."[98] A modern scholar, W. H. C. Frend, says, "His assertiveness and quick fire of rhetorical questions could hardly have won him friends. Added to this he was tactless toward colleagues. Visiting bishops were not entertained as they thought they ought to be. Too much promotion was given to monks."[99] These references are to his tenure as bishop of Constantinople.

Chrysostom spoke fearlessly and perhaps without tact, especially when he was addressing the nobility. It was his ultimate undoing when in Constantinople he spoke of the empress: "Again Herodias raves; again she rages; again she dances; again she asks for the head of John [Chrysostom] upon a charger." His reward for his courage and forthright candor was exile and death, but not before he said this in his final sermon:

> The waters are raging and the winds are blowing but I have no fear for I stand firmly upon a rock. What am I to fear? Is it death? Life to me means Christ and death is gain. Is it exile? The earth and everything it holds belongs to the Lord. Is it loss of property? I brought nothing into this world and I will bring nothing out of it. I have only contempt for the world and its ways and I scorn its honors.[100]

Augustine

Augustine of Hippo (d. 430) was not only the most distinguished and influential theologian of the early Latin church; he also represents the flowering of its preaching. Just as the great Cappadocian fathers were schooled in the art of oratory by pagan teachers, so also Augustine devoted his early life to rhetoric, and he served as a professor of rhetoric at his hometown of Thagaste, then at Carthage, and finally at Milan where he was baptized by Ambrose. He preached on a regular basis for thirty-nine years from his ordination as presbyter in 391 until his death in 430.

Augustine composed a treatise with the title *De Doctrina Christiana*, which is somewhat misleading, as it speaks primarily of exegesis, hermeneutics, and of the relationship of educated Christians to their culture. The fourth book is concerned extensively with preaching. It has been considered the earliest homiletics textbook of the church. Despite his training in rhetoric, Augustine cautions against its abuse:

> We must beware of the man who abounds in eloquent nonsense, and so much the more if the hearer is pleased with what is not worth listening to, and thinks that because the speaker is eloquent, what he says must be true. . . . A man speaks with more or less wisdom to the extent he has made more or less progress in the knowledge of the Scripture, not just in knowing them but especially in understanding them correctly. . . . It is more important to speak wisely than eloquently.[101]

He says that if a preacher has not learned rhetoric, there is no reason to take up its study, because the best oratory can be learned from Scripture itself. He then demonstrates how St. Paul closely followed Cicero's rules of oratory in 2 Corinthians 11:16-30: "Are they Hebrews? So am I. Are the Israelites? So am I." He subjects other biblical orations to the same analysis and finds them all following Cicero's rules of rhetoric. He does not deny the importance of eloquence, but the content of the message and the edification of the hearers is more important than the form. The first task of a preacher is to be understood:

> A man who speaks with the intention of teaching should not think he has said what he intended . . . if he is not understood. Although he has said what he himself understands, he has not yet spoken to the man who has not understood him. . . . But the manner in which he speaks is important in order that he may produce the effect [of pleasing]. Just as the listener must be pleased in order that he may be kept listening, so he must be persuaded in order that he may be influenced to act.[102]

Augustine recognized three styles of preaching—the restrained, moderate, and grand. "While the preacher speaks of great matters, he ought not always be speaking of them in a majestic tone, but in a subdued tone when he is teaching, and temperately when he is giving praise or blame."[103] But when he is trying to persuade or move to action, he must speak "with power calculated to sway the mind." Ideally all three styles should be used according to the occasion. The same text may be taught in a subdued manner, with moderate rhetoric when urging its importance, and "powerfully when we are forcing a mind that is averse to the truth to turn and embrace it."[104]

Unlike the great Greek pulpit orators, Augustine's sermons were short, seldom more than thirty minutes, and many which we have would have taken only fifteen minutes to deliver. He sometimes ended the sermon abruptly, leaving the conclusion for another day. "I believe I have talked long enough," he says in one sermon, "but I have not come to the end of the Gospel lesson. If I should complete the rest, I would tire you, and I fear that what you have learned would be lost: therefore this must be enough for *caritas vestra*."[105] He often referred to his hearers as "your love," much as preachers of not long ago may have said "dearly beloved." He ended an Epiphany sermon by saying, "It is proper that an old man's address should not only be serious but also short."[106] But on another occasion he uncharacteristically spoke for two hours and concluded abruptly:

> I have forgotten how long I have been speaking. The Psalm (Ps. 72) is ended, and I attribute my perspiration to the fact that I have delivered a long address, but I cannot do enough to answer your enthusiasm. You have a violent effect upon me. Ah, if you only showed the same enthusiasm in grasping the kingdom of heaven.[107]

Augustine encouraged pastors to use the sermons of other preachers, especially if they lacked the skill or time to write their own:

> There are, indeed, some men who have a good delivery, but they cannot compose anything worth delivering. Now, if such men take what has been written with wisdom and eloquence by others, and commit it to memory, and deliver it to the people, they cannot be blamed. For in this way many become preachers of the truth, which is certainly desirable.[108]

The Christian preacher should pray before preaching. "He ought to pray for himself and for those he is about to address before he attempts to speak. And when the hour has come that he must speak, before he opens his mouth, he must lift up his thirsty soul to God, to drink in what he is about to pour forth, and be himself filled with what he is about to distribute."[109] Augustine emphasized the need for a preacher to be "himself filled with what he is about to distribute." He suggested that the best rhetoric was the preacher's own excitement about what he was saying, and his own conviction that it was true.

He concludes his book on preaching with the reminder that the pastor's way of life could not be dissociated from his words. "If the preacher lacks eloquence, let him live in such a way that he will not only prepare a reward for himself but will also furnish an example for others. Let his beauty of life be, as it were, his most powerful ceremony [sermon]."[110]

Augustine preached not only at the Sunday Eucharist, but he also offered sermons several times during the week, and during periods of fasting, such as Lent, he spoke daily. He did not write out his sermons in advance but spoke extemporaneously, and almost all those which we have are from stenographic accounts. On one occasion he improvised a sermon on an unexpected text when the lector by mistake read another Psalm than the one appointed for the day. "There are very few instances in the history of preaching where the extant manuscripts give us as vivid a picture of the oral sermon as we receive from the record of Augustine's sermons."[111] Preacher and congregation seem to be in constant dialogue.

As in the East, there was frequent applause. We should remember that these sermons, in both the East and West, were delivered with the preacher seated in this chair and the people standing. But apparently the people did not stand still; they moved about, and often conversed among themselves in whispers. This contributed to a sense of informality and an ambience foreign to modern churches where the congregation is seated in pews. As late as the sixteenth century and the time of the Reformers the people still stood or moved about during the sermon. This informal atmosphere helps us to understand the applause, or shouts of approval, or silence of disapproval, or in some cases hisses and groans, which seem to be a part of the vitality of early Christian preaching.

Augustine loved his people, his *caritas vestra*, but that did not prevent him from being critical of them, as Chrysostom in Antioch. In a sermon to the catechumens he spoke of "those confused multitudes whose bodies fill the churches," and he warned his hearers against persisting in pagan practices, "because you see so many so-called Christians loving evils of this sort, participating in them, defending them, and persuading others to continue in this kind of life."[112]

In a remarkable Christmas sermon, Augustine says that on Christmas day the church was thronged with the multitudes, and he chose not to waste his time expounding profound doctrinal truths to those who were indifferent to the faith, but he only preached an introduction to his present sermon, inviting the Christmas crowd to return and listen to its conclusion during the following week:

> You will recall, my dear people, that on Christmas morning we postponed the question which we had proposed to solve; because many, even those who find the Word of God burdensome, were with us to celebrate the festivities usual on that day. But now, I suppose, only such have come here as desire to hear a sermon. We are not, therefore, speaking to hearts that are deaf, nor to minds that are bored.[113]

Augustine had a weak voice, and on days when the church was filled there was much noise with people milling about. One Epiphany, he simply quit in the middle of his sermon because he could not be heard. "Many people have come here today not to listen to a sermon but to help us celebrate the feast. So I invite those people who want to listen to the rest of what I have to say to come back tomorrow. In this way I shall avoid giving short measure to the zealous, and I shall not weary the indifferent."[114] Augustine was critical of festival crowds. He noted that Christian celebrations involved too much drinking. "Feast days are drinking days." Even the newly baptized are warned on Easter morning not to appear drunk when they return to the church for Vespers later in the day.[115]

Augustine followed the typological exegesis we have seen in Chrysostom and the Antiochene church. One of his favorite types is Adam/Christ and Eve/Mary:

Let each sex see its own honor, let each confess its own guilt, and let both hope for salvation. When man was about to be deceived, it was through woman that the potion of destruction was administered to him: so, when man is to be restored, let it be through woman that the cup of salvation is presented to him. Let woman make good the sin of man deceived through her, by giving birth to Christ. Hence, too, women were the first to announce the resurrection of God to the apostles. The woman in paradise announced death to her husband; and so, too, the women in the church announced salvation to the men. The apostles were to announce Christ's resurrection to the nations; women announced it to the apostles. Therefore, let no one misrepresent the fact that Christ was born of a woman. The Deliverer could not have been defiled by the sex; and as its Creator, He could not but show it favor.[116]

In an Easter sermon, Augustine welcomed the newly baptized by using the bread of the Eucharist as a type of their process of entry to the church:

We have become his body, and through his mercy we are what we receive. . . . You were brought to the threshing floor of the Lord; by the labors of oxen, that is, of those preaching the Gospel, you have been threshed. When as catechumens you were being temporarily deferred, you were under observation in the granary. Then you were enrolled; the grinding process, achieved by fastings and exorcisms, began. Afterwards you came to the font; you were sprinkled and you became one [with the whole loaf]; by the application of the burning heat of the Holy Spirit you were baked and you became the bread of the Lord.[117]

He continues by referring to the wine as a type of unity, having been created through the juice of many grapes. So also must the newly baptized contribute to the unity of the church and avoid schism or heresy.

We have an example of Augustine's effective use of rhetoric from another Easter sermon (we have forty-one sermons from the Easter season):

Let us sing Alleluia. Then the word of Scripture will be realized. . . . "Death has been swallowed up in victory." Let us sing Alleluia. "O death, where is your sting?" Let us sing Alleluia here in the midst of trial and temptation. Let us sing Alleluia for man is guilty, but God is faithful. . . . O blessed Alleluia of heaven! No more anguish or adversity.

Here on earth, praise mingled with fear, but in heaven praise without fear. Here on earth the one who sings must die, but in heaven he who sings, lives forever. Here he sings in hope, there he sings in love. Here it is Alleluia on the way, there it is Alleluia on the spot. Now let us sing Alleluia to lighten our burden. Sing like a man upon a journey, but keep time as you keep step. Sing to sustain your effort and do not give in to laziness. Sing in tune and march to the tune you sing. . . . March in step and don't turn back. Onward, onward to Christ![118]

Another example of oratory combined with humor is from a call to repentance:

When are you going to reform? When are you going to change? "Tomorrow," you say. Behold, how often you say: "tomorrow, tomorrow"; you have really become a crow. [The words "tomorrow, tomorrow," in Latin, cras, cras, approximate the cawing of a crow.—Ed.] When you make the noise of a crow, ruin is threatening you. For that crow whose crawing you imitate went forth from the ark and did not return.

I beg you by the name which has been invoked upon you, by the altar to which you have approached, by the sacraments which you have received, by the future judgment of the living and the dead, I beg you, I put you under obligation in the name of Christ, not to imitate those persons whom you know are such as I describe. May the sacraments of him who did not wish to come down from the cross, but who did wish to rise from the tomb, endure.[119]

Augustine was a diligent and passionate preacher. We have 363 sermons considered genuine, in addition to many treatises which may have been homilies, including 124 treatises on John's Gospel and a large number on the Psalms. If we include the treatises, his extant homiletical productions approach one thousand. "No worthier representative of the prophetic office appeared in the history of the church before the time of the Reformation than the bishop of Hippo."[120]

4 The Care of Souls

Gregory the Great wrote in his *Pastoral Care* that "the government of souls is the art of arts."[1] Pastoral life and practice in the early church, as in every age since, has been devoted to a greater or lesser degree to the care of souls. By this is meant the concern for the spiritual and physical welfare of individual Christians on a personal and intimate level, or in contemporary parlance, on a one-to-one basis. We have already discussed the role of the pastor in the developing office of the ministry; we have witnessed the pastor's life with the congregation as an administrator, dispenser of charity and justice, and as an exemplar of holiness; and we have considered the pastor's role as a teacher and preacher to large or small groups of people. But in addition to these tasks, the clergy also devoted time to the care of individuals in their various spiritual and emotional crises. At least since the time of Gregory (600) this has come to be known as the care of souls.

One difficulty in pursuing this topic is the lack of primary sources, because we have no verbatim accounts of pastoral conversations with those who sought counsel. We possess a large number of letters involving pastoral care, and from them we are able to discern the issues and how they were dealt with. There is little secondary literature with its primary focus on pastoral care in the early church, but some recent works help to fill this need: William A. Clebsch and Charles Jaekle, *Pastoral Care in Historical Perspective;* John T. McNeill, *A*

History of the Cure of Souls; and H. Richard Niebuhr and Daniel Williams, *The Ministry in Historical Perspective*.[2] Thomas C. Oden's *Care of Souls in the Classic Tradition* is a superb analysis of the work of Gregory the Great as it relates to contemporary standards of pastoral care.[3]

In our review of the care of souls we shall first consider what the early church believed to be the basic qualifications for one who assumed the role of spiritual advisor. What follows is a vignette of the variety of situations that called for pastoral care and a brief account of the responses offered. Letters of consolation abound in early Christian literature, a corollary to the funerary sermons we have already considered. In this segment we will look at the manner in which pastors offered consolation in times of personal disaster or loss. The literature on the discipline of the Christian life, which includes confession and penance, is voluminous and it was an activity that consumed a great deal of pastoral time and effort. Meanwhile, from monastic groups there emerged the role of spiritual director for individuals who sought spiritual guidance. Finally, since Gregory's *Pastoral Rule* is in a class by itself in the field of pastoral care, we shall consider his approach to the task, and with acknowledgment to Thomas Oden's analysis, suggest Gregory's timeliness for today.

Pastor as Counselor

We have already considered some of the primary qualifications required of a pastor in the early church, especially that of holiness, as he was to serve as an example to the congregation (chap. 2). In addition to exemplary conduct and a knowledge of the Scripture, he who wished to engage in the care of souls required skills and a disposition specifically related to this task.

Polycarp (150) advises presbyters in their relationships with those under their care to "refrain from all anger, partiality, and unjust judgment, not hastily believing evil of anyone, nor being severe in judgment."[4] The caution against partiality, anger, and harsh judgments is often repeated in early Christian advice to the clergy. Chrysostom recognizes the possibility of a counselor becoming angry by the revelation of wrongdoing, and he advises against it. A hot temper clouds one's judgment. "The soul's eye is darkened as in a night battle, and cannot distinguish friend from foe, or worthlessness from worthy."[5] He also cautions against showing partiality in one's relationships to members of the church, especially in a counseling situation. And yet it is necessary to differentiate among the various maladies that come to his attention, and not to treat every situation in the same way. "It is impossible to treat all his people in one way, any more than it would be right for the doctors to deal with all their patients alike, or a helmsman to know of only one way of battling with the winds."[6]

Not only should the pastor be impartial and temperate, but he must avoid unjust and harsh penalties to the penitent. "It is to be feared that if a man is punished too severely, he may be swallowed up with overmuch sorrow. Great care is needed to ensure that what was meant to help does not become the occasion of greater loss. For the vengeance for sins which he commits after such treatment is shared by the surgeon who lances the wound unskillfully."[7]

Chrysostom continues the analogy of soul care to that of medicine, a favorite analogy that we find throughout this literature, comparing the pastor to a physician. But doctors do not ordinarily seek out the sick. "The decision to receive treatment does not lie with the man who administers the medicine but actually with the patient."[8] Because people cannot be improved by the use of force, a great deal of tact is required, "so that the sick may be persuaded of their own accord to submit to the treatment of the priest, and not only that, but to be grateful to them for their cure. . . . The man does not exist who can by compulsion cure someone else against his will."[9] Therefore it is necessary for the pastor to be aware of the spiritual condition of every member of his church so as to be able to bring those in need to spiritual health in a winsome and engaging manner. Changing the metaphor, "the shepherd needs great wisdom and a thousand eyes to examine the soul's condition from every angle."[10]

Gregory of Nazianzus, to whom Gregory the Great is much in debt for his *Pastoral Care,* continues the imagery of the physician by pointing to the varieties of illness, each of which demands a different type of treatment:

> Place and time and age and season and the like are the subjects of a physician's scrutiny; he will prescribe medicines and diet, and guard against things injurious, that the desires of the sick may not be a

hindrance to his art. Sometimes he will make use of the cautery or the knife or more severe remedies; but none of these . . . is so difficult as the diagnosis and cure of our habits, passions, lives, wills, and whatever else is within us, by banishing from our compound nature everything brutal and fierce, and introducing and establishing in their place what is gentle and dear to God, and not allowing the superior to be overpowered by the inferior.[11]

Gregory continues by making a further application. Some sin is so hidden within the depths of the soul that the sinner is not conscious of it, yet its presence continues to affect one's life. The counselor must devise means to bring it to the surface. Other sins are paraded as virtues, and still others are denied. In the latter case, when the one who is suffering is confronted with his malady, he responds by "tightly closing up his ears, obstinate in refusing to be treated with the medicine of wisdom, by which spiritual sickness is healed."[12]

Origen offered this sound advice to people who were seeking pastoral guidance, and by implication, advice to counselors as well:

See, then, what holy scripture teaches us, that it is not right to bury sin in our hearts. . . . But if a man become his own accuser, in accusing himself and confessing he vomits out his sin, and dissipates the whole cause of his sickness. Only, look around carefully to find the proper person to whom to confess your sin. Prove your doctor first, the man to whom you must disclose the reason of your weakness, that he be one who knows how to sympathize with a sufferer, to weep with a mourner, one who understands the word of sympathy, and then if he, a man who has thus shown himself a learned and merciful doctor, tells you to do anything, or gives you any advice, do it.[13]

Origen was not especially fond of the clergy, and in offering this advice he was suggesting that if any Christians felt their pastors were incapable of giving competent and sympathetic care, they should seek a spiritual director, ordained or not, who would serve their needs.

Jerome warns the counselor against "having a tongue or ears that itch: that is, do not defame others or listen to people who defame others. . . . It belongs to your office to visit the sick, to know their households, and the married women and their children, and not to disregard the secrets of distinguished men. Therefore it belongs to your office to keep not only your eyes guarded, but also your tongue."[14]

Although the confidentiality of pastoral care did not become part of canon law until the medieval period, in the early church it was assumed. Jerome heaps scorn upon those clergy whose confidences are shared with every home he visits. Ambrose counseled that every pastor should have a door to his mouth, that it may be shut when need arises, and let it carefully be barred. Let his tongue be subject to his mind, that it may be held in check with a tight rein.[15]

Together with the analogy of medicine and the physician as an appropriate image for the pastor, we find that of shepherd and flock frequently utilized. Sometimes they are both used in the same paragraph. The shepherd, of course, has ample biblical precedent, and at the beginning of the third century the prayer for the ordination of a bishop in the *Apostolic Tradition* of Hippolytus lists "to feed your holy flock" as the first task of the ordained. The *Didascalia Apostolorum* (before 250) underscores the need for pastoral attention to individuals. "Thus, O bishop, you must also visit the one that is lost, seek the one who has wandered, and restore the one who is afar away. . . . Lead not with violence; be not vehement, nor judge sharply, nor be merciless."[16] Cyprian in his numerous letters to the clergy regularly refers to the shepherd imagery. An anonymous fifth-century writer from Alexandria offers this advice: "You who are entrusted with Christ's spiritual flock must be long-suffering, and should seek after great stability. . . . You, the shepherd, know this; you should not reject the sheep, nor separate it from the flock; but whenever you find a sinner, call him apart. Reprove some things, encourage him in others, and remind him a second and a third time to abstain from evil."[17]

Bernard Cooke points out that comparing the clergy with a shepherd has only one constant, and that is seeking the good of the flock. But that is ill-defined, and it depends historically upon what those in this office at a given time judge to be for the good of their flock, and therefore it is subject to manipulation.[18] Appealing as we find the pastoral image, in the course of time it led to an authoritarian interpretation of rulership and governance. Chrysostom cautioned against making too literal an identification of shepherds with clergy, as "shepherds have full power to compel the sheep to accept the treatment if they do not submit of their own accord . . . but you cannot treat men with the same authority with which the shepherd treats a sheep."[19] Yet the same writer insists that within the church the difference between the shepherd and sheep is as great as that between rational and irrational creatures. Other analogies of the relationship between clergy and laity in addition to physician and shepherd were those of parent and child, ship captain and crew, military leader and soldiers, and athletic coach and team.

Although these images of the pastoral role in counseling were subject to a paternalistic or even authoritarian imbalance, early Christian literature abounds in warnings to the clergy not to abuse their trust. The shepherd analogy can be understood to mean that we are all sheep, clergy and laity alike, under the Good Shepherd. Gregory of Nazianzus continues a word to the clergy: "A man must himself be cleansed before cleansing others; himself become wise, that he may make others wise; become light, and then give light; draw near to God, and so bring others near; be hallowed and then hallow them; be possessed of hands to lead others by the hand, possessed of wisdom to give advice."[20] Throughout this literature the clergy are cautioned that theirs is a position of great responsibility and not of privilege, "as they who must give account" for the souls under their care.

There were few printed guides for pastoral counseling in the early church, although occasionally we find suggestions. The earliest specific treatment is Gregory's *Pastoral Care*, but two hundred years earlier, Ambrose, bishop of Milan (d. 397) wrote *On the Office of Ministry*, in which he explained that "office" should be understood as "duties," which was heavily in debt to Cicero. It has been called "the first great Western textbook of Christian ethics," in which he finds biblical support for the four classical virtues of wisdom, justice, fortitude, and temperance.[21] Cicero had written a book with the same title in which he had expounded the ethics of Stoicism, which Ambrose christianized. The work presents an exhaustive philosophy of ethics (ninety double-columned pages in the *Nicene and Post-Nicene Fathers*, vol. 10) and may not have been especially helpful for pastoral counselors dealing with specific issues. In it he speaks of conscience and free will, of the nature of blessedness and goodness, of virtue, of political and social ethics, of wealth, of the ordered life (*decorum*), and a host of other ethical topics. F. Homes Dudden offers this summary of book one of Ambrose's work:

> The modest man's life exhibits a harmonious order; all his actions are becoming. This charming quality is apparent in the very tone of his

voice, in the measure alike of his speech and of his silence; in his gestures and gait, in his dignified yet unpretentious attire. It is shown also in his relations with the other sex, in his prayers to God, in the courtesy and urbanity of his ordinary conversation, and in his "manly gravity" [a typically Roman trait] which he preserves even in his relaxations. Such a man is humble, gentle, mild, serious, and patient; he preserves measure in all things; his quiet countenance and speech show that there is no vice in his life. [22]

Although this work does not relate directly to the practice of pastoral care, it offers an ideal of accepted Christian morality, which provided a standard for Western clergy in guiding the lives of the faithful.

In summary, early Christian clergy were very much aware of some basic principles of pastoral care, and as we shall see, were actively engaged in that practice. These principles included empathy with the parishioner, an awareness that surface symptoms may reveal deeper maladies, the delicate nature of counseling relationships, the need for wisdom and discretion, and the dangers of abusing a relationship of confidence and dependence. But it was not an exact science. Chrysostom warned that "some guesswork must be made about the disposition of sinners." [23] Yet he who undertakes such work must train for it with the diligence and discipline of an athlete about to compete in a contest.

Guiding and Sustaining the Faithful

In their excellent study of the history of pastoral care, Clebsch and Jaeckle arrange their material according to eight periods over the course of two millennia of Christian history. They suggest that in the early church the primary motif up to 180 was that of sustaining; during the time of persecution it was reconciling, and under the imperial church it was guiding. [24] Useful as this approach may be, the material here is arranged topically according to the nature of problems to which pastoral care was addressed, inasmuch as the wide range of issues requiring such attention was present in every age.

The large number of martyrologies extant from the time of persecution was intended to encourage the faithful to persevere in time of trial, holding up the witness of those who had died for their faith as heroic examples of the faithfulness of God. Of Polycarp it was said, "his martyrdom all men are eager to copy, in that it came to pass according to the Gospel of Christ. Through his patience he overcame the unrighteous ruler, and thus received the crown of incorruption."[25] Polycarp's death was according to Christ's prediction of suffering, and now he enjoys the company of the apostles, all just persons, and that of Christ himself. The Scillitan martyrs of Africa (180) were "crowned with martyrdom together, and reign with the Father and Son and Holy Spirit forever and ever."[26] The heroism of the martyrs approaches recklessness. Ignatius's courting of martyrdom is well known. "I am more truly learning discipleship. May I have the joy of the beasts that are prepared for me. I pray they may be prompt with me. I will even entice them to devour me promptly. . . . Let there come fire and cross . . . that I may attain to Jesus Christ."[27] Cyprian at his beheading gave his executioners some money because they were speeding him on to his eternal reward. When Justin was interrogated by the authorities, he was asked whether he thought that by his death he would gain rewards. He replied, "I do not [merely] think, I know and am fully persuaded."[28]

Such accounts of heroism were widely circulated among Christians as an encouragement to remain faithful, yet not all were possessed of such fortitude. We read that in Lyons and Vienne they were divided. "Some were manifestly ready for martyrdom, and fulfilled with zeal the confession wherein they gave witness; but others were manifestly unready and untrained and still weak."[29] On this occasion ten apostatized, not only to the sorrow of those who remained steadfast, but to their own sorrow as well. As to pastoral care, we can only imagine the difficulties confronting the clergy in ministering to those about to die and their families, in addition to assisting those who had denied Christ but who wished to remain Christians.

We have some idea of care for the martyrs in several pastoral letters addressed to them. Tertullian writes a warm and encouraging letter to the catechumens imprisoned in Carthage in 202. He reminds them that the Holy Spirit has been with them in the past, and will not fail them now.[30] The world is a prison of sin and false promises, putting on far greater chains than those they now wear. "The prison now offers to the Christian what the desert once gave to the prophets," a secluded place where God will be manifested (2:8). He recognizes the hardships of prison life, but he compares it with the harsh training of soldiers preparing for battle (3:1). The flesh is weak, but the spirit is strong.

He calls to memory others who have heroically given witness before them. The martyrs may object and say, "our fear of death is not so great as the fear of torture," to which he replies by offering more examples of other martyrs in addition to the rewards of paradise (4:7). He also points to others who in the course of their lives endured suffering totally apart from Christian witness, and they persevered. He also asks for a charitable attitude toward those who have apostatized, suggesting that the martyrs pray for them. It is Satan, not the Roman government, that is tempting them to fall, and their present circumstance should be seen as a contest with the Evil One (3:5).

Fifty years after Tertullian, Cyprian wrote a letter, *On Facing Martyrdom*, to a congregation suffering under the Decian persecution. It suggests that even in prison they received the Eucharist daily. "A severer and fiercer fight is now threatening for which the soldiers of Christ ought to prepare themselves, with uncorrupted faith and robust courage, considering that they drink the blood of Christ daily, for the reason that they themselves also may be able to shed their blood for Christ."[31] He cites numerous biblical references. The time is coming when they who kill you will think they are offering true worship. "When the time has come, you may remember that I told you" (John 16:2-4). Biblical examples include Abel, the three children of the fiery furnace, Daniel, the Maccabees, and the Holy Innocents. The contest is with Satan. "The Adversary is enraged and threatens, but there is One who can deliver us from his hands. . . . God looks upon us in the warfare and fighting in the encounter of faith; his angels look upon us, and Christ looks on us." The ultimate example, of course, is the crucified Christ, whose disciples we are. He returns to the fortification provided by the Eucharist, "that the hand which has received the Lord's body may embrace the Lord himself, hereafter to receive from the Lord the reward of heavenly crowns." In conclusion he encourages them to steel themselves against their impending death and to take heart. He also suggested that they find consolation not only in their certain bliss in eternity but also in the fiery doom that awaited their persecutors. Thus did early Christian pastors attempt to offer solace and counsel to those who faced death for their Christian witness, a situation that was repeated countless times even to our generation. The content of the sustenance included the examples of others, the example of Christ and his predictions of suffering for his disciples, the contest as one with Satan and not with the persecutors, the false values of this world, and the eternal joys of the blessed.

Not all Christians were required to face martyrdom, and for those who continued to live in this world the pastor faced other challenges. One of the most compelling was in the area of sexual ethics and marital counsel. The Christian church presented a moral ethic completely at odds with the culture, as we have seen (chap. 2). Monogamy and fidelity in marriage, as well as sexual purity outside marriage, presented the clergy with a formidable case load of counseling.

Under Roman law, marriage was a civil and private ceremony. As early as 110, Ignatius insisted that Christians have their marriages blessed by the bishop. "It is right for men and women who marry to be united with the bishop's approval. In that way their marriage will follow God's will and not the promptings of lust."[32] The church also emphasized the free consent of the partners. By 200, Christian marital blessings took place in a eucharistic context.[33] Not only was marriage sacred, but engagement to be married was considered inviolable. Pope Siricius of Rome at the end of the fourth century declared that any man who married a woman who had been betrothed to another had "profaned" his marriage.[34]

Chrysostom takes a dim view of excessive festivity at a Christian wedding. "Let us celebrate marriage without flute or harp or dancing; for a groom like ours is ashamed of such absurd customs. Nay, let us invite Christ there, for the bridegroom is worthy of him. Let us invite his disciples . . . [The groom] will learn to train his own sons in this way, and they theirs in turn, and the result will be a golden cord."[35]

The ideal family was understood to be patriarchial, with the father as the head. Chrysostom writes that God intended the family not to be a democracy, "for equality often brings strife," but a monarchy. After the father, the wife serves as lieutenant and general, followed by the children in the third rank, and then come the servants. Among the children there is rank according to age and sex, "since among the children the female does not hold equal sway." Chrysostom appealed to the priority of Adam over Eve in creation, but to prevent Adam from viewing his wife as inferior to him, "God honored her and made them one." The childbearing role of Eve was intended to keep Adam from pride in his own priority. The entire family pyramid was not a matter of inferiority or superiority, but one of order. He finds it distressing when the woman dictates to the man, but intolerable when the children control their parents.[36]

Augustine related the peace of society to peace in the family. Unless the families of the empire are stable, there can be no tranquility in the city. "The order and harmony of rulers and ruled must directly be actualized from the order and harmony arising out of creative guidance and commensurate responsibility in the family"[37] But paternal authority did not mean dictatorship. Victorinus Afer, a fourth-century commentator, urged the husband to be ready to suffer all things for his wife, just as Christ loved the church. The husband, who represents the spirit, and the wife, who represents the soul, are to be indivisibly joined in marriage as Christ and his church.[38]

We do not have many direct letters of counsel on marriage from the early church. Among those extant is one from Augustine to Ecdicia, a married woman who had left her husband and son, and had joined a convent of nuns under a vow of chastity. Augustine blamed her for forcing her husband into adultery: "You undertook this state of continence, contrary to sound doctrine, before he had given his consent. He should not have been defrauded of the debt you owed him of your body before his will joined yours in seeking the good which surpasses conjugal chastity."[39] He continues by emphasizing the patriarchal position that she should be submissive to him, but more poignantly, How could she leave her young son without a mother? "As you have seen fit to consult me, I have written this, not with the intent to break down your virtuous resolution by my words, but because I am grieved by your husband's conduct, which is the result of your reckless and ill-considered behavior. You must think now very seriously about reclaiming him"[40] This long letter (nine pages in English) concludes with the opinion that the child can be raised properly only with "a union of hearts" between the parents. For Augustine, a devout champion of monasticism, this must have been a difficult letter to write. And we are not informed of the circumstances that prompted Ecdicia to leave her husband, other than that he considered her impressionable, naive, and the victim of misguided piety.

But Augustine did not always champion the cause of the husband. He urged wives to defend their honor and to stand firmly upon their Christian rights. In a sermon he told the women of his congregation:

> Let the women listen to me. Let them show jealousy toward their husbands. I will not urge husbands to show jealousy toward their wives,

because I know well enough that they will do that without prompting
from myself. I do not want the Christian wife to be overpatient; on the
contrary, I want her to be a jealous wife. I say this with all emphasis.
I order it. I command it. Your bishop commands it. And Christ commands it through me. I say this and I command it to you. Do not suffer
it if your husbands make themselves guilty of unchastity. Appeal against
them to the church. In all things be subject to your husbands, but where
this matter is concerned defend your cause![41]

On another occasion a close friend of Augustine in his youth had
lost his wife through his infidelities, and after a series of mistresses
he wrote to his old friend for consolation. Augustine sent him a
blistering reply in which he commented on his presumption to appear
as an aggrieved party, to appeal to old friendships, and to do this
with a bishop of the church! If he wished to be reconciled with his
virtuous wife, he must begin to lead a chaste life himself.[42]

The early church developed in a society that understood the family
as a patriarchal unit, with the father and husband as the head of the
household, and the wife and children as being submissive to him.
Despite this structure, the clergy did not hesitate to insist on marital
fidelity and on the demand that the father/husband conform to Christian virtue and discharge his duties in a responsible manner. This
evidence comes more from sermons on the family than from direct
counseling—sermons that rebuke men for infidelity and drinking and
gambling, which robs their spouses and children of support.

Augustine counseled against early marriages. In a commentary on
Psalm 149, a psalm of praise to Yahweh, he found it expedient to
express his aversion to marriage by the young or immature. Van der
Meer paraphrases Augustine:

Heed me, young people, he says, marriage is an iron fetter; other fetters
can be loosed by us here in the church, but not this one. I say this lest
you think you can seek asylum here with us and have your marriage
dissolved. We, your bishop, rivet this fetter with double rivets, but you
are not compelled to put your foot into it. What says the Apostle? "If
thou art tied to a wife, seek not thy freedom, but if thou art free, seek
not a wife." As against this, he looked upon the young married state
as unsuitable for men of uncontrolled character.[43]

We have already commented on the church's concern for raising
children properly in considering Chrysostom's *Address on Vainglory*

and the Right Way to Bring up Children (chap. 3). In addition to what has been said, the author compares the raising of children to an artist's care for creating beauty on a blank canvas, or a sculptor fashioning a statue from a block of stone. But parents have a nobler task in creating wondrous statues for God (chap. 22). It is imperative for children to have rules to guide them and to be clear about them. "Uphold them if they are being transgressed, for it is useless to draw up laws if their enforcement does not follow" (chap. 26). But the rules should be fair and reasonable, and infractions should not frequently be punished with blows, for that is self-defeating. Love is far more effective than fear. Furthermore, there must be consistency in the raising of children. Inasmuch as a number of people are involved in childrearing, including servants and slaves, there must be an agreement among them of expectations, "so all of them together may be his guardians" (chaps. 30–33). This essay on raising children (thirty-seven pages in English) touches on a multitude of issues, including kindness to slaves, justice, observance of nature, sobriety, continence, responsibility, diligence, respect, establishing priorities, the use of time, and much more. Basic to the parental task is showing the child love and offering it security.[44]

The *Apostolic Constitutions* of the fourth century also offer advice to parents and clergy for raising children, but it is more severe in that it counsels chastening with the rod. "Smite his loins sore while he is little." The authors of this treatise offer less counsel than Chrysostom on the methods of childraising and focus more on parental responsibilities, warning parents against neglect of their children. Since children learn from example more than from words, it is mandatory that parents be good models, for they must give an account on the day of judgment for their stewardship of parenting.[45]

In addition to offering sustenance to those under persecution and guidance to families, the clergy were involved in many other issues requiring pastoral attention. High on the list of clerical responsibilities was the visitation of the sick. Hippolytus early in the third century advises that "the bishop [pastor] should be told who are sick, so that, if he wishes, he may visit them. It is a great consolation for a sick person if the high priest is mindful of him"[46] Hippolytus also informs us that following the weekly Sunday Eucharist, the sacrament was taken by the deacons to all those who were sick or homebound. Chrysostom points out that visits to the sick require special discretion and skill due to the infirm condition of the patient. "Sick men are hard to please and given to languor. Unless every attention and care is lavished on them, the smallest neglect is enough to cause the patient great distress."[47] The object of such visitation is to offer the sick relief, especially for their spirits, rather than add to their distress.

The New Testament often refers to miracles of healing performed by Jesus or his disciples. The office of healer, apart from the ordained clergy, continued in the early church as we find it in Hippolytus, where hands are not laid upon one who claims to have such a gift, as "the deed shall make manifest whether he speaks the truth."[48] The same writer offers a prayer of blessing over oil with which the sick are to be anointed, "that you would grant health to those who use it and partake of it, so that it may give comfort on all who taste it and health on all who use it."[49] Sick visitations of women were often carried out by deaconesses or widows who anointed the patient with oil. Before the fourth century there is no evidence that sick visitations with the Eucharist and the unction were believed to effect a physical cure, but they were for the spiritual fortitude of the patient. Thereafter we find belief in physical cures associated with relics and the shrines of the martyrs.[50] Pope Innocent II in 417 decreed that the sick in every congregation must be anointed with oil. By this time such visitations were made either by the pastor or by others who were designated for this purpose, both men and women. Ministry to the sick, then as today, was considered a primary obligation of pastoral care. The Christian church initiated the establishment of charitable institutions for any who were in need, and this included the first hospitals, as witness the Basilead of Basil of Caesarea.

The pastor was not only to visit the sick but others as well, including widows, mourners, and the healthy. Chrysostom points to "an extensive round of daily visits," demanded by the pastoral office. This work, he cautions, has the potential for great misunderstanding, as some will feel neglected while others are flattered at the pastor's visit, not because of their piety but because of the honor. And he warns against selective visitation of the wealthy contributors or an overzealous solicitude for widows.[51]

One of the best known letters of counsel was that sent by Ambrose of Milan to the Emperor Theodosius after the massacre at Thessalonica in 390. The bishop wrote to him after pleading in vain to deal mercifully with the people. At the time, the imperial capital was at Milan, which placed the emperor within Ambrose's jurisdiction. Upon hearing the news of seven thousand people who were killed, Ambrose went into seclusion and wrote a masterpiece of tact and firmness:

> Listen, august emperor, I cannot deny that you have a zeal for the faith; I confess that you have the fear of God. But you also have a natural vehemence, which, if anyone endeavors to sooth it, you quickly turn to mercy; and if anyone stirs it up, you allow it to be roused so much that you can scarcely restrain it. . . . There took place in the city of Thessalonica that of which no memory recalls the like, which I was not able to prevent taking place, and which you yourself by revoking it too late, you consider to be grave.[52]

Then he offers the example of several Old Testament kings who exhibited sorrow for their sins. "I urge, I beg, I exhort, I warn; for it is grief to me that you who were an example of unheard of piety, conspicuous for clemency, should not mourn that so many innocent people have perished." Although the emperor had succeeded in conquering many people and nations, he had not yet conquered himself. He expresses his own gratitude for many favors shown to the church, and pleads that the emperor now have the piety to do penance for his sin. He concludes by saying that he found it impossible to preside over the Eucharist in the emperor's presence, which was a tactful way of announcing Theodosius's excommunication.[53] The emperor expressed his sorrow and was eventually reconciled to the church.

Letters of pastoral counsel abound from the early church on a host of issues. Some are from clergy to clergy. Ambrose wrote to a newly ordained pastor about various subjects, including the prohibition of lending money at interest, something the church opposed for at least sixteen centuries. "If a Christian has money, he should give it out as if he did not expect to get it back, or at least to get back only the principal he loaned. In this transaction he reaps no small interest in grace. . . . What could be harsher than to give your money to someone who has none, and to demand twice as much back?"[54]

Augustine exchanged several letters with Count Boniface, the imperial commander for North Africa who asked whether a Christian could be a soldier. "You do not need to fear that someone in military service will be unable to please God." David was a soldier, and God blessed him; Cornelius was likewise blessed. "Your primary aim should be peace; war should be fought only out of necessity in order to ensure that God will remove the cause and allow all to live in peace." The ultimate goal of a soldier should be seeking peace.[55]

We have 368 letters of Basil of Caesarea dealing with a variety of issues. In one he writes to creditors of a widow to remind them that she had paid her late husband's loan on time, therefore the interest was to be canceled; to another he scolded that his letters were both rare and brief, probably because he was up to no good—"Truly we do want letters"; to a woman who had broken her vow of chastity; to Athanasius of Alexandria a request for "men strong in sound doctrine" to assist in the struggle against Arianism; to a bishop of Neocaesarea he wrote that "you have made innovations in the faith and have talked in the manner contrary to sound doctrine"; and to another he suggests "you have abandoned your common sense" by terminating the monastic life.[56] We gain an insight into the range of pastoral guidance from a list offered by Augustine. "Disturbers are to be rebuked, the low-spirited to be encouraged, the infirm to be supported, objectors confuted, the treacherous guarded against, the unskilled taught, the lazy aroused, the contentious restrained, the haughty repressed, the good approved, the evil borne with, and all are to be loved."[57]

One principal theme we can see reflected through all these examples of pastoral sustenance and guidance is that of unity—unity of Christian life and practice, unity of faith, unity with Christ, and the unity of the church. There is no case where this concern is not reflected in the counsel given. This assumes that there was an absolute and universal ideal that was known, recognized, and could be appealed to. In general terms this was true; sin was recognized as sin, apostasy as apostasy, and sometimes heresy as heresy. But to offer counsel in every case required a knowledge of the individual, the circumstances, and a personal relationship. Ambrose's excommunication of the emperor was far removed in time and place from Tertullian's letters to the martyrs, but in each situation there was an appeal to fidelity to Christ, to the expectations of the baptized life; and in each case there was evidence of a pastoral recognition of the counselee's circumstances, that which today we call empathy. We turn now to that genre of early Christian epistolary activity known as letters of consolation.

Letters of Consolation

Letters of consolation were usually concerned with death but also with exile and other misfortunes. Jerome wrote a number of such letters, the earliest being to his friend Paula, on the death of her oldest daughter, Blesilla, who died within three months of her conversion. She had been a beautiful woman of twenty who had caused Paula and Jerome much worry because of her high life in Rome. After a seven-month marriage she became a widow and continued to enjoy the aristocratic social scene until the steady admonitions of Jerome, assisted by a sudden illness, brought her to conversion, rigorous mortifications, and a life of prayer. "Who can recall with dry eyes the glowing faith which induced a girl of twenty to raise the standard of the cross, and to mourn the loss of her virginity more than the death of her husband?" Jerome recalls her keen intellect, fluent in Greek, Latin, and Hebrew, and the rival of Origen in theology (!):

> When at last her spirit was delivered from the burden of the flesh, and had returned to him who gave it; when after her long pilgrimage, she had ascended up into her ancient heritage, her obsequies were celebrated with customary splendor. People of rank headed the procession, a pall made of gold cloth covered her bier. But I seemed to hear a voice from heaven saying, "I do not recognize these trappings; such is not the garb I used to wear; this magnificence is strange to me."[58]

What began as a tender recollection of Blesilla and words of assurance that she had been received into paradise with joy, now turns into a rebuke for Paula, who, overcome by grief, had collapsed at the funeral. Tears have their place; did not Jesus weep for Lazarus? But one need not permit grief to control one's life. "My agony is as great as yours." True sorrow should be reserved for unrepentant sinners who are certainly languishing in hell fire. True Christians should rejoice and give thanks at the death of loved ones. We do not know whether Paula was comforted with this rebuke: "Have you no fear lest the Savior say to you, 'Are you angry, Paula, that your daughter has become my daughter?' With rebellious tears do you begrudge me the possession of Blesilla?" Finally, Jerome appeals to the scandal Paula is causing Blesilla herself, enjoying the company of the saints, to see her mother carrying on in this way. "She is not my mother who displeases my Lord."[59] Undoubtedly Jerome had good intentions, but in terms of today's standards of therapy for the grieving, he was wide of the mark.

Jerome shows much more insight in a letter he wrote to Heliodorus on the death of his nephew, Nepotian, an officer who had become a priest. He acknowledges the propriety of grief, referring again to Jesus at Lazarus's death, but it is not the sorrow of those without hope. "We know, indeed, that Nepotian is with Christ and that he has joined the choir of the saints." He contrasts pagan hopelessness with the certainty offered in Christ's resurrection. Next he offers a eulogy of the virtues of the departed both as a person and as a priest. After rehearsing his strong faith and deeds of charity, he adds: "Nepotian took pains to keep the altar bright, the church walls free from soot, and the floor duly swept. He saw that the doorkeeper was constantly at his post, that the doorhangings were in their places, the sanctuary clean, and the vessels shining. The careful reverence he showed to every rite led him to neglect no duty small or great." Then Jerome recalls the disasters besetting the empire, from whose evils Nepotian was now removed. The letter is marked throughout with deep and sincere feeling, with the curious inclusion of at least six quotations from the Latin poet Vergil, as part of the consolation.[60]

Another consolatory letter barely warrants the description. It is to Pammachius, a Roman senator, at the death of his wife, Paulina, daughter of Paula. It was written two years following her death and contains little about her, but there is commendation of Pammachius himself, because following his wife's death he embraced monasticism and wore his black habit to the senate. Of Paulina he says, "not presuming to aspire to the virginity of her sister or the continence of her mother," she chose the lower path of being a wife and the mother of children. Jerome undoubtedly believed he was offering her praise when he wrote that he had it on good authority that "she only desired children that she might bring forth virgins to Christ."[61] Perhaps he believed he was offering the widower comfort when he pointed out that because of his wife's death he was now a monk. In a much longer letter to Eustochium on the death of Paula, Jerome repeats his views of the ideal Christian. "In the laudatory characterization of Paula we discover the ascetic ideal of Jerome in all its ruthless intensity."[62]

In addition to several funeral orations, we have one letter of consolation from Gregory of Nazianzus written on the death of an unknown "sister," who was "the true consort of a priest." It appears to be written to her husband, for Gregory speaks of their life together, "and was honored by you with that fair funeral honor which is due such as she." She was truly sacred and worthy of the great sacrament, an indication she had been a deaconess. He encourages her husband to console himself with the same promise of hope with which he comforts others who mourn. He speaks of the numerous people she had known and ministered to, who now call her blessed, and he concludes by reminding his reader that we shall not for long have either to rejoice or to suffer.[63]

In Chrysostom's "Letter to a Young Widow" we have a sympathetic and perceptive approach to grief, which displays some remarkable insights we have come to believe are modern.[64] He explains his delay in writing to her:

> I abstained from troubling you when your sorrow was at its height, and the thunderbolt had only just fallen upon you; but having waited an interval, and permitted you to take your fill of mourning, now that you are able to look out a little through the mist, and to open your ears to those who attempt to comfort you . . . I offer you some contributions of my own.
>
> While the tempest is still severe, a full gale of sorrow is blowing, he who exhorts another to desist from grief would only provoke him to increased lamentation. But when the troubled water has begun to subside, and the fury of the waves is abated, one can spread the sails of conversation.

Chrysostom has been told by her servants and other women "qualified for this office" (i.e., deaconesses), that she was ready for conversation. "Under any circumstances, the female sex is the more apt to be sensitive to suffering." He tells her he is aware of the host of new problems she is facing, not the least of which are matters of business and finance. Furthermore, a young widow is vulnerable "not only to those who aim at getting her money but also those who are bent upon corrupting her modesty."

For these reasons she may find the role of widow distressing and seek an early second marriage. She is cautioned against doing this. Widowhood is highly honored among Christians, "its luster shines on brightly, keeping its own value." Just as her devout husband had been her protector, so now God will be her help. God has seen her through rough waters; how much more will God help in calmer times.

Then Chrysostom turns to speak of her late husband. "There have been few like him, so affectionate, so gentle, so humble, so sincere, so understanding, so devout." His death is not death, but a kind of emigration and translation from the worse to the better. She should rejoice that under the temptations he met with wealth and power he remained unscathed, and has departed in safety and honor. Chrysostom implies that they are still married (therefore to avoid a second marriage) and their union will resume forever when she meets him again; "no longer in that corporeal beauty which he had when he departed, but in luster of another kind, and splendor outshining the rays of the sun." Perhaps he will return to visit her in visions (advice not recommended today).

Then the writer lists all the calamities they had been spared in their marriage, recounting the misfortunes of others due to wealth, pride, barbarian invasions, sickness, and war. It is the time when the Goths were spreading havoc in the East, and Chrysostom describes the difficulties that face citizens of wealth and position, such as she and her husband had enjoyed. Even apart from the political upheavals, wealth by itself is a snare to the soul. The widow, therefore, should be trained gradually to loosen her hold of earth and gradually move in the direction of heaven. The best way to save her possessions is to send them to "that good husband of yours, where neither thief, nor schemer, nor any other destructive thing will be able to pounce on them." The implication is that she should bestow them on charity and take up the role and the work of widows. He concludes by encouraging her to "desist from mourning and lamentation, and hold on to the same way of life as his . . . and then there will be a union of soul with soul more perfect, and of a far more delightful and far nobler kind."

We do not know what happened to this young widow. Although we today would not have offered her the same counsel about remarriage or the indissolubility of a first marriage despite the death of a spouse, given the fourth-century context it was arguably sound advice. By remaining a widow she retained her independence; by remarriage she placed herself under the domination of a husband who had full control of her life. Chrysostom suggested it was better for her to find security with the church and enjoy a respected role in society and meaningful work as a widow.

When Ambrose became bishop of Milan (374), his brother, Satyrus, devoted himself entirely to the management of Ambrose's secular affairs. The brothers were very close, and when Satyrus died four years later, Ambrose composed two essays, one for the funeral and one a week later, which spoke of the resurrection. These have come to us as a single composition.[65] Although technically the first is a sermon and not a letter of consolation, the essays were circulated with the intent of providing comfort for mourners. In a style of address we have already witnessed among the Eastern pulpit orators, Ambrose often addresses the deceased directly. "If there was at any time a discussion between me and my hold sister [Marcellina] on any matter, we used to take you as judge, who would hurt no one, and anxious to satisfy each, decided to as to let each depart satisfied" (1:41). But apart from personal references to Satyrus, Ambrose emphasized the resurrection of Christ as the pioneer of salvation, and he frequently cited Scripture. "I seek again, then, O Sacred Scripture, thy consolations." In his first book he expounds on twenty-five texts of the Bible for his consolation. Then he concludes:

> But why should I delay thee, brother? Although the sight and form of thy lifeless body, and its remaining comeliness and figure abiding here, comfort the eyes, I delay no longer. Let us go to the tomb. But first, before the people I utter the last farewell, declare peace to thee, and pay the last kiss. Go before us to that home, common and waiting for all, and certainly longed by me before all others. Prepare a common dwelling place for him with whom thou hast dwelt. . . . And now to Thee, Almighty God, I commend this guileless soul [1:78, 80].

His treatise on the resurrection is more theological than personal. He writes that if heaven and earth can be renewed, who should doubt that humankind can be renewed, and it is on its account that heaven and earth were made. "This is the course and fundament of justice, that as actions are common to both body and soul—for what the soul pondered the body effected—both shall come to the judgment and both shall either be given over to punishment or preserved for glory" (2:87).

Emperor Valentinian II was assassinated at age twenty (392). Only two days before news arrived of his death, he had sent messengers

to Ambrose delivering his request for baptism. Ambrose sent Emperor
Theodosius a letter of consolation together with his funeral oration,
which contained these thoughts about young Valentinian dying without
having been baptized:

> I hear you lamenting because he had not received the sacrament of
> Baptism. Tell me, what else could we have, except the will to it, the
> asking for it? He too had just now this desire; and after he came into
> Italy it was begun, and a short time ago he signified that he wished to
> be baptized by me. Did he, then, not have the grace which he desired?
> Did he not have what he eagerly sought? Certainly, because he sought
> it, he received it. What else does it mean, "Whatever just man shall
> be overtaken by death, his soul shall be at rest"? (Wisdom 4:7)[66]

In a letter to Faustinus, who was mourning the death of his sister,
Ambrose repeats some of the themes common to early Christian counsel at death, themes in debt to the Stoics: death is common to all,
the departed are offended by our tears, and if we are truly Christian
we should rejoice rather than mourn. We have seen such counsel
given by Jerome to Paula at the death of Blesilla with offensive
intensity. But in the letter to Faustinus, Ambrose touches on the
problem of pathological grief. "I knew very well that you would lament
with bitter grief the death of your sister, yet not in such a way as to
estrange yourself from us, but to come back to us. Although mourners
have not joyous consolations, they are always necessary ones."[67] Ambrose recognized the need for mourning, he who had suffered intensive
grief at the death of his brother, Satyrus. But Faustinus had "gone
off to a mountain retreat, to a cave amid the haunts of beasts, spurning
all part in the affairs of men and, what is more serious, disregarding
even your own good judgment."[68] Solitude in mourning was acceptable,
but not to the point of cutting off all communication with friends, and
that by going off to a cave and living among the wilds. He is not harsh
with him, but invites him back. "What need is there for us to grieve
if now it is said to the soul, 'Thy youth is renewed like the eagle's'?
Why do we lament the dead when the reconciliation of the world with
God the Father has already been made through the Lord Jesus?"[69]
He encouraged him to believe what he had always believed, and not
to permit his "exceedingly great grief" to cause doubt. For our Lord
Jesus became sin to take away the sin of the world, and therein was

the sure reward of paradise. He concludes with the words: "Farewell, and love us, for we love you."

The proper burial of the dead was of great concern to the early Christians. Indeed, in the first and second century the church was looked upon by the Roman government as another burial society (*collegium*) among many in the empire. By Roman law the dead had to be buried outside the walls of a city, and as early as the third century Christians owned their own cemeteries, including catacombs at Rome. Hippolytus (215) insists that the charges were not to be severe, and that the pastor was to defray the expenses from the common treasury for those who could not pay.[70] In the time of persecution the martyrs' graves were given special reverence. We find this first with Polycarp, where the faithful gathered annually at his grave on the anniversary of his death, to celebrate the Eucharist.[71] Under the imperial church when Christianity became the official religion of the empire it became customary to hold a funeral agape or meal at the gravesite on the anniversary of one's death, a practice borrowed from pagan Rome, which led to abuses (see chap. 2).

We have little information about early Christian funerals apart from the funeral orations. We know that the Eucharist was central to the service, with its strong eschatological dimensions, which are alluded to in the sermons. We also find eucharistic imagery throughout the catacomb frescoes—the feeding of the five thousand, the Last Supper, the multiplication of bread and fishes, and pictures of the blessing of bread and chalice—which indicate a strong association of Holy Communion with the burial of the dead. There was a procession from church to cemetery in which the casket was carried on the shoulders of the pallbearers. Then, as today in many countries, mourners wore white.

The letters of consolation reveal a number of facets of pastoral care. The fact that we possess a large number in this genre indicates that apart from delivering funeral sermons, clergy wrote letters to people who were grieving or who were in need of counsel. This was not only because in some cases the recipients lived at some distance, but in many cases they lived in the same city. The letters were written so that the sender could gather his thoughts in an organized manner, knowing the recipient would read and reread its contents, share it with friends, and make copies for others. The letters also reveal the concern of clergy for discharging their functions as curators of souls, however competently this may have been done. In offering consolation to mourners, they utilized themes common to humanity, but never without reference to Christ's resurrection, his conquest of death, and the hope of eternal life.

Reconciling the Penitent

We have already described the origins of the penitential system in the church (chap. 2). For the sake of the sinner and out of zeal for the purity of the church, those who were guilty of major offenses (apostasy, adultery, murder) were required to make public confession of their guilt and undergo a public penance, which automatically excluded them from receiving the Eucharist. Penitents were variously graded according to their progress until the pastor judged they were ready for readmission and the reception of the Eucharist. This was done in a public absolution before the congregation. The entire process was known as *exomologesis*, or confession, and it was permitted only once following one's baptism. It was administered only for sins that were considered especially serious. Lesser sins were atoned for through almsgiving and by praying the Lord's Prayer, "forgive us our sins." In addition to offering pastoral care through guidance, sustenance, and consolation, the clergy were actively engaged in reconciling penitents to the church, or the process of discipline.

Tertullian represents a rigorist position in the application of discipline. He is writing during the time of persecution when large numbers of the faithful apostatized, and he was equally severe on those who were guilty of immorality. He developed his advice in a work *On Penitence*, written about 203.

Only one penance is permitted following baptism. Because the basis for repentance is the fear of the Lord, writes Tertullian, it is clear that committing a second sin following penance indicates that there is no longer a fear of the Lord. Therefore the sinner has no more recourse to grace. "In truth, it is nothing but wilful disobedience which destroys the fear of God."[72] Inasmuch as grievous postbaptismal sins are forgiven only once, it follows that baptism should not be hastily offered or given without thorough preparation. For this reason, Tertullian was opposed to infant baptism.

Regarding public penance, Tertullian explains:

> Exomologesis, then, is a discipline which leads a man to prostrate and humble himself. It prescribes a way of life which, even in the matter of food and clothing, appeals to pity. It bids him to lie in sackcloth and ashes, to cover his body with filthy rags, to plunge his soul into sorrow, to exchange sin for suffering. Moreover, it demands that you know only such food and drink that is plain; this means it is taken for the sake of your soul, not your belly. . . . In proportion as you have had no mercy on yourself, believe me, in just this same measure God will have mercy upon you.[73]

But most people avoid such public exposure (as well we can imagine) because of the shame. Yet no human is better or above another. We are all sinners in God's sight, and no Christian who witnesses the humility of penitents dare think of himself as superior. But as with medicine, there can be no cure without pain. "Why are you tardy to approach what you know heals you?"[74] After vivid description of hell, he suggests it is only rational and good sense to try to avoid it, at whatever cost to self-esteem.

Tertullian fairly reflected the mind of most theologians of the first five centuries in his demand for public confession and reconciliation of sinners guilty of serious faults. But in his Montanist days he found himself in opposition to Bishop Callistus of Rome (217–23), for by that time Tertullian refused penance to any who were guilty of the three capital sins. In the course of time the less rigorous view of Rome prevailed, probably due to the pressures of the large numbers who lapsed under persecution and to the impossibility of maintaining absolutely rigid standards with the growing numbers of converts to the faith. In defense of his action, Callistus appealed to the parable of the tares (Matt. 13:24-30) and the mixed assortment of animals in Noah's ark.[75] What may be considered the more evangelical attitude is reflected in Cyprian's comment, "We allow adulterers an opportunity of penance and grant them absolution."[76] Although Cyprian's moderate view became the norm, the old rigorism still showed itself at the Council of Elvira (303), which is memorable for the large number of canons ordering lifelong excommunication without the hope of reconciliation even at death.

The Council of Nicea (325) addressed the issue of restoring the penitent in several of its canons. Excommunication in one diocese was to be recognized by the entire church (can. 5), and we assume the same was true for readmission. Clergy who had been guilty of the Novatian heresy could be readmitted to their clerical status confessing the true faith, but they were to serve under the direction of other clergy (can. 8). Clergy who had lapsed under persecution were to be deposed from office, and if such had been ordained because the bishop was unaware of their apostasy, the ordination was declared void (can. 10). Any persons who had denied Christ without the threat of harm or loss or property were to be dealt with mercifully (can. 11), and all penitents, regardless of their status, were to be offered the Eucharist if they were at the point of death (can. 13). Cathechumens who had lapsed were assigned a three-year penance (can. 14).

Beginning with the mid-fourth and early fifth century our knowledge of the penitential system becomes clearer. In the East, Basil described the length of penance imposed for various sins and established the principle that clergy convicted of adultery were to be deposed.[77] Epiphanius said that there was only one "perfect repentance" (i.e., baptism), but he believed that God would welcome guilty persons back to the fold in consideration of their good works.[78] At Constantinople the number of penitents was so large that the bishop delegated his responsibility to a special penitentiary priest (or priests) who supervised the penitents, but the office was suppressed about 397 when abuses by the priest were discovered.[79]

Ambrose composed two books *On Repentance*, which were prompted by the rigorous practices of the Novatians. In dealing with penitent sinners, gentleness is the highest virtue. "He who endeavors to amend the faults of human weakness ought to bear this very weakness on his own shoulders, let it weigh upon himself and not cast it off."[80] Using the analogy of a shepherd, he points out that just as carrying a wounded sheep imposes a burden on the shepherd, so also the sin of the penitent is a burden to be borne by the pastor. Penance is offered out of love for the sinner, not anger. There is no sin so great that it is beyond God's mercy. The "unforgivable sin" (Matt. 12:32) is that of unfaith, but as long as there is the faintest glimmer of faith, we should nourish and tend it, just as the Good Samaritan brought healing to the man who was found almost dead. King David is a good example of one who was guilty of apostasy, adultery, and murder, yet who found mercy with God. In his second book, Ambrose is critical of the mechanical or perfunctory discharge of penance, because God requires true sorrow of the heart. It is necessary to remove shame from penitence by reminding the congregation that all are sinners, and among God's greatest saints there have been notorious sinners (i.e, David) whose very penance contributed to their sainthood. Ambrose defends the prevailing custom of permitting only one opportunity for penance, and it should be public.

Augustine's writings are filled with allusions to penance, which he divides into three categories. First, there is repentance for sins committed before baptism. In the case of children, "the faith of those by whom they are presented prevails."[81] Second, there is repentance for the lighter daily sins, "whose committal runs through our entire life." This occurs through praying the Lord's Prayer daily as well as practicing almsgiving and fasting.[82] Thirdly, there is repentance in the proper sense of the term—that is, "the more serious and painful repentance in which they are properly called penitents in the church."[83] These are those who on account of grave sins have been excluded from Holy Communion. Such must make confession to the bishop who assigns to them an appropriate "satisfaction." Repentance is understood as a continuation of one's baptism.[84]

By the end of the fifth century we find these features relating to penance. First, it was permitted only once, and that for grave sins. Because there was no second opportunity for repentance, many people postponed their *exomologesis* until late in life. There was no agreement on which sins were mortal. Basil's list is fairly long, and Augustine vaguely says that any sin against the Ten Commandments requires public penance.[85] Others, such as Gregory of Nyssa, kept the earlier list of three—apostasy, adultery, murder. Given the imprecision of what constituted a mortal sin, we can assume the clergy exercised considerable pastoral discretion in making this determination.

Second, there was the confession proper. In earlier years this was made publicly, and Ambrose recommends that it be made before the people, but he also permitted a private confession. Origen also allowed the penitent to confess privately to the pastor, "to declare his sin to a priest of the Lord and to ask for the cure,"[86] and Augustine, as we have just seen, recommends that confession "be made to the bishop." It appears that a public confession was preferable, and the private conversation with the pastor was a concession to human frailty. We can certainly assume that even prior to a public confession there had been private pastoral counsel.

Whether the confession was private or public, the actual penance was invariably public, if for no other reason than withdrawal from Communion would be observed by all. In addition to this there were austerities to be observed, which included fasting, weeping, wearing a hair shirt, not cutting one's hair, donning sackcloth and ashes, and wearing the dress of mourners. Penitents also were assigned a special place in public worship and were required to leave with the catechumens before the liturgy of the Eucharist. The duration and severity of the penance was at the discretion of the pastor, but there were several guidelines for their consideration. The Council of Ancyra (314) in dealing with apostates assigned them one year as hearers, three years as kneelers, and two as costanders. The Council of Nicea called for a total of eleven years of penance for those who had lapsed under persecution. The Synod of Laodicea (after 434) simply suggested a period of penance in proportion to the guilt.

After undergoing the prescribed penance, the sinner was given public absolution. By the fifth century this was often done on Maundy Thursday. The Gelasian Sacramentary, which originated in the fifth century, offers a detailed description of this rite as it was observed in Rome, including prayers, prostrations, admonitions, the kiss of peace, and the reception back into full communion with the faithful.[87]

How and when did the once-in-a-lifetime penance become repeatable and confession and absolution become private? Scholars are still divided or uncertain about this question. Although there is ample evidence of private confession at an early time, it was always accompanied with public absolution, and it was limited to one time only. The sacramental absolution appears to have been the sole privilege of clergy. When Hunneric, the Vandal, expelled many of the clergy from North Africa in 483, Christians appealed to him: "Who will now minister to us the office of penance, and by reconciliation loose those who are bound in the chains of their sins?[88] Caesarius of Arles (d. 542) urges his readers to "go to the priest that you may be reconciled."[89]

But confession to a priest was not obligatory. It appears in some writers that in the entire process of *exomologesis*, penance itself was of primary importance rather than the confession or the absolution. Gennadius, a priest of Marseilles (d. 496), devotes one chapter of his *On Ecclesiastical Doctrines* to this problem. He points out that confession of sin to God alone is sufficient for the average Christian, and an alternative to public penance is adopting the religious life.[90] Julianus Pomerius suggests that Christians may discipline themselves:

> If they become their own judges, and thus as it were the avengers of their own iniquity, let them exercise against themselves a voluntary penalty of severe chastisements; so they will exchange everlasting punishments for temporal penalties, and will extinguish the conflageration of eternal fire by tears flowing from a true remorse of heart.[91]

This self-inflicted excommunication had sacramental efficacy and was a valid penance in the sight of God. Caesarius of Arles wrote in the same vein, arguing that it was better to adopt this kind of penance than to leave everything to a final death-bed confession.

This is not yet the same as frequent private confession and absolution before a priest. For this development we must look to the monastic life, specifically to the Celtic monks who played a prominent role in introducing the practice of private confession. This is a development that is just beginning at the dawn of the medieval church (600), and which will be discussed further in the following section. In terms of pastoral care in the early church, we have ample evidence that the clergy were actively engaged in private conversations with troubled sinners, either to encourage them to proceed to public penance or to offer counsel.

There is some question about the nature of absolution. On the one hand we have seen that some believed that only a priest could forgive sins, presumably because such authority had been given him at the time of his ordination. But Gregory the Great taught that the absolution of God preceded that of the priest, and the priest simply declared what was an accomplished fact. "This lifegiving of the Lord is recognized already in the confession of sin itself before the official sentence."[92] In the earliest extant formulations of reconciliation, there is only a prayer of thanks to God and the laying on of hands. Bernard Cooke observes that the priestly role in absolution remained a point of controversy for many centuries, "whether the action of the church (i.e., priest) in the reconciliation of sinners is petitionary, declarative, or causative. Does the church assure the penitent that his sins are forgiven, or does it act as God's instrument in this forgiveness?"[93] According to some modern scholars, we do not find a definitive priestly declaration in which he says, "I forgive you," until the twelfth century.[94] This would account for the recommendation of Caesarius of

Arles and Julianus Pomerius for every Christian to exercise self-examination, imposing one's own penance, leaving the absolution to trust in God's promises.

The Spiritual Director

When Origen advised his fellow Christians to "look around carefully to find the proper person to whom to confess your sin," he did not necessarily have in mind the selection of someone who had been ordained. In his view, one primary requisite for any who served as a spiritual counselor was the ability to understand the situation of the person seeking direction, but above all to possess a high degree of virtue and wisdom. Origen himself was a respected teacher of the church long before his controversial ordination, and he had little respect for many of the clergy. Instead of acting as religious examples and sympathetic physicians of souls to their congregations, he said they were worldly minded, looked for advancement, were easily flattered by their parishioners, and were less professional than others in the secular world.[95] We recall that it was Origen who said it was "ridiculous" to believe that any bishop could absolve sins simply by virtue of his office if he did not also display exemplary spirituality. For Origen, personal spiritual qualities, including virtue, wisdom, and experience—the gnostic ideal of "perfection"—were of greater significance in offering pastoral guidance than was the mere possession of the pastoral office. For Origen, "all that is necessary, and in a certain sense indispensable, for the Christian is a teacher, a guide, a friend to educate him. . . . There is no moral progress without the person of the spiritual helper, without the living example and the loving participation of someone who is perfect."[96] Origen reflects an attitude closely associated with the earlier prophets and teachers of the second century, who for a time took precedence over the clergy, and whose authority was derived from their sanctity of life.

In Von Campenhausen's masterful work, *Ecclesiastical Authority and Spiritual Power in the First Three Centuries*, those who represented "spiritual power" were at first prophets and teachers, followed by ascetics and monks, including women as well as men, especially that large company of spiritually sensitive persons known as mystics. Origen referred to these nonordained persons as the true priests and

Levites of the new people of God, which is itself a priestly race.[97] The end of the persecutions and the increased secularization of the church found many devout Christians seeking the solitude of the wilderness to pursue a more austere way of life in monasticism or the hermitage. This movement not only produced a considerable body of literature on pastoral care, but many of the desert fathers and mothers were actively sought out as spiritual advisors by Christians from the cities. St. Anthony (d. 356) complained about the large numbers of people who came out to visit him, and moving deeper in the desert several times did not stop the flow of visitors. Yet it is doubtful that he was ever ordained a priest. Among his numerous counselees was Athanasius, the celebrated bishop of Alexandria, who also wrote his biography.

Part of the rationale for seeking out those who were perceived as possessing extraordinary holiness was the belief that their healing, forgiveness, and spiritual counsel would be more effective than that of the clergy at home, who, as Origen's melancholy account suggests, did not present themselves as examples of piety. George H. Williams writes about this phenomenon: "It is one of the anomalies of the evolution of the monastic ideal that they who withdrew to the wilderness, for the most part dispensing with the ministries of the organized parishes and thinking of themselves as laymen, were presently to become the tutors and models of the secular clergy."[98] The monastic submission to the rule was construed as a type of ordination, and in time the monastic ideal became a model for the church with momentous consequences for pastoral life and ministry.

One of the most significant developments in the "monastisization" of the church was in penitential practices. This came not from the deserts of Egypt or Syria, but from the Celts who lived beyond the boundaries of the Roman empire. The pre-Christian Welsh and Irish religious traditions included the functions of a spiritual and moral director who served as a guide for souls, or a soul-friend. The Celts of Gaul practiced a spiritual discipline that included penance, catalogues of virtues and vices, excommunication, and restoration, which we find recorded in Julius Caesar's *Gallic War*.[99] In pre-Christian times it was expected that everyone would have a spiritual guide. Following the introduction of Christianity, these practices continued in the Celtic monasteries—that is, the practices of private confession to a soul-friend followed by absolution. St. Gildas (d. 570) informs us that the discipline practiced in his day included private confession, private penance, and private reconciliation.[100] This was reserved for monastic houses, but much earlier, St. Finnian of Clonard (c. 530) informs us that such frequent and repeatable confession and absolution was available for students and laymen who desired to do penance.[101] Thus the laity could receive the same privileges of private confession as the monks. A modern scholar of the history of penance, O. D. Watkins, comments on this development:

> The outstanding significance of the Celtic monastic systems of penance for the student of the history of penance is that whereas on the continent of Europe the rule throughout the West is public penance and public reconciliation, in the Celtic procedure the public character has been taken away from penance and reconciliation alike. The change is of momentous importance. It marks the beginning of the modern revolution in penitential procedure.[102]

It appears, therefore, that the roots of the Celtic system are found in the spiritual director or soul-friend of the Druid system, because one did not confess to anyone in general but to one's spiritual guide, whose authority lay not in an official position but in his skill as a spiritual counselor. "Confession of sins was looked upon as a saving ascetic exercise, one which could have much of its impact even if the confession was given to a lay person."[103] A layperson would not confer a sacramental absolution validated by ordination, but then our sources are vague about a "sacramental" absolution even by priests, who often simply reminded the penitent that God had forgiven him, as we have seen was Gregory's position.

Private confession and absolution continued to be resisted in the West, where the third Council of Toledo (589) condemned it as an *execrabilis praesumptio*. This clearly indicates that it was coming into use on the continent, especially in religious houses. S. Donatus, Bishop of Besancon in the early seventh century, writes that nuns were confessing their sins to their abbess.[104] Although this example is from outside the period of the early church, it indicates the continuing practice of penitents seeking the guidance of spiritual directors. The transition from the early practice of a single penance that was public, to that of frequent private confessions, which became the norm in the late medieval period, is not clear. It appears there was a coalescence of at least three influences. First is the practice of the early church with its once-in-a-lifetime public *exomologesis,* accompanied with private pastoral counsel given to the penitent. Second was the revival of the Origenist tradition, which encouraged Christians to seek a pastoral relationship with a spiritual guide. This practice found its fruition in the fourth and fifth centuries when the monks of Egypt, Syria, and Palestine were sought after for spiritual counsel. The third influence, and the most significant, came from the Celtic monastic practices, which in turn were a continuation of pre-Christian religious traditions developed in Wales and Ireland involving the counsel of soul-friends. How these forces converged into the practice of private confession and absolution remains a question of scholarly inquiry. For our purpose it is sufficient to recognize the importance attached to a confessor, a soul-friend, by the early church. Despite Origen's criticism of the clergy, there is little evidence the Christians who were seeking a confessor were anticlerical. The spiritual guide was one whose saintliness and sagacity commended itself to the care of souls, and for this task the monks appeared to be the best suited, whether or not they were clergy.

Although in many cases the appeal of ascetics and monks to serve as spiritual advisors was a reaction to worldly clergy, this development was also one dimension of a growing idealism of asceticism, which reached unprecedented popularity in the church of the fourth and fifth centuries. It was fed by the need for examples of heroic faith now that the age of martyrdom was ended.[105] "Something of the days of persecution was being recaptured in the call to idealism, joyful service, and self-renewal."[106] But the ideal was not without its darker side, as it also represented a revival of the Manicheistic dualism that disparaged matter, including the body, marriage, and the pursuits of legitimate worldly interests. Augustine, a monk himself, heaped scorn on the exhibitionism of the new heroes. They spent too much time in begging and in visiting each other, these long-haired eccentrics. "Is it necessary for them to be so completely idle that they cannot get a haircut?"[107] Ragged and dirty clothing, he said, was often deceptive, as it covered a pride and hypocrisy of the worst kind, wolves in sheep's clothing. Chrysostom, himself a monk for a time, viewed the new popularity of monks as spiritual sages with some misgivings:

If anyone admires a solitary life and the avoidance of crowded society, I admit that it is a sign of patient endurance, but not sufficient proof of all-around spiritual prowess . . . we need not give lavish or excessive praise to the monk . . . nothing is as useless for church government as this inactivity and detachment, which other people regard as a form of self-discipline.[108]

The extremes were reached in fanatical devotion to spiritual heroics by the crowds of admirers attracted to the "stylites" or pole-sitters, monks who isolated themselves on small platforms raised up to thirty feet from the ground, and who remained there for weeks at a time. But these were eccentrics, and they did not represent the mainstream of monasticism, which contributed much to life and literature of the church in the late patristic period.

The new wave of asceticism produced literature that would influence the practice of pastoral care for centuries. One of the most distinguished writers was John Cassian (d. 435), a monk of Marseilles. His two principal works were the *Institutes*, which established the rules for monastic life, and the *Conferences*, which recall his conversations about spiritual life with the great leaders of Eastern monasticism. Although he wrote primarily for monks, the care of souls found useful in the monasteries became the standard for the laity as well. He popularized the idea that there were specific deadly sins:

There are eight principal faults which attack mankind; first is gluttony, secondly fornication, thirdly avarice or love of money, fourthly anger, fifthly dejection, sixthly acedia or listlessness and low spirits, seventhly boasting or vainglory, and eightly pride.[109]

Later, Gregory the Great revised the list to seven principal vices. With perceptive theological insight he placed pride at the head of the list as being the "mother" of all sin, followed by envy, anger, dejection, avarice, gluttony, and lust.[110]

Cassian continues by describing the circumstances of each sin. Some, like gluttony and fornication, require external objects or people. Some sins are physical and some are mental. "It is extremely useful for those who aspire to purity to begin by withdrawing from themselves the material which feeds these carnal passions."[111] He suggests that one of the best cures for sin is to seek the company and friendship of honorable people, who will rebuke us when we have done wrong. In this he recognizes the powerful influence of peer pressure and of the salutary effect of one's friends, provided they are carefully chosen. Each of the eight capital vices attacks persons in different ways. Each person should discover his own besetting sin and direct his main attack against it, not trying to cope with all eight at one time. To do this one needs the resources of prayer, meditation, and (we assume) a spiritual guide. "For it is impossible for a man to win a triumph over any kind of passion unless he has first clearly understood that he cannot possibly gain the victory in the struggle with it by his own strength and efforts."[112] And having gained a measure of victory, one should not succumb to pride in having done so, but exercise constant vigilance against its reoccurrence. Cassian's influence was also paramount in establishing the manifestation of conscience in spiritual life. Throughout his writings, Cassian speaks of the value of the moral life as a contributing factor toward one's salvation, and in this he is viewed as a father of the Semi-Pelagianism that opposed Augustine's doctrine of grace.

Maximus the Confessor (d. 662) was another monastic writer on spiritual counsel. Although he writes a few years later than our definition of the early church (600), his *Four Hundred Chapters on Love* recapitulate the wisdom of the desert fathers who preceded him. Among his four hundred chapters he writes:

- The passion of greed is revealed when one is happy in receiving but unhappy in giving. Such a person cannot be a good steward.
- A person definitely wants to be healed if he does not put up any resistance to the healing remedies. These are the pains and hurts brought on by many different circumstances. The one who resists does not know what is being worked out here nor what advantages he would draw from it.
- Be on guard lest the vice that separates you from your brother be not found in your brother but in you.
- Do not recall in time of peace what your brother said in time of hurt, even though the offensive things were said to your face, or were said to another about you and you heard them afterward, lest in retaining grudges you revert to pernicious hate for your brother.
- Friends are abundant—that is, in times of prosperity. In times of trial you can barely find one.[113]

Wisdom of this kind was produced in significant quantity by the desert fathers, and it was used by clerical advisors for many centuries.

Alongside books of counsel we find the emergence of "penitential disciplines," which were books containing prescribed penances for specific sins, intended to assist the clergy in assigning appropriate penances for moral infractions. These first appeared among the Celtic Christians in the sixth century, but their use and development lies beyond our period of study.

The desirability of every Christian relating to a spiritual director is found as early as Origen in the third century, but its implementation gained impetus with the emergence of monasticism in the fourth and fifth centuries. This period also produced literature on soul care, which formed the basis for pastoral counseling for a millennium and beyond. Largely under the influence of the Celtic monks, public penance was transformed into private confession and absolution, which included private counsel by the pastor. The amount of literature extant from the desert fathers of the fourth and fifth centuries on the care of souls indicates a concern, indeed a passion, for the spiritual growth of individuals and for competent and sympathetic pastoral care.

Gregory the Great—*Pastoral Care*

Gregory (d. 604) had a distinguished career before he became pope in the year 590. He was the son of a wealthy senator, and when he became prefect of Rome he sold his vast properties and gave the proceeds to the poor. He founded seven monasteries and resided in one himself before he reluctantly permitted himself to be named one of the seven deacons of Rome. After a few years in Constantinople as the pope's ambassador, he returned to Rome as abbot of his former monastery, and in 590 he was elected bishop of Rome during a time of military, economic, and political disasters in the West. He is known for his political success in securing freedom for the Western church from the Eastern emperor, for the mission of Augustine to Canterbury in England, and for the beginning of Gregorian chant. His greatest contributions were made in his writings, of which *Pastoral Care* (*Liber Regulae Pastoralis*) was by far the most influential in the following centuries. King Alfred of England translated it into Anglo-Saxon, and it was customary in the Middle Ages that at the elevation to the episcopate, every bishop was given a copy to guide him in his cure of souls. Not only is it the earliest work devoted entirely to pastoral counseling, but its insights into the human condition and pastoral guidance remain remarkably relevant in today's world. We are in debt to Thomas C. Oden, *Care of Souls in the Classic Tradition*, who has analyzed Gregory's methods in light of modern therapeutical practice, and has found him to be very contemporary indeed.[114]

The work, which Gregory composed immediately upon becoming bishop of Rome, is divided into four sections: (1) the difficulties of the pastoral office and its requirements; (2) the life of a good pastor; (3) how to deal with the various kinds of maladies of people; (4) the pastor should be mindful of his own weaknesses.

"The governance of souls is the art of arts" (1:1). It requires wisdom and humility. People who are utterly ignorant of spiritual precepts are often not afraid of professing themselves to be physicians of the heart. "They crave to appear as teachers and covet ascendancy over others" (1:1). He warns against clergy who delight in managing other people's emotional lives and who find delight in wielding such power. Those who are vested with the appearance of holiness often destroy others by word and example. Too often the physician is distracted by a host of extraneous matters and is unable to give adequate and responsible concentration to the individuals who seek his aid. "This is not to censure the office itself, but to fortify the weak heart against coveting it." (1:4). But just as those who are unfit often covet the office, those who are best qualified avoid it, which is equally perverse. During the days of persecution, clergy were often the first to suffer or die, so the office attracted more spiritual leaders. Under the freedom of the church, the office often attracts those who desire instant authority and status by virtue of ordination (1:8).

The pastor must himself be a person of stability. "If in his practice ailments still thrive in him, with what presumption does he hasten to heal the afflicted while he carries a sore on his own face?" (1:9). He concludes the first section by describing the character necessary for a counselor: a spiritual life, not tempted by wealth, setting an example, sympathetic, experienced, one who is at peace with himself. He continues by describing those unfit for the office: unstable habits, having an excessive interest in the private lives of others, one who himself is burdened with too many worldly cares, the one who is beset with wicked thoughts while he offers counsel, even though he may not act on them (1:11).

In the second part Gregory discusses the life of the pastor. He first offers a summary of the topics he will treat:

> It is necessary, therefore, that he should be pure in thought, exemplary in conduct, discreet in keeping silence, profitable in speech, in sympathy a near neighbor to everyone, in contemplation exalted above all others, a humble companion to those who lead good lives, erect in his zeal for righteousness against the vices of sinners. He must not be remiss in his care for the inner life by preoccupation with the external; nor must he in his solicitude for what is internal, fail to give attention to the external [2:1].

Gregory clearly insists on a "double standard" of behavior between pastor and people. He should not merely be virtuous, but outstandingly so. As to discretion in speech, not only ought he know how to keep secrets, but he should also know when to speak candidly, lest he give an uncertain sound out of fear. And even when a word should properly be spoken, it should be done carefully, not with an excess of words or carelessly or slovenly, because even when the pastor says what must be said, the people may not hear it, because of the way in which it is spoken (2:4).

He has a word for style of leadership, recognizing that "all men cannot be on an equal footing," so there must be leaders and followers. The pastors should "find their joy not in ruling over men but in helping them . . . not kings of men but shepherds of flocks." Flattery is a professional hazard, especially "when he believes himself to be such as he hears himself proclaimed to be." It is also important to distinguish between the sin and the sinner, recognizing that pastors are the equals of the people they correct, not superior to them. One must avoid discipline that is too rigid and loving-kindness that is too lax. "In other words, gentleness is to be mingled with severity; a compound is to be made of both, so that subjects may not be exasperated by too great harshness, nor enervated by excessive tenderness" (2:6).

Next Gregory touches on a subject that has engaged modern concern—workaholism. He chides clergy who equate busyness with accomplishment, whose lives are governed by reacting to external pressures rather than by controlling their own time. And when there is no need at the moment for external activities, "they hanker after them day and night with the surge of a disordered mind":

> For they take it as a pleasure to be weighed down by such activities, and regard it laborious not to be laboring in earthly concerns. And so

it happens that, while they rejoice in being weighed down with tumultuous worldly business, they disregard those interior matters which they ought to be teaching others. [2:7]

But there are clergy who piously devote themselves to contemplation and thereby believe they are doing well, but they neglect the exterior life of the congregation. Clergy who are isolated from the flock by their study should not be surprised when their words are not heeded by the faithful. There is also a very fine line between accepting flattery and being loved, for the love of the people is essential to effective pastoral care. "It is difficult for one who is not loved, however well he preaches, to find a sympathetic hearing. Wherefore, he who rules ought to aim at being loved, that he may be listened to." Love of the pastor is not for the sake of the pastor, but for the sake of the Word (2:8).

The third section of the *Pastoral Care* is by far the longest. It contains thirty-six "case studies" of care, each one dealing with extremes or opposites. We find advice on dealing with the poor and rich, the joyful and sad, the impatient and patient. Gregory uses this method in order to emphasize the need for contextual counseling, as the method will depend upon the malady. Also, men, women, and young people are to be admonished in different ways, as are the old and the young. On the poor and the rich, he says, one should not harbor stereotypes; the rich man may be humble and the poor man proud. In dealing with a man of power, one should be indirect and tell a story, as Nathan did to King David, and let the man's own intelligence draw the proper conclusions. As to the wise and the dull, the "former are more readily converted by arguments from reason; the latter are often converted better by examples" (3:6).

Thomas Oden offers an analysis of Gregory's advice on counseling the timid and the assertive in which he clearly anticipated some forms of transactional analysis. The timid person has developed a behavior of such modesty that it leads to self-effacement, whereas his counterpart has developed such self-confidence as to become arrogance. "Gregory had an extraordinarily clear intuitive awareness of such dynamics in his analysis of the pastoral care of the timid and the assertive."[115] To the timid person, Gregory offers the sixth-century version of assertiveness training, and the arrogant must be shown how they are overplaying their hand and defeating their purposes. "The former [arrogant] esteem everything they do to be singularly excellent, the fainthearted think what they do is extremely despicable, and therefore their spirit is broken in dejection" (3:8).

On counseling the impatient and the patient, Gregory describes the former with keen insight. They are impetuous, neglecting to curb their spirit, only to feel regret when later they realize what they have done. "The less patient a man proves to be, the less instructed does he show himself to be" (3:9). Gregory understands that the demanding person, arrogant and boastful, "advertising himself," may have a deep-seated feeling of inferiority, which feeds his need for recognition. But the excessively patient person is sometimes wronged, but they do not recognize it at the time. "But when after a time they recall what they have suffered, they become inflamed with resentment and seek out reasons for revenge, and by withdrawing the meekness displayed in their endurance, they turn it to malice" (3:9). Here Gregory displays a keen knowledge of human nature. The patient person who has suffered an indignity, "because he has lost his case in open conflict, he is all on fire to lay hidden snares." He may grossly exaggerate the supposed wrong done to him, and permit it to consume his mind. He may denounce himself for having lacked the courage at the moment of the insult to "requite insult for insult." Although people may admire the patient person for his virtue, inwardly he may be harboring the malice of resentment from previous insults. The pastoral counselor must recognize that what appears on the surface of a person's behavior may not be the real person (3:9).

Gregory suggests how to admonish the quarrelsome and the peaceable. There may be parishioners who display admirable qualities of character, but they are contentious and tend to "lose the gift of concord, which is the greater gift." For these he reminds them of the words of James: "But if you have bitter zeal, and there be contentions in your heart, glory not" (James 3:14f.). The evils of discord are great, and they nullify whatever other good qualities a person may have. Furthermore, reconciliation with one's neighbor is a precondition for reconciliation with God (3:22).

On the other hand, peaceable persons may harbor other vices. It is no virtue to be peaceable in the face of evil or wrongdoing. "The peaceful are to be admonished not to fear disturbing their temporal peace by breaking out into words of reproof. Further, they are to be admonished to maintain inwardly their love unimpaired, that peace which outwardly they disturb by giving reproof" (3:22). Sometimes the peace-loving are so complacent in their lives that they lack zeal for the life to come, so peace is both to be loved and condemned.

Gregory continues in this way through thirty-six "case studies" of pastoral care, in which he reveals a perceptive knowledge of human nature and the various nuances and shades of virtue and vice that confront the pastoral counselor. In all his advice there is the caution not to accept appearances at face value. Virtue, such as patience, may be a disguise for underlying malice, and vice, such as arrogance, may be a cloak for a very troubled soul. He concludes his work with a short reminder to clergy, who are constantly advising others, not to disregard their own spiritual health. "Let him not, while he is helping his neighbors, neglect himself; let him not, while lifting up others, fall himself." He returns again to an earlier admonition against pastoral pride. He concludes his manual on pastoral care by saying, "I have tried to show what a pastor should be like. I, miserable painter that I am, have painted a portrait of an ideal man; and here I have been directing others to the shores of perfection, I, who am still tossed about by the waves of sin."

Throughout the vicissitudes of early Christian pastoral life, which witnessed extensive discussion on the pastoral office and questions of authority, as well as heated controversies over Christology, the Trinity, and doctrines of salvation and human sin, the ultimate significance of theology found its meaning in the care of souls. Early Christian pastors addressed themselves to this daily task with the same degree of zeal or indifference, responsibility or lethargy, competence or incompetence, as their successors of every age. But as these examples have demonstrated, there was no lack of devoted energy given to pastoral care among early Christian pastors. "The governance of souls is the art of arts."

5 The Pastoral Role of Women

In recent years a great amount of literature has been produced concerning the role of women in the early church. Not all these studies have equal value, because too often they have a polemical intent born of current interests in the role of women in the modern church. On the one hand we find those who view antiquity with dismay as fostering a subservience upon women, which the church has yet to overcome. On the other hand are those who interpret ancient texts in such a way as to give women far greater equality than was the case. Others associate the leadership of women in the early church with heretical sects, suggesting that the sects may have been declared unorthodox partly because of the role that women played in them. It is difficult to offer a dispassionate assessment of women in the early church without the danger of making a direct leap to the twentieth century in terms of moralisms, examples, precedents, or alarms.

The intent of this chapter is to concentrate on the pastoral role of women. We know that they did not share in the episcopal or presbyterial ministry of males, although some have claimed to find a notable exception or two. In terms of pastoral functions by way of recognized officeholders, to which women were appointed and ordained, we are limited to the office of deaconess and widow. However, before such offices became commonplace, we also find women serving in various ministerial capacities since the time of Jesus and the apostles.

The New Testament

Unlike the Judasim from which Christianity grew, women were included as full members of the Christian community. Whereas Judaism required a minimum of twelve circumcised males to form a legitimate synagogue, there were no such requirements in the church. Before his conversion, Saul was intent on arresting both women and men indiscriminately (Acts 8:3, 9:2). The focus of preaching was to men and women alike, as in Berea, where many believed, "not a few Greek women of high standing as well as men" (Acts 17:12). Jesus attracted a number of women as his followers. "The Twelve were with him and also some women . . . Mary Magdalene, and Joanna, and Susanna, and many others who provided for them out of their means" (Luke 8:1-3). The indication is that these women offered provisions for Jesus and the Twelve from their own possessions. Joanna was the wife of a court official in Herod's palace and was certainly a woman of some means. When Luke writes that these women were with Jesus together with the Twelve, we can assume they traveled with him and shared in the ministry of evangelism.

Not only did women accompany Jesus during his ministry, but they were also prominent during his passion, death, and resurrection. Abandoned by his disciples, the women stayed on during his execution and burial, and they were the first witnesses to the resurrection. In addition to these listed above, the Gospels also mention Mary, the mother of James and Joseph, and the mother of the sons of Zebedee (Matt. 27:56) and "the other Mary" (Matt. 28:1); Mary, the mother of James the Younger and of Joses and Salome (Mark 15:40); and the mother of Jesus (John 19:25). Mary Magdalene appears in every Gospel listing of women, and except in John, is always listed first.

St. Paul concludes the letter to the Romans with a long list of women who had worked with him. At the head of the list is "our sister Phoebe, a deaconess of the church at Cenchrae . . . for she has been a helper of many and of myself as well" (16:1). It has been questioned whether "deaconess" is a proper translation for *diakonos*, thereby implying a recognized office in the church, or whether one should not simply refer to Phoebe as a servant of the church. To me it appears to be a title and not simply a general term of service. In any case she was singled out for her assistance to the apostle and many others as well. Paul next refers to Prisca and Aquila as his "fellow workers" in Christ Jesus, to whom "all the churches of the Gentiles give thanks" (16:4), and he sends greetings to Mary, "who has worked hard among you." Others who have served as workers for the Lord are Tryphaena, Tryphosa, and Persis. Here (Rom. 16:12) Paul uses the word *kopian* (work), which he reserves for the task of evangelism, whether by himself or others. Then Paul greets the mother of Rufus, whom he calls his own mother as well (16:13), in addition to greeting Nereus and his sister. In Philippians he refers to Euodia and Syntyche "who have struggled together with me in the Gospel" (Phil. 4:2).

The early house churches, crucial to the success of the gospel, were often provided by women. Lydia offered such hospitality in Philippi after she was baptized with her entire household (Acts 16:14), and Nympha opened her home in Laodicea (Col. 4:14). Mary, the mother of John Mark, also offered her home for Christian gatherings (Acts 12:12). "In short, there is no doubt that Paul often benefited from the cooperation of women in his apostolic labors and that the women did not prove themselves less fervent than the men in spreading the Good News."[1]

We have seen that the earliest triad of ministries in the early church was that of apostle, prophet, and teacher (see chap. 1; 1 Cor. 12:28). There is strong evidence that alongside the ministry of prophets there existed one of prophetesses or female prophets. Joel announced that at the end of time, after the pouring out of the Spirit, women as well as men would prophesy (Joel 3:1-2). We read of the four daughters of Philip the Evangelist ("one of the seven") who prophesied (Acts 21:9), and St. Paul cautions that women who prophesy must have their heads covered (1 Cor. 11:4-5). The function of prophecy was apparently one exercised in the public worship of the congregation. In the case of women, this seems to be contrary to St. Paul's demand that women should be silent in the assembly (1 Cor. 14:34-35). Furthermore, we have the example of Anna, daughter of Phanuel, who is mentioned by Luke as a prophetess, who was "continually in the temple, worshiping day and night in fasting and in prayer" (Luke 2:36-38). Jean Daniélou resolves the difficulty of the prohibition against women speaking in public and the clear indication that there were prophetesses who spoke in the public assembly by suggesting that prophecy was largely limited to prayer.[2] In the 1 Corinthians text Paul speaks of "every man or every woman who prays or prophesies." In 1 Timothy, admittedly later and non-Pauline, women are still permitted the privilege of public prayer, with the caution that they should be dressed modestly (1 Tim. 2:8-9). Women prophets, therefore, were definitely included among the recognized leaders of the early churches. Their function was largely restricted to public prayer and to the example of leading an ascetic life.

In the course of the second century the role of prophets and prophetesses became absorbed in other ministries, although Von Campenhausen finds a continuation of their "spiritual power" throughout the early church and into later periods by way of monasticism and mysticism.[3] It is probable that the prominent role given to prophecy in general and to prophetesses in particular within Montanism discredited this second-century movement in the eyes of the orthodox. Maximilla and Priscilla were especially active in the prophetic movement. Among the nineteen Montanist oracles gathered by P. de Labriolle, seven belong to the prophetesses.[4] Some Montanists believed that since Eve was the first to eat of the tree of knowledge, women were more likely than men to be recipients of divine wisdom and revelation.[5] Yet even Tertullian, that indefatigable critic of women, did not relent in his Montanist days and permitted prophetesses only the privilege of prayer in public; any other revelations given to them must be disclosed to male clergy in private.[6] He found fault with Marcion for permitting women to serve as leaders in his sect, thus ignoring the Pauline "law" opposed to the practice.[7]

Within second-century heretical groups the role of women was not only prominent among the Montanists, but they held special place within Gnosticism as well. The exact role of women in Gnosticism is not certain or uniform; some Gnostics denigrated women just as some orthodox affirmed them. But Irenaeus, among others, is dismayed by the attraction the Gnostics held for women. "Even in our own district of the Rhone valley," the gnostic teacher Marcus had attracted "many foolish women" from Irenaeus's own congregation, including the wife of one of his deacons.[8] In some gnostic groups women gained prominence as leaders—prophets, teachers, priests, and even bishops. This practice was undoubtedly influenced by the gnostic description of God in both masculine and feminine terms. In some gnostic literature Mary, the mother of Jesus, Mary Magdalene, Martha, and Salome play a conspicuous role. Sometimes women are the channels of revelation, or in the case of Simon Magus's female companion, Helena, they are the object of worship. Elaine Pagels, in *The Gnostic Gospels*, has commented on the role of women in the gnostic sects, but her conclusions have received a critical review by Susanne Heine, *Women and Early Christianity*.[9] There is no question that some gnostic sects place considerable emphasis on the feminine dimension of God and on feminine leadership in their sects, but other gnostics went to the other extreme to denigrate everything feminine and to view women as the source of evil. Heine questions whether Gnosticism can even be called a Christian heresy and whether it may have been completely alien to the Christian movement.

Regarding the pastoral role of women in the New Testament, some comment must be made about the clear statements that forbid women the exercise of leadership in the public assembly (apart from prophecy). The texts are well known. St. Paul insists that women should keep silent in the church (1 Cor. 14:34); if there was anything they should know, women may ask their husbands at home. In 1 Corinthians 11, the apostle writes that the head of the woman is the man, and that women may prophesy provided their heads are covered. In pseudo-Pauline literature (Col. 3:18) wives are to be subject to their husbands, and the husband is the head of the wife (Eph. 5:23). In 1 Tim. 2:11-12 such injunctions are repeated; women are forbidden to teach publicly or have authority over men. In the Pauline letters the goal is harmony and unity, both of the married couple and of the church. The husband is not to rule as a despot but with compassion and love. Christians took over pagan models of domestic life that served the economy of the household. Overall, "the Christians of that time adapted to social reality. The motive can be taken to be that expressed in 1 Tim. 3:7—the respect of those who are outside the church."[10]

As the first century moved toward the second, the church was becoming more settled, attracting to itself some wealthy aristocratic converts, including women. We read of Joanna, the wife of Herod's official, who was definitely wealthy, giving generously to Jesus' disciples. Lydia was a successful businesswoman, and Paul is on familiar terms with those of Caesar's household, and Romans 16 indicates that this included many women. It seems plausible to assume that the church, in trying to avoid the appearance of being socially disruptive, requested that women not assume roles that were at variance with accepted norms in pagan life. Toward the end of the first century we repeatedly hear admonitions to live "a sober, upright, and godly life in this world" (Titus 2:12), and a "quiet and peaceable life, godly and respectful in every way" (1 Tim. 2:2). A modern commentator on the Pastoral Epistles suggests restrictions were placed upon women's leadership in the church in order to present the church as a respectable institution. "Being a Christian is expressed in a way which brings it close to 'reasonable' and exemplary bourgeois behavior. One may compare the frequency of such key words as modesty, honesty, piety, sound teaching, good conscience, and the catalogues of duties, virtues, and vices."[11] In this regard the church was more influenced by Roman conservatism than by the gospel. Certainly another factor in the role of women in the early church in addition to the Greco-Roman culture was the legacy of Judaism, in which women did not play an active leadership role. There were only four Old Testament prophetesses—Miriam, Deborah, Hulda, and Naodiah. Apart from these, the Old Testament was suspicious of the goddesses and priestesses of the surrounding cults, and imposed ritualistic impurities upon women in terms of acceptable worship.

Given these restrictions, women played a decisive role in New Testament ministries, assisting both Jesus and the apostles in the work of evangelism, serving as faithful witnesses to Christ's death and resurrection, giving generously of material goods as well as opening their homes to facilitate the church's mission. They served as prophets in their prayers within public assemblies. Before the end of the first century, we find more definite organization given to groups of women serving in a pastoral role, and these are the widows.

Widows*

Initially the widows were not considered an "order" within the church but were simply the recipients of charity, those women who

---

*A recently published study of widows appeared too late for its scholarship to be included in this essay, Bonnie Bowman Thurston's *The Widows: A Women's Ministry in the Early Church* (Minneapolis: Fortress, 1989). The author covers the material were cared for by the community (Acts 6:1-2; 9:39). The Epistle of James insists that "religion that is pure and undefiled before God and the Father is this: to visit orphans and widows in their affliction, and to keep oneself unstained from the world" (James 1:27). These widows had no means of support available to them. In 1 Timothy it is mentioned three times that widows who had children or grandchildren should be supported by them so as not to burden the church, which saved its resources for "real widows."[12] "She is a real widow [who] is left all alone. . . . If anyone does not provide for his relatives, and especially for his own family, he has disowned the faith and is worse than an unbeliever" (1 Tim. 5:5, 8).

Among the subapostolic writers, Hermas gives prominence to the need to care for widows, and he warns against "pernicious men who abusing their ministry, plunder widows and orphans."[13] Ignatius made it a reproach against some heretics that they neglected widows and those who were in distress.[14] Polycarp, in a passage that will be repeated often by subsequent writers, refers to widows as "an altar of sacrifice"—that is, the object of sacrificial charity.[15] Widows were registered with the church, but not before the age of sixty, having been married once, and who had raised their children in the fear of God and had demonstrated hospitality" (1 Tim. 5:9-10). Younger widows, in whom it was feared the fires of passion still burned too brightly, were urged to marry and bear children, even though the church theoretically frowned on second marriages. Widows, therefore, were simply indigent older women who needed support. Nothing is said so far about a ministry exercised by these women. Their numbers could be large. Bishop Cornelius of Rome wrote in 250 that the Roman church had fifteen hundred widows and others in distress on the church rolls, and Chrysostom late in the fourth century reckons there were three thousand widows registered at Antioch.[16]

Such widows inevitably came to prominence in the church because of the qualifications of sanctity required of them. They became models of the virtuous life, as Polycarp says, "discreet in their faith pledged

---

up to A.D. 325 during the period when the role of widows achieved its greatest prominence. Thurston's conclusions support those offered here, but in greater detail and with a helpful introductory chapter on the role of widows in the Jewish, Hellenistic, and Roman context of the early church. In addition, she offers a very good analysis of "The Widow as Altar: Metaphor and Ministry."

to the Lord, praying unceasingly on behalf of all, refraining from all slander, gossip, false witness, love of money—in fact, from evil of any kind."[17] Hippolytus, writing in 215, speaks of the appointment of a widow and adds the note that she should not be ordained, "because she does not offer the oblations nor has she a liturgical ministry, but she is appointed for prayer."[18] The same author includes widows with virgins, since the former also took a vow of celibacy upon their appointment. He states that "widows and virgins shall fast often and pray on behalf of the church."[19]

Tertullian, a contemporary of Hippolytus (c. 200), is the first to include widows among the clergy—that is, within the "order" (ordo) of the clergy. "How many men and how many women in ecclesiastical orders owe their position to the practice of continence. They have preferred to be wedded to God."[20] In his treatise On Monogamy Tertullian lists the representatives of the church whose approval must be sought by those about to be married, a list that includes the bishop, presbyters, deacons, and widows.[21] Furthermore, we read in Tertullian's treatise On the Widows that they occupied special seats in the church service, and penitents seeking to be reconciled were required to prostrate themselves before the presbyters and widows.

Following Tertullian, the Alexandrian fathers included widows among the clergy. Clement of Alexandria writes: "Innumberable commands such as these are written in the Holy Bible and directed to chosen persons, some to presbyters, some to bishops, some to deacons, others to widows."[22] Origen speaks of special obligations required of widows, priests, and the bishop, and he writes that second marriages prevent aspirants from assuming ecclesiastical dignities—namely, that of bishop, presbyter, deacon, and widow.[23] We have already seen that the special vocation of widows was to prayer, fasting, and chastity. Origen adds others—to teach younger women to be sober, to love their husbands, to raise their children, to be modest, chaste, to be good housekeepers, to be submissive to their husbands, to be kind, to practice hospitality, to wash the feet of the saints, and to fulfill in all chastity all the other duties which are ascribed to women in Scripture.[24] Thus we find that widows are also given the task of teaching younger women and serving them as examples of virtue and charity.

An early third-century document from Syria, the Didascalia Apostolorum, offers an extensive description of the qualifications and duties of widows. It permits widows to be appointed to the "order" at the younger age of fifty, indicating the existence of an ecclesiastical order, but younger widows who are not yet enrolled should nonetheless be "taken care of and helped."[25] Following the suggestion of 1 Tim. 5:14, this document permits younger widows to seek a second marriage, but any marriage beyond a second is forbidden. The Christian faithful are to support widows with their gifts; they are not to be given directly but through the bishop, although the names of donors should be told the recipients that they may pray for their benefactors. The primary task of widows is prayer: "a widow should have no other care save to be praying for those who give and for the whole church."[26] They are especially forbidden to teach or to baptize, and they are warned against an apparent abuse among widows, that of amassing more gifts than are required for their needs. There is also a warning against being a "busybody" who flits from house to house carrying gossip, because "the altar of God never strays about everywhere but is fixed in one place."[27] Although earlier the *Didascalia* lists prayer as the sole duty of widows, another task was added to those already mentioned in that widows are to visit the sick, pray for them, and lay their hands upon them. "They were recognized as having a special power of intercession in prayer, and their laying hands on the sick was considered to be effective."[28] Earlier both Tertullian and Clement of Alexandria referred to the widows' participation with the clergy in the healing of sinners and the comforting of those in distress.[29]

Roger Gryson offers a summary statement of the role of widows as outlined in the *Didascalia Apostolorum:*

> Widowhood appears as a privileged opportunity for spiritual progress. Accentuating the special features of the "real widow" in First Timothy, the author neatly draws the outlines of a spiritual ideal composed of two essentials—continence and prayer. For widows over fifty, agreement with this ideal was sanctioned by entering the "order of widows." Younger widows were invited to embrace the same ideal. . . . The right to material help was no longer tied to "enrollment" in a group of widows but was accorded to every widow, as well as to all in need.[30]

In a letter to a young widow named Ageruchia, Jerome expands on the virtues of widowhood, especially urging the young widow to refrain from a second marriage. Although St. Paul had permitted a second marriage (1 Cor. 7:39), it was only as a precaution for those who were too weak to follow vows of chastity. In a curious exegesis of the parable of the seeds (Matt. 13:8), Jerome suggests the hundredfold referred to virginity, sixtyfold to widows, and thirtyfold to married people. After his strong opinions against second marriages, he writes, "Do I condemn second marriages? Not at all. Do I expel twice married persons from the church? Far from it."[31] Nevertheless, he considered second marriage a remedy for scandal. He followed a conventional opinion in the early church, which interpreted the death of a spouse as an indication from God not to seek another spouse. He follows the same logic in a letter to Furia, encouraging her to maintain her widowhood, because through the death of her husband God had shown the divine will toward her.[32] By discouraging second marriages, Jerome sought to enhance the role and status of widows in the church, but this was due not primarily for the office of widows, for it was a reflection of Jerome's deprecation of sex and marriage.

Several church orders from the beginning of the fourth century refer to the role of widows in the church, indicating that by this time they constituted an established institution with pastoral responsibilities. In the *Apostolic Church Order* from Egypt early in the fourth century, we find the stipulation that in every church "three widows shall be appointed, two who persevere in prayer . . . and one in the service of those who are sick."[33] C. H. Turner is of the opinion that this text is "the first beginning of the transformation of the widow into an active ministry."[34] Turner finds the same institutionalization of widows in the *Didascalia*, which he dates as contemporary with the *Apostolic Church Order*, but which I have assigned to 250. As to the third widow who cares for the sick, we are told that "this implies not only material assistance but religious ministrations as well."[35] Although the text does not indicate what such ministrations may have been, the *Didascalia* earlier spoke of prayer and the imposition of hands. In the small rural churches of Egypt in the early fourth century, it was usual to have three presbyters and three deacons. The fact that the *Apostolic Church Order* also suggests there be three widows implies that they were also included as representatives of the church or as clergy.

The *Canons of Hippolytus* is a pseudepigraphical collection coming from Egypt in the mid-fourth century, and it contains several rubrics concerning widows. They are not to be ordained, as ordination is reserved for men. Their duties are limited to prayer, fasting, and the care of sick women. "The function of the widows is important, because of all their duties: frequent prayer, care for the sick, and frequent fasting."[36] Here as before, the only distinctly public ministry exercised by the widows is that to the sick, since fasting and prayer was also recommended to all the faithful. At the same time one must recognize that visitations of the sick, then as today, could include a host of activities—anointing with oil, washing linens, food preparation and feeding, running errands, prayer and Scripture reading, serving as confidant, relieving anxieties, and whatever else may have been required to be of assistance. It was a ministry that today is often carried out by full-time clergy or staff in larger congregations.

Sometime in the mid-fourth century a council was held at Laodicea in Phrygia, modern Denizle in Turkey, whose canons have come down to us in two separate collections (1–19 and 20–59). Of interest to us is canon 11, which reads: "Senior women [or female presidents] are not to be appointed in the church."[37] The Greek term *presbytidas* may be rendered the equivalent of the male *presbyteras* or presider, priest, elder. Hefele believes these were senior deaconesses, but the evidence is against this. Gryson, citing other authorities, believes the *presbytidas* refers to senior widows who had established themselves as leaders, who had special seats in front of the assembly and were honored because of their age.[38] The intent of this canon, apparently, was to counteract any pretensions such widows had to assuming the functions of presbyters, which may be taken as evidence that in some churches such developments were taking place. It is certain that some widows were respected above others, had a prominent seat in the service of worship, and were given a title.

From the late fourth century we have received the largest collection of ecclesiastical law in antiquity, known as the *Apostolic Constitutions*, most likely originating in Syria. Of its eight books, the first six are based on the *Didascalia Apostolorum*, and book seven contains the *Didache*. From the material unique to the collection, we see the further development of the order of widows in the third- and fourth-century church.

As in the preceding documents, widows in general were the object of the church's charity, or the "altar of God" as Polycarp had written. But some widows were "appointed" (*katistathsai*) to the "order of widows" (*to chērikon*). As before, they were to remain continent, and the minimum age was again sixty, whereas in earlier documents it had been reduced to fifty and then forty. Following 1 Tim. 5:8 we read of the "real widows" who had brought up their children as God-fearing, had practiced hospitality, and were diligent in good works. Besides practicing continence, they were to persevere in prayer.[39] They were considered to be "consecrated to God."[40] Earlier documents had absolutely forbidden widows to teach, but the *Constitutions* permit widows with sufficient understanding to teach women outside the public assembly. The document places a higher value on virginity than on widowhood, consistently naming the former before widows, and the widows received Holy Communion after the virgins, who received after the clergy. But in this document, unlike the *Didascalia*, widows may no longer visit the sick. Their primary vocation seems to have been ascetical—living a life of celibacy and engaging in prayer. The repeated references to "virgins and widows" indicate that by the end of the fourth century the office of widows was merging with that of virgins. Jean Daniélou suggests that by this time the role of widows was in decline, and by the end of the fourth century the "office" as such disappeared: "It died of its own ambiguities."[41]

Yet such a "death" was not immediate or readily apparent, at least not uniformly in every place and time. The *Testamentum Domini Nostri Jesu Christi*, a fifth-century Syrian document, devotes four chapters to widows and gives them considerable prominence. The number of widows was established at thirteen, and they were set aside with a prayer in the same style as one for deacons and presbyters. They stood with the clergy at the Great Thanksgiving. "Let the bishop stand first in the middle, and the presbyters immediately behind him on either side, and the widows immediately behind the presbyters on the left side, and the deacons also behind the presbyters on the right hand side."[42] Following in descending order of importance are the readers, deaconesses, and subdeacons. According to this scheme it is the widows who parallel the deacons and not the deaconesses. The widows referred to are not all those of the church but the thirteen specially appointed, who are called "those who sit in front," who together with the presbyters and deacons are definitely included among the clergy. They lived together in a house next to that of the bishop.

According to the *Testamentum Domini*, the function of these specially appointed widows was "to instruct those women who do not obey, to teach those who have not learned, to convert those who are foolish."[43] They also had the oversight of women in the assembly, "counseling those things which are proper" and chastening the disobedient, as well as enforcing appropriate dress. "Let [them] also visit those [women] who are sick; on each first day of the week let [them] take one deacon or two to help them."[44] This document also permits such widows to be young women, as it stipulates that those who are menstruating ought not approach the altar. These widows, although not ordained, were appointed with a ritual and a solemn prayer by the bishop, invoking God for "the spirit of power to this thine handmaid, and strengthen her with thy truth. . . . Grant to her, O Lord, the spirit of meekness and of power, and of patience and of kindness . . . so that she may endure her labors."[45] A significant difference between the earlier *Apostolic Constitutions* and the *Testamentum* is that in the former document the widows are subject to the deaconesses, whereas in the latter document the reverse is true, deaconesses were supervised by the widows, who definitely shared in the pastoral care of the souls.

It is probable that by the fifth century the distinction between widows, virgins, and deaconesses was not all that precise, and that one or the other was dominant in various places. The Gallican practice in the fifth century required that taking the vows of widowhood implied entrance into a monastery, and it was accompanied by the adoption of a unique form of dress. Ultimately the order of widows merged into that of women under vows who lived in a community.[46] Widows remained the object of charity, and as cloistered religious under vows their vocation of prayer and example of virtue remained, but their pastoral role was assumed by others. At the time the office of widows was in decline, that of deaconess was gaining in popularity and distinction.

Deaconesses

In Rom. 16:1, St. Paul commends to the Roman Christians, "Phoebe, our sister, who is also a deacon (*diakonon*) of the church at Cenchrae . . . for she has been my helper and that of many others as well." There is some doubt whether the *diakonos* referred to here represents a developed office or whether it simply means that Phoebe's service was that generally expected of all Christians. Gryson suggests the latter, and that *diakonos* is best translated simply as minister in the sense of service.[47] But he also cites with approval the judgment of A. Oepke that Phoebe represents a situation "where the original charisma is becoming an office."[48] If this is correct, we may say that the female deaconate is of apostolic origin.

However, deaconesses were unknown in the West before the fifth century and they were not accepted by Rome before the end of the eighth century.[49] They appear to be an office unique to the church in the East—that is, Syria and Greece. Some scholars have suggested that the women referred to in Pliny's correspondence with the Emperor Trajan were deaconesses. The governor found it necessary to torture two Christian women whom he calls *ministrae*, but we cannot know for certain whether this was an office corresponding to the later deaconess. The status of the female diaconate is not clear before the third century.

The earliest reliable evidence to deaconesses comes from the *Didascalia Apostolorum*, a Syrian document dating from approximately 250, which describes the functions of a third-century deaconess: "Wherefore, O bishop, appoint thee workers of righteousness as helpers who may cooperate with thee unto salvation." The bishop is to appoint men (deacons) to assist men, "but a woman for the ministry of women. For there are houses whither thou canst not send a deacon to the women, on account of the heathen, but mayest send a deaconess."[50] In many other matters the office of a woman deacon is required. One of these was assistance at baptism, where a deaconess was needed to anoint the women candidates, "because it is not fitting that [naked] women should be seen by men." The priest may anoint only a woman's head, but the deaconess anointed her body. Yet the actual baptism itself was conducted only by the male priest.

The deaconess was also given the responsibility for teaching the women the rudiments of the faith following the baptism. "For this cause the ministry of a woman deacon is especially needful and important. For our Lord and Savior was also ministered unto by women ministers." Despite the fact that women were still prohibited from public teaching, the deaconesses were charged with instructing women, presumably in private. Another task was visiting women. "For a deaconess is required to go into the houses of the heathen where there are believing women, and to visit those who are sick, and to minister to them in that of which they have need, and to bathe those who have begun to recover from sickness."[51]

The document reiterates the need for women to serve women, and men to serve men, with male and female deacons to be appointed by the bishop and to be under his direct supervision. Gryson suggests that deaconesses were limited in their duties to assistance in Baptism, to visitations of the sick, and to the instruction of newly baptized women.[52] But LaPorte points out that under the general rubric of "many other matters," a deaconess "was a kind of social worker of the church," which included the distribution of charities to widows and generally seeing to the needs of women.[53] The *Didascalia* clearly distinguishes deaconesses from widows, referring to the former as types of the Holy Spirit, and to the latter (following Polycarp) as types of the altar. "The deaconess shall be honored by you in the place of the Holy Spirit, and the presbyters in the likeness of the apostles, and the orphans and widows . . . in the likeness of the altar."[54]

Although we have said that there is little evidence for the office of deaconesses before the *Didascalia*, mention is made of them in the Alexandrian fathers of the third century. Clement explains St. Paul's statement in 1 Cor. 9:5 ("Have we not the right to take a woman around with us as a sister, like all the other apostles?") to say that women were co-workers with the apostles. "It was through them that the Lord's teaching penetrated also the women's quarters without any scandal being aroused."[55] Then Clement adds, "We also know the directions given about women deacons, which are given by the noble Paul in his second letter to Timothy" (perhaps 2 Tim. 3:11).[56] Origen, in commenting on the role of Phoebe, writes that "even women are instituted deacons in the church," and that "women who have given assistance to so many people and who by their good works deserve to be praised by the Apostle, ought to be accepted in the diaconate."[57] Gryson, in an extensive commentary on these texts, insists that Clement and Origen are dealing only with theoretical considerations and not with concrete situations and a living practice in third-century Alexandria. Both fathers use the past tense to explain biblical texts that refer to women associates of the apostles, but there is no evidence of deaconesses who are contemporary with the Alexandrians. "When they spoke of the ministries of their era, deaconesses were never mentioned among the ministers of the church."[58] Therefore at this stage of our inquiry we are left with the conclusion that deaconesses constituted an order in the churches of Syria and Greece by the mid-third century, and their duties included the visitation of Christian women in their homes with particular attention to the sick, they assisted in baptism, they instructed the newly baptized women, and they probably did much more in the ministry to women—that is, "many other matters."

Chronologically, the next witness to deaconesses comes from canon 19 of the Council of Nicea (325). This canon deals with the readmission to the church of the heretical Paulinists whose trinitarian ideas were considered to be heterodox. Paulinist deaconesses could be readmitted if they were rebaptized (on the assumption that a heretical trinitarian baptism was invalid), and if they lived moral lives. The canon continues, "and we mean by deaconesses those who have assumed the habit, but who, since they have no imposition of hands, are to be numbered only among the laity."[59] This reveals to us that deaconesses were accepted as a recognized order in the church and that they wore distinctive clothing. A further intriguing question is raised by the council's insistence on their lay status, pointing to the possibility that under the Paulinists they may have been considered clergy.

The *Apostolic Constitutions* is a collection of ecclesiastical law dating from the last half of the fourth century, and most likely from Syria. The eighth book of this collection reveals a "most fundamental change" in the position of deaconesses.[60] Although we have assumed, given the high valuation on celibacy of that time, that deaconesses would be virgins, we now have evidence. "Let the deaconess be a pure virgin; or at the least, a widow who has been but once married, faithful, and well esteemed."[61] As in earlier times, the deaconess was to visit sick women, but in addition to this she was to relay messages from the bishop, a task also given to deacons. "This duty is pointed out in the instruction to let both of them [deacons and deaconesses] be ready to carry messages, to travel about, and to serve in many things."[62] The deaconesses were also to keep order among the women in the assembly, a task that heretofore had been assigned to the widows. "Just as the deacon did for the men, she had to see that women arriving at church found a place, whether they were rich or poor, and that younger ones on occasion gave up their places to older ones."[63] They also distributed charities to the widows, and widows were obliged to obey them.[64] This indicates a decline in the prominence of widows and the growing importance of the deaconesses.

Another function of the deaconess described in the *Constitutions* is that of intermediary between clergy and women. "Let not any woman address herself to the deacon or bishop without the deaconess."[65] Although she is to be "honored in the place of the Holy Spirit," she remains under the supervision of the deacon. Even though her duties in many respects paralleled those of the deacon, the deaconess was not permitted to assist at the altar, as did the deacons, or distribute Communion to the sick. Nevertheless, there is a decided advance in the status of deaconesses over previous documents in the ritual and prayer of ordination by which they were placed into office:

> O bishop, thou shalt lay thy hands upon her in the presence of the presbytery and of the deacons and deaconesses, and shalt say:
> O Eternal God, the Father of our Lord Jesus Christ, the Creator of man and of woman, who didst replenish with the Spirit Miriam, and Deborah, and Anna, and Huldah: who didst not disdain that Thy only-begotten Son should be born of a woman; who also in the tabernacle of the testimony, and in the temple, didst ordain women to be keepers of Thy holy gates, do now Thou also look down upon Thy servant, who is to be ordained to the office of a deaconess, and grant her Thy Holy Spirit, and "cleanse her from all filthiness of flesh and spirit" (2 Cor. 7:1), that she may worthily discharge the work which is committed to her to Thy glory, and the praise of Thy Christ, with whom glory and adoration be to Thee and the Holy Spirit forever. Amen.[66]

As with other clergy, deaconesses received the imposition of the bishop's hand and prayer, whereas widows and virgins did not receive such an ordination. This prompts Gryson to suggest that "it is indisputable that deaconesses were part of the clergy. Their participation with the clergy and with them alone in the eulogies, i.e. in the distribution of the unconsecrated loaves of bread offered by the faithful for the Eucharist, clearly supports this fact."[67] Another commentator, M. Martimort, believes that "the ordination of deaconesses was truly sacramental."[68] They occupied a position in rank between that of deacons and subdeacons.[69] Despite such an elevated rank, deaconesses were not permitted to teach publicly or to baptize.

A late fourth-century letter of Basil to Amphilochius touches only marginally on the office of deaconess. If she committed fornication, she could be restored after seven years of penance. However, if a deacon was found in the same sin, he was to be deposed. This may lead to the conclusion that deaconesses were not considered by Basil to be of the same rank as clergy.[70] Turner, however, writes with fulsome appreciation for the role played by deaconesses in the late fourth century. "As the fourth century wears on we find the deaconess enjoying a position of high distinction in the churches of the Eastern empire. The devout women who run parishes are no invention of modern days: their activities in the patristic age were on an even larger scale."[71] As evidence, he cites a letter of Basil to two deaconesses of Samosata, daughters of a count, whom he addresses as "your orderliness," in which he expounds on the doctrine of the Trinity. He also refers to the *History* of Theodoret, which tells of two deaconesses in Antioch at the time of Julian (361–63), one of whom supervised a community of young women dedicated to virginity, and both women were clearly wealthy and accustomed to independent thinking and action.[72]

Chrysostom (d. 407) offers some comments on the ministry of women in general but little of deaconesses in his commentary on Romans 16. Of Phoebe he writes: "[Paul] mentioned her before all the rest, and called her sister. . . . Moreover, he added to her rank by mentioning her as deaconess. . . . Let us imitate, both men and women, this holy woman."[73] He points out that Prisca exceeded Aquila in piety, and that neither their marriage nor their occupation was a hindrance to being effective evangelists. It was to Prisca's credit that she instructed her husband in the gospel and made him into an effective teacher. In a separate homily on Prisca and Aquila, Chrysostom writes: "When a man is not a believer and the plaything of error, Paul does not exclude a woman's superiority, even when it involves teaching."[74] He suggests that Paul's prohibition against women teaching had to do with public proclamation from the pulpit, "but he does not forbid exhorting and advising in private."[75] He points out that women are by nature required to be the instructors of their children, and as to husbands, "when she is the wiser, [Paul] does not forbid her teaching and improving him."[76]

In his comments about "Greet Mary," Chrysostom marvels at the spirit and independence of the women around Paul, who were often wealthy and traveled freely about. "The women of those days were more spirited than lions."[77] Of Junia he writes, "Oh how great is the wisdom of this woman that she should be counted worthy of the appelation of apostle."[78] Although Chrysostom displayed great admiration for the women of the first century, his views on some fourth-century women were considerably reserved. In his treatise *On the*

Priesthood he complains that some "have become invested with so much power that they can appoint or eject priests at their will."[79] He continues by noting that some women have obtained such a large privilege of free speech as to rebuke clergy and censure them more severely than masters do their servants.

Despite such general warnings, there was one deaconess, Olympias, whom Chrysostom held in high esteem and for whom he had warm affection. No less than seventeen of his extant letters are addressed to her, including four from his exile in which he addresses her as "My Lady, the most reverend and divinely favored deaconess, Olympias."[80] She must have been a truly remarkable woman, for Gregory of Nazianzus, sometime patriarch of Constantinople, also took a great interest in her, speaking of her in his letters as "my own Olympias" and delighting to be addressed by her as "father."[81] Palladius's *Lausiac History* gives a brief and eulogistic account of her life, but we have a much longer *Life* from an anonymous fifth-century writer who either knew her or those who had known her. She was the daughter of a pagan count of the empire through whom she inherited considerable wealth when she was orphaned. An uncle brought her up as a Christian. After a brief unhappy marriage, she became a deaconess and took the vow of chastity. She built a convent that housed two hundred fifty women. No visitors, male or female, were permitted to come into the house, "the only exception being the most holy patriarch, John [Chrysostom], who visited them continuously and sustained them with his most wise teachings."[82] She spent her time and wealth for the sick and the poor, as well as giving lavish donations to the churches in Greece, Asia Minor, and Syria. Chrysostom warned her against her indiscriminate liberality, which earned him the hostility of some avaricious bishops. For herself, however, she chose a life of austere asceticism. In addition to her benefactions to the church and her example of virtue, she spent time in teaching Christianity to pagan women. Her biographer writes that she "supplied widows, raised orphans, shielded the elderly, looked after the weak, had compassion on sinners, guided the lost, and had pity on all . . . she was a precious vessel of the Holy Spirit."[83]

Theodore of Mopsuestia (d. 428) understood the order of deaconesses to be of apostolic origin. He points out that in 1 Timothy 3:8 Paul gives the qualifications of deacons, so that when in v. 11 he writes, "The women likewise must be serious," it can only refer to the women deacons. He suggests that the word *hōsautōs* (in like manner) can only refer to women who do the same work as deacons. The reason Paul gives the age of sixty for the admission of deaconesses was to prevent younger women from becoming dependent on the church's welfare. Theodore encourages younger widows to remarry, and such a second marriage would not constitute an impediment if later they chose to be enrolled as widows or deaconesses.[84] Theodoret of Cyrus (d. 458) followed Theodore's reasoning, that 1 Tim. 3:11 refers to deaconesses, and that younger widows may remarry without fear of censure.[85]

In canon 15 of the Council of Chalcedon (451) we find legislation regarding deaconesses. The canon reads: A woman shall not receive the laying on of hands (*cheirotoneisthai*) as a deaconess under forty years of age, and then only after searching examination. And if, after she has had hands laid on her and has continued for a time to minister, she should despise the grace of God and give herself in marriage, she shall be anathematized and the man united to her.[86] Here the minimum age has been lowered to forty, and we find the same verb used, *cheirotonein*, which is regularly applied to the ordination of male clergy. This verb was also used of the deaconesses in the *Apostolic Constitutions*. Lowering the age to forty may represent something of a compromise, because we know that much younger women, such as Olympias, were being received as deaconesses. At the time of her profession she may not have reached the age of twenty. The canons of Chalcedon do not speak of the functions of the deaconess.

In the legislation of Justinian we have further evidence of the growth and significance of the female diaconate. In a section of his *Code* dating from 535 he fixed the number of clergy assigned to the church of Hagia Sophia in Constantinople. There were to be no more than forty priests, one hundred deacons, and forty deaconesses in addition to lesser officials. Here the deaconesses are clearly numbered among the clergy, as elsewhere in the legislation, where "male and female deacons" are mentioned together.[87] Like other clerics, deaconesses are ordained (*cheirotonia*), with a minimum age set first at fifty and then lowered to forty. They were required to be virgins or widows married only once, with severe penalties for violating the vow of chastity, ranging from capital punishment to seclusion in a monastery. Like the other clergy, they received their living from the church. They lived either in a community or alone, but if they shared lodging it had to be with close relatives who were beyond reproach. And like the male clergy, deaconesses enjoyed the privilege of the bishop's tribunal and of receiving pensions from ecclesiastical institutions, and if they died without legitimate heirs, the church of their ordination received their legacy.[88]

While the female diaconate flourished in the East, it was unknown in the West, or if known, either assigned exclusively to the first century or else prohibited. The anonymous fourth-century writer called Ambrosiaster knew of such an office, but he believed it existed only among heretics.[89] Pelagius, in commenting on Rom. 16:1, writes about Phoebe at Cenchrae that "just as now, in the Eastern regions, one sees women deaconesses."[90] The fourth-century Priscillian heresy in Spain attracted large numbers of women, and in opposing this group, the First Council of Saragossa (380) opposed women in any kind of leadership role. "The Fathers of this council had no knowledge at all of the existence of deaconesses in the East."[91] Canon 25 of the First Council of Orange (441) reads: "Deaconesses are absolutely not to be ordained; and if there are still any of them, let them bow their head under the benediction which is given to the congregation."[92] However, the need to proscribe deaconesses is surely evidence of their existence, and this appears to be confirmed by the repetition of the proscription nearly eighty years later in Gaul at the Council of Epaon, canon 21: "We completely suppress throughout our territory the consecration of those widows who are often called deaconesses."[93] Several years after this we find a similar proscription by the Second Council of Orleans (533), canon 18: "It has been decided that henceforth no woman may any longer receive diaconal benediction, due to the frailty of her sex."[94] These later Western attempts to curb the institution of deaconess were contemporary with the full flowering of the female diaconate in the East, as witness the legislation of Justinian.

The office of deaconess may have been of apostolic origin (see Rom. 16:1 and 1 Tim. 3:11), but we know little of it before the third century. It is largely limited to Greece, Asia Minor, and Syria, where it grew in acceptance and prestige, deaconesses being included among the clergy with the same ordination as deacons and the laying on of hands by the bishop. Among them were some highly respected women such as Olympias. Their pastoral duties included assistance at the baptism of women, the instruction of women, both as evangelists to pagans and as catechists to Christian women. They also visited the sick and performed works of charity for the poor, orphans, and widows. The deaconesses greeted the women at the assemblies, were responsible to maintain decorum among them, and they served "in many other things." The minimum age for the office began at sixty, but in later years it was reduced to fifty and forty, with some exceptions being made for younger women. They assumed the vow of perpetual celibacy, wore distinctive clothing that identified them as a deaconess, and in some cases they lived in community. They were not permitted to advance to the priesthood or to preside at Baptism or the Eucharist, and they were not permitted to preach in public, though private instruction was a significant aspect of their vocation. They also served as intermediaries between the women of the congregation and the male clergy. Given these varied tasks, and in light of the large numbers of deaconesses recorded in Eastern Christianity up to the sixth century, we can say with assurance that deaconesses served in a demanding pastoral capacity with sacrifice, grace, and distinction.

Women in the Service of the Church

The pastoral role of women was exemplified primarily by widows and deaconesses. Both institutions were recognized as an order, with rituals and prayers of ordination, and at times both were recognized as being included among the clergy. But there was also a large number of women who may not have been included in these orders who nevertheless came to play a prominent role in the service of the church and who should be included among those who functioned pastorally in the early years of Christianity. These women include primarily virgins as a group as well as several outstanding leaders who emerged from this group as examples of piety and energetic activity.

The special honor paid to the unmarried state has its roots in St. Paul (1 Corinthians 7). The earliest postcanonical literature that refers to virgins is from the letter of Ignatius to Polycarp (c. 110): "If anyone is able to maintain chastity to the honor of the flesh of the Lord, let him maintain it without boasting. If he boasts he is undone, if his vow be known further than to the bishop, he has lost his purity."[95] Polycarp himself wrote to the Philippians that virgins must live with a blameless and pure conscience.[96] Both these references make it clear that men as well as women are the intended audience, but most references to virgins in the early church have only women in mind. The next reference is a short sentence from Justin Martyr who speaks of "many men and women sixty and seventy years old . . . who have kept themselves uncorrupted."[97] Hippolytus (c. 215) notes in the *Apostolic Tradition* that "hands shall not be laid upon a virgin, for it is her purpose alone that makes her a virgin."[98] This indicates that virgins were not ordained or given any formal status in the church, and that it was only women who were under consideration.

Tertullian, a contemporary of Hippolytus, wrote the earliest treatise dealing with virgins in *The Veiling of Virgins*. To the casual reader this title may suggest that the author was recommending that women who had taken a vow of celibacy should wear a veil as a mark of their distinction, as this became the rule in later centuries. The very opposite was the case. Contemporary etiquette called for all women to wear a veil in public, regardless of marital state or age. Some Christian virgins, however, were dispensing with the veil, claiming that their vows gave them the liberty of appearing in the public service without the veil. Tertullian writes that this is not only a false use of freedom, but by their desire to be noticed as having taken the vow they were guilty of the very pride Ignatius had warned against when he said that only the bishop should be informed of the vow. Virgins should remain anonymous as a sign of humility, but an unveiled virgin desires "to be notable and marked as she enters the church."[99] It appears ironic that the veil, which in later years became a distinctive sign of the women in religion, should in its origin serve the opposite purpose. Elsewhere Tertullian alludes to the large number of "virgins who are married to Christ," by the year 200.[100]

Tertullian's protégé, Cyprian, follows a different line of thinking in his treatise *On the Dress of Virgins*. They should dress plainly, avoid all jewelry and cosmetics, and if they are wealthy they should support the poor. He addresses them with fulsome praise: "the flower of ecclesiastical seed, the grace and ornament of spiritual endowment, a joyous disposition, the wholesome and uncorrupted work of praise, God's image answering to the holiness of the Lord, the more illustrious portion of Christ's flock, the glorious fruitfulness of mother church."[101]

The question may well be asked, Is it appropriate to speak of virgins as serving a pastoral function in the early church? Unlike the widows or deaconesses, they do not appear to have been assigned any specific tasks other than to maintain their vow of chastity. Perhaps the most significant function they performed was to serve the church as a sign of the coming of God's kingdom, living testimony that God's grace was active in their lives, and they were examples that a countercultural life dedicated to discipline was possible. Methodius of Olympas (d. 312) alludes to the exemplary life of the virgins as being beneficial to the entire church in his *Banquet of the Ten Virgins*, a dialogue in eleven discourses in praise of the virginal life. They are signs of the advancement of humanity toward perfection since the coming of Christ, they are Christ-figures in their celibacy even as they are called the brides of Christ, they are human types of the angelic host, they are examples of perfect consecration and devotion to God, and they are eschatological signs of the coming kingdom. And if one should ask for more practical benefits from their presence, Methodius suggests that the virgins by their vows are combating demons, the offspring of the dragon of Revelation 12, which is of no small value to the church and society. [102] Certainly another eminently valuable contribution was their intercessory prayer, which was more efficacious than that of other Christians. From the time of Methodius (c. 300) the number of virgins in the church multiplied dramatically. Given the high honors accorded them, it is curious that the *Didascalia Apostolorum* from the mid-third century never once mentions virgins, although it sets value on the continency of widowhood and is averse to second marriages.

At the end of the third century virgins did not yet constitute an order in the church, nor do we read of them being cloistered in convents. [103] For the most part they lived in their own homes under the general supervision of the bishop. Cyprian warns virgins against the dangers of such an independent way of life, for he complains that "the church frequently mourns over her virgins, she groans at their scandalous and detestable stories." [104] It is not surprising that some did not live up to their ideals of asceticism by frequenting raucous marriage feasts or by visiting the public baths. To those who dressed in colored woolen clothing, he repeated Tertullian's warning that had God intended for us to wear such garments, God would have made scarlet or purple sheep. [105]

Chrysostom, writing at the end of the fourth century, indicates that despite the availability of convents, many virgins still lived at home, but this presented a danger. By this time the supervision of virgins fell to the priests, and in his treatise *On the Priesthood* Chrysostom writes about the burden such supervision entailed. For one, "a great number of women, full of innumerable vices, have intruded into the ranks of these holy ones."[106] He suggests that women under the vows of celibacy should not walk abroad unnecessarily or often, not speak at all without good reason, and they should not "be allowed to be perpetually dashing into the marketplace."[107] A natural father can easily watch over his daughter, but the spiritual father (priest) has a much more difficult task. He cannot live with her, but without a male protector the virgin finds numerous excuses to venture outside the home. "I cannot enumerate all the anxieties caused by virgins. The fact is that when they are enrolled, they cause extraordinary trouble to the man who is entrusted with this administration."[108] Some virgins, male and female, found a middle way between living alone and in a monastic community by living together, a male and female virgin. Even at its most ideal level such arrangements clearly had the potential for scandal and broken vows. The Council of Nicea (325) legislated against the practice. "The great synod has stringently forbidden any bishop, presbyter, deacon, or any one of the clergy whatsoever to have a *subintroducta* [woman under vows] dwelling with him, except only a mother or sister or aunt or only such persons as are beyond all suspicion."[109] Not only had Cyprian warned against such an arrangement already seventy-five years earlier, but other fathers repeated the warning in succeeding years. Late in the seventh century the warning is offered again at the Quinisext Council.

We have seen that Chrysostom referred to virgins who were "enrolled," which indicates that they now constituted a publicly recognized order. We cannot say for certain when such a recognition of status as an institution within the church, comparable to widows and deaconesses, came to be. But in the *Apostolic Constitutions* (c. 350), virgins are mentioned with the widows on six occasions, to be honored as figures of the altar. Furthermore, the virgins occupied a special place in the assembly, and they are mentioned in the prayers together with the readers, singers, widows, and orphans.[110] This definitely suggests the recognition of the virgins as an order. The same author writes: "About virginity we have received no commandment; but we permit it as a vow to those who wish it, only urging this upon them, that they do not make a profession rashly. . . . For one who has made a profession, doing works that are worthy of her profession, must show that her profession is true, and that it is made to give her leisure for religion."[111] Under Constantine the Empress Helena assembled the virgins in Jerusalem and waited on them at supper.[112] Constantine directed provincial governors to make annual provision for them as well as for widows.[113] Vows were clearly no longer made in secret with only the bishop's knowledge, but virgins were prominent and well known in the community.

Cyril of Jerusalem (c. 350) speaks of the "order of virgins" (*to tagma tōn parthenōn*) with the advice, "let the rest of the people follow them . . . who are enrolled in the angelic books."[114] By the end of the fourth century the veil, which had earlier been urged by Tertullian to encourage anonymity, was now bestowed upon virgins in a public ceremony. Jerome states that in addition to the veil, which he maintains designated the recipient as a bride of Christ, a dark colored dress was required.[115] Basil of Caesarea refers to the veiling taking place in a public ceremony, "before God and angels and men, the venerable gathering of clergy, the holy band of virgins, the assembly of the Lord, and the church of the saints."[116] The ceremony took place at Easter. Augustine implies there was a feast at the veiling of the virgins.[117]

The age of virgins varied widely, with Basil suggesting a minimum of sixteen; Ambrose refers to a dispute about age and advises that the candidate's "sobriety" was of greater significance than age, but in the fifth century civil law decreed that the minimum age be set at forty.[118] Later legislation distinguished between various stages of the vocation of religious life, reducing the age at entry to twenty-five or less.

As indicated earlier, the order of widows was absorbed by that of the virgins by the fifth century, and they were cloistered. Their vocation was that of contemplation, asceticism, and prayer, although we read of some liturgical functions as well, chiefly the singing of Psalms and hymns in the convent and assembly. J. LaPort records occasions where choirs of consecrated virgins were established to lead the singing in public assemblies for worship and at burials. Citing J. Chabot, there is also the intriguing possibility that virgins served as lectors as well, because the lessons were often sung, and singing was the responsibility of the virgin cantors.[119]

The earliest virgins tended to live alone in their homes or with relatives, although Tertullian knows of the existence of life in community.[120] By the fourth century such communities became more common, and eventually became the rule. One of the early communities for women was built by Pachomius, the founder of cenobitic monasticism, in Upper Egypt. Placed under the direction of his sister Maria, the convent attracted over four hundred women so that two more had to be constructed. Shortly after Pachomius's foundation, Shenute established a convent with eighteen hundred women. We read of the Pachomian establishment that "the women lived on one side of the river opposite the men. When a virgin died, the others laid her out for burial, and they placed it on the bank of the river. The brothers [monks] would cross on a ferry-boat and carrying palm leaves and olive branches bring the body over and bury it in the common cemetary."[121] The women occupied themselves in prayer, worship, and meditation, and they made clothing for the monks and themselves. On Sundays a priest and a deacon crossed to the convent to preside at the Eucharist.

A large number of prominent women emerged from the communities that flourished in the fourth century. In addition to serving their own growing communities as administrators and examples of piety, these women often played a significant role in the life of the church. Among these was Macrina, the sister of Gregory of Nyssa and Basil of Caesarea. We have an account of her life written by Gregory, who informs us that after the death of the man to whom she was betrothed, she took a vow of celibacy and started a community within her home, living as an equal with her maid servants. She influenced the development of her four brothers, including Peter, who became a famous hermit, and Naucratius, who was active in serving the elderly. When Basil returned from his philosophical studies at Athens, "he was enormously puffed up with pride over his rhetorical abilities," says Gregory, "yet Macrina drew him with such speed to the goal of philosophy [i.e., Christianity], that he renounced worldly renown."[122] Gregory also testifies to her competence as a theologian: "She went through arguments in detailed manner, speaking about natural phenomena, recounting the divine plan hidden in sad events, revealing things about the future life as if she were possessed by the Holy Spirit."[123] Gregory was so impressed with her theological acumen that it seemed to him he was standing inside the heavenly sanctuary. Such lofty words from one who has been called the "father of Christian mysticism" suggest that Macrina may have been a primary catalyst in Gregory's theological development.

Jerome's close friend, Paula, one of the best known women of the fourth century, was a wealthy Roman matron married to a senator. His early death left her a widow at age thirty-three with five children, whereupon she took the vow of celibacy. After visiting the monasteries in Egypt and Palestine, she settled in Bethlehem in 385 where she used her wealth to build a convent for women, over which she presided, and a monastery for men under Jerome's supervision, as well as a hospice for pilgrims. She had already learned Greek and now undertook the study of Hebrew to enable her to sing the Psalms in their original words. Besides administering her own community, she concerned herself with Jerome's welfare, which was no simple task. After her death, her daughter, Eustochium, supervised the convent. We have an account of her life and virtues in Jerome's eulogy to her (Letter 108). Jerome describes the austerities of the convent:

> In the early morning, at the third, the sixth, and ninth hours, in the evening and at midnight, they chanted the Psalter in order. None of the sisters was allowed to be ignorant of the Psalter, and daily they were to learn something from the Holy Scriptures. . . . All dressed the same. . . . Aside from food and clothing she permitted no one to have anything. . . . She used to censure [bodily adornment] by saying, "A clean body and a clean dress imply an unclean soul."[124]

After describing her strenuous journeys, Jerome marvels: "Her zeal was amazing, and her endurance scarcely believable in a woman."[125] Among her good works were the care of the poor and the dying, the visitation of the sick, and feeding the hungry. She also offered hospitality to the many pilgrims who thronged to Bethlehem, saying that in the place where the Holy Family found no room it was not fitting that strangers should suffer the same hardship. She discussed biblical texts with Jerome in their original languages, in all respects his equal in scholarship.

Jerome's several female friends included Marcella, whom he had met while he as still living in Rome. She learned of the communal life when Athanasius visited the city during his second exile, and she enthusiastically adopted its austerities. She gained a reputation for theological scholarship in her dialogues with Jerome, whom she sought out for instruction in the Scriptures. We are told by Jerome that in their conversations she did not appear in awe of his considerable reputation, but to every suggested interpretation of a text she would offer an opposing view, "not for the sake of being contentious, but so that by asking she might learn solutions for points she perceived could be raised in objection."[126] After Jerome left for Bethlehem, Marcella continued her theological studies and often was asked to resolve difficult questions by pretending that her solution was that of Jerome, when in fact it was her own. Jerome marvels at her wisdom in assuming the role of a teacher under the guise of claiming his authority, "lest she seem to inflict an injury on the male sex and on those priests who were inquiring about obscure and doubtful points."[127] In Marcella we have an example of a woman who served the church as teacher of the clergy, but unfortunately we do not possess any examples of the substance of their discussions.

Another formidable woman was Melania the Elder, a redoubtable but somewhat imperious person. Married to a high-ranking Roman official, she was widowed at age twenty-two. She used her wealth to hire a ship filled with women and children to sail to Egypt. There she spent six months visiting the most outstanding hermits in the desert. When some of these monks were banished to Palestine during the Arian controversies, she ministered to them from her own resources. The consul of Palestine had her jailed, but she forced him to release her, with apologies, by revealing her aristocratic background and connections in Rome. After the monks were recalled from exile, Melania built a convent in Jerusalem and lived there for twenty-seven years heading a company of fifty virgins. Nearby lived Rufinus of Aquileia, the controversial translator of Origen and bitter opponent of Jerome. Palladius refers to many works of charity Melania supported with Rufinus, besides convincing four hundred heretical monks of the deity of the Holy Spirit, thereby restoring them to orthodoxy. When she was sixty years old, she returned to Rome to strengthen her granddaughter, Melania the Younger, who despite being married, had decided to renounce the world. She not only convinced her to take vows but convinced her parents as well—that is, Melania's own son and daughter-in-law.[128] Paulinus of Nola also comments on the life of Melania the Elder and her activities in Palestine, her lavish donations to the church, and her zeal for the ascetic life. He describes her return to Rome, contrasting the glitter of wealth displayed by her children and their friends with her own "emaciated little horse, worth less than a donkey . . . but the grace of Christian humility outshone such empty magnificence."[129]

Melania the Younger, granddaughter to the Elder, was forced into a marriage with a prominent Roman, but Palladius writes that she was so "stung" by the stories about her grandmother that she was unable to cooperate in the marriage. Two sons died in infancy, and Melania, unhappy in her seven-year marriage (married at thirteen) convinced her husband to take vows of continence with her. They gave lavishly of their wealth to various churches—ten thousand pieces of gold to Egypt, the same amount to Antioch, fifteen thousand to Palestine, and ten thousand to the churches in the islands. An index of her wealth, if Palladius is correct, is that she freed eight thousand of her slaves who desired freedom and the rest she gave to her brother.[130] Stories such as these reveal the extent to which the ascetic ideal had captivated some of the Roman aristocracy, primarily women, and that the church was the beneficiary of their largesse.

Fabiola, another friend of Jerome, provides us with a further example of women who served the church. She divorced her first husband on grounds of his adultery and married a second. After the death of her second husband, she believed it was necessary to do penance for the second marriage, as the first husband was still living. She gave her considerable wealth to the poor, and we are told by Jerome that "she was the first person to found a hospital, into which she might gather sufferers out of the streets, and where she might nurse the unfortunate victims of sickness and want." He continues by offering a graphic description of the loathsome nature of the diseased—flesh alive with worms, noses slit, cleaning up the incontinent. She was especially attentive to the dying—a fourth-century Mother Teresa.[131] She also gave generously to the clergy and the monks, and then went from island to island assisting the needy. She followed her ministry in Rome by embarking for Palestine where she continued her work among the needy. That is where she met Jerome and, like Paula and Marcella, engaged him in animated theological discussions on Scripture texts. When Palestine was threatened by the Huns, she returned to Rome where she died in poverty (399) but hardly unrecognized. "On that day Rome saw all her peoples gathered together in one, and each person present flattered himself that he had some part in the glory of her penitence."[132]

Etheria, probably from Spain, was a remarkable woman who has left us a diary of her travels through Egypt, Palestine, Edessa, Asia Minor, and Constantinople sometime late in the fourth century. She possesses considerable intelligence with power of observation and sheer stamina, demonstrated by climbing Mt. Sinai, visiting scores of holy places, and traveling by land and sea, most likely by herself, around the eastern Mediterranean. In the first part of her diary she describes numerous holy places. She tells of her visit to Mt. Sinai: "In this place there is now a church, though not a very large one, because the place itself, the summit of the mountain, that is, is not very large. Yet this church has great charm all its own. When through God's will we had reached the mountaintop and had arrived at the church door, there was a priest . . . to meet us. . . ."[133] She continues by saying the Communion was celebrated with other hermits in the area, and they offered her fruit before making the descent. She depicts with some detail the other peaks and valleys in the area, a visit to Moses' burning bush, and the site of the Golden Calf.

The second part of the diary portrays the liturgical practices of various churches, primarily in Jerusalem and its environs. She offers us a full account of the daily offices, the services of Holy Week, Easter, Pentecost, and Epiphany. About observing Maundy Thursday she writes: "As soon as it begins to be the hour of cockcrow, everyone comes down from the Imbomon singing hymns and proceeds to the very place where the Lord prayed. There stands a tasteful church. The bishop has a prayer fitting to the day and place, followed by a hymn and a reading from the Gospel."[134] At Gethsemane over two hundred candles give light in the early morning, and after these devotions the assembly processes through the city to the place of Golgotha for the veneration of the cross. By this time it is midday, and the people are dismissed to return to their homes to prepare for the Good Friday vigil, which will begin later in the day. In this way Etheria works through the major festivals of the church year, giving us a detailed account of early liturgical practices and the development of the church calendar. Her work is a unique contribution in the service of the church.

Together with the company of virgins, deaconesses, and widows, women such as Paula, Marcella, and two Melanias, Fabiola, Maria (sister of Pachomius), Etheria, and Olympias are representative of a large group of women who served the church in pastoral roles. They are worthy successors of Phoebe, Lydia, Prisca, and Joanna, and forerunners of such later saints as Bridget of Sweden, Catherine of Sienna, and Teresa of Avila. At the same time, we must recognize that the fourth-century women mentioned here were not typical of Christian women, being set apart by their wealth and aristocratic social position. Also, given the outburst of ascetical fervor of these times, one could scarcely gain position in the church apart from adopting a celibate life-style, whether one was man or woman. And we cannot ignore the fact that, despite the fervor and devotion exemplified by multitudes of women, the office of priest remained closed to them. Elizabeth Clark, however, suggests there is positive value in their example: "Our age, with its more democratic interests, should not scorn these accounts for their nontypicality: they are the single strongest evidence that male patristic writers could, and did, overcome their prejudices and see women as worthy bearers of the new religious ideals."[135] Any account of pastoral life and practice in the early church must recognize the considerable contributions made by multitudes of women who functioned in a pastoral role in the service of the church.

Notes

Chapter 1: The Pastoral Office

1. Scholars do not agree whether the Twelve actually were companions of the historical Jesus or whether the designation is a creation of the early church. I believe the evidence supports the former thesis, that they were in fact with Jesus before his death. See B. Rigaux, "The Twelve Apostles," *Concilium* 4/4 (1968): 4–9; A. Hultgren, unpubl. essay, "Forms of Ministry in the New Testament," Consultation on Expanding Forms of Parish Ministry, 1978.

2. Karl H. Rengstorf, *Apostolate and Ministry*, trans. P. D. Pahl (St. Louis: Concordia, 1954), 26.

3. Jerome D. Quinn, "Ministry in the New Testament," *Lutherans and Catholics in Dialogue*, vol. 4, "Eucharist and Ministry" (U.S.A. National Committee of the Lutheran World Federation, 1970), 100. Jean Daniélou, *The Theology of Jewish Christianity* (Chicago: Regnery, 1964), 350: "There is a missionary priesthood as distinguished from a stable one attached to one place, that of the *apostoloi*. The various roles assigned to these *apostoloi* are all related to this primary distinct vocation. They are essentially preachers, and this aspect of their ministry is indicated by the term prophet and *didascolos*. As prophets they announce the kerygma to pagans; as *didascaloi* they prepare those pagans who have decided to receive baptism."

4. Eusebius, *Ecclesiastical History*, 7246.

5. Rudolph Sohm, *Kirchenrecht* (2 vols.; Leipzig: Dunker and Humblot, 1892 and 1923) and *Wesen and Ursprung des Katholizismus* (1909; repr.,

Darmstadt: Wissenschaftliche Buchgesellschaft, 1867); Adolph von Harnack, *The Constitution and Law of the Church in the First Two Centuries* (German ed., 1910; New York: Putnam's Sons).

6. A contemporary revision of Harnack's thesis is by Hans von Campenhausen, *Ecclesiastical Authority and Spiritual Power in the Church of the First Three Centuries* (London: Adam and Charles Black, 1969). The author supports the two triad theory but sees it in much less rigid or exclusive terms than does Harnack.

7. Clement of Rome, *Letter to the Corinthians*, 64.

8. Ibid., 60. He makes no direct equation between the Old Testament hierarchy and that of bishop, priest, deacon, but the inference is clear.

9. Edwin Hatch, *The Organization of the Early Christian Churches* (Bampton Lectures at Oxford, 1880, lect. 5), argues that 1 Tim. 4:14 says the gift came *meta*, i.e., together with the laying on of hands, whereas 2 Tim. 1:16 says the gift came *dia*, i.e., through the hands. He believes greater weight should be placed on the *meta* in that the gift was not conferred through the hands but was already present.

10. Cf. G. Kittel, *Theological Dictionary of the New Testament* (Grand Rapids, Mich.: Wm. B. Eerdmans, 1974), 9: 428–34. Kittel believes the laying on of hands is unique to the Judeo-Christian tradition.

11. Ibid., 429.

12. Ibid., 432. The example of Simon Magus in Acts 8:18 is evidence that the laying on of hands is not to be misused as magic.

13. *Teaching of the Apostles*, 11–13.

14. Ignatius, *To the Magnesians*, 6–7.

15. Ibid., 13; *To the Trallians*, 3.

16. Clement of Rome, *To the Corinthians*, 42.

17. Ibid., 44.

18. Irenaeus, *Against Heresies*, 3:3:3.

19. Tertullian, *Proscription against Heresies*, 32.

20. *Library of Christian Classics*, vol. 1, ed. Cyril C. Richardson (Philadelphia: Westminster, 1953), 125. Cf. Tertullian, *Prescription against Heresies*, 32:2.

21. Bernard Cooke, *Ministry to Word and Sacraments* (Philadelphia: Fortress, 1976), 419. Hippolytus, *The Apostolic Tradition*, 2, speaks of more than one bishop in attendance and laying hands upon a new bishop, although only one bishop pronounces the consecratory prayer.

22. Hippolytus, *The Apostolic Tradition*, 1:2.

23. A. C. Piepkorn, "A Lutheran View of the Validity of Lutheran Orders," *Lutherans and Catholics in Dialogue*, vol. 4, "Eucharist and Ministry," 209–26. Piepkorn argues primarily on the basis of the synonymity of presbyters with bishops in the first five centuries.

24. Edward J. Kilmartin, "Ministry and Ordination in Early Christianity," *Ordination Rites Past and Present*, ed. Vos and Wainright (Rotterdam, 1980), 60. "The *cheirotenei* signifies the bestowal of the spirit which empowers the ordinand for certain fundamental functions in the community, above all liturgical ones. Only the bishop has the power to communicate the Spirit to the ordinand, and he receives this by ordination," 59. Hastings, *Encyclopedia of Religion and Ethics*, 542, "There is no trace of an imperative formula like 'Receive the Holy Ghost,' such as we find in the medieval and modern books in the West."

25. *Didascalia Apostolorum*, trans. R. Connolly (Oxford, 1929), 4:1–6; 8:1–4; 9:1, 2, 5.

26. Cf. C. H. Turner, "Cheirotonia, Cheirothesia, Epithesis chairōn," in the *Journal of Theological Studies* 24 (1922–23): 496–504; see also Kittel, *Dictionary*, 9:437.

27. Tertullian, *Prescription against Heresies*, 41.

28. Cf. David Powers, *Ministers of Christ and His Church* (London, 1969), 31–34. But we find a vigorous disclaimer in J. H. Bernard, "The Cyprianic Doctrine of the Ministry," in H. B. Swete, *Early History of the Church and Ministry* (London, 1918): "In truth it is a perversion of history to regard the authority of the bishop over his presbyters as a development which was unknown in early times, and which only came into prominence after the days of Constantine, when the church was 'established.' The facts point in the opposite direction. The 'evolution of the presbyterate' rather than the 'evolution of the episcopate' is the process which history offers to our view," p. 236.

29. Ibid.

30. L. E. Elliot-Binns, *The Beginnings of Western Christendom* (London, 1948), 318.

31. Jerome, *Letter 146:* "The apostle clearly teaches that presbyters are the same as bishops. . . . Afterward one was chosen who was placed above the others as a remedy for schism. The presbyters always chose one of their number, placed him in the higher rank, and named him bishop."

32. Hatch, *Organization*, 79.

33. Cyprian, *Epistle 67:4*.

34. Idem, *Epistle 55:8*.

35. Idem, *Epistle 67:3*.

36. Idem, *Epistle 67:5*.

37. Idem, *Epistle 3:3:* "The Lord chose the apostles, that is, the bishops." Cf. Council of Carthage, 256: "We have succeeded to the apostles and govern the church with the same authority as they," in Swete, *Early History*, 139.

38. Cooke, *Ministry*, 419.

39. Cyprian, *Epistle 70.*

40. Idem, *On the Lapsed,* 17.

41. Origen, *Commentary on Matthew,* in John T. McNeill, *History of the Cure of Souls* (New York: Harper and Row, 1951), 132.

42. Cyprian, *Epistle 69:11.*

43. Idem, *Epistle 75:9.*

44. Hans von Campenhausen, "The Origin of the Idea of the Priesthood in the Early Church," in *Tradition and Life in the Church* (London: Collins, 1960), 220–21.

45. W. H. C. Frend, *The Rise of Christianity* (Philadelphia: Fortress, 1984), 401.

46. Eusebius, *Ecclesiastical History,* 6:43:11.

47. *The Ministry in Historical Perspective,* ed. H. Richard Niebuhr and Daniel Williams (New York: Harper and Row, 1956), 45.

48. Origen, *Homily 6* (on Lev. 7:35—8:13), 3.

49. Cited by Niebuhr and Williams, *Ministry,* 42. See W. Telfes, "Episcopal Succession," *Journal of Ecclesiastical History* 3 (1952): 1–13.

50. Hans von Campenhausen, "Origin," 222.

51. T. M. Lindsay, *The Church and the Ministry in the Early Centuries* (New York: A.C. Armstrong and Sons, 1902), 279.

52. *Codex Theodosianus,* 16:2:1–2 (A.D. 313 and 319) cited by Frend, *Rise of Christianity,* 487. In 346, clergy and their children were exempted from fiscal obligations with regard to the cities.

53. Eusebius, *Ecclesiastical History,* 10:5:23. The privilege of using the imperial mail horses was also available for the Council of Nicea and subsequent councils, leading the Roman historian Ammianus Marcellinus to complain about the serious disruption this caused the postal services.

54. Council of Arles (314) canons in *A New Eusebius,* ed. J. Stevenson (London: S.P.C.K., 1957), 322–25.

55. Council of Ancyra (314) in *Nicene and Post-Nicene Fathers,* ed. Philip Schaff (Grand Rapids, Mich.: Wm. B. Eerdmans, 1st pub. 1899), vol. 5, *The Seven Councils,* 71.

56. Council of Neocaesarea, *The Seven Councils,* 79, 84.

57. Council of Nicea, *The Seven Councils,* 8ff. Hefele is actually citing Greek commentators. He writes, "The Latin church acted otherwise. It is true that with it also the people have been removed from episcopal elections, but this did not happen until later, about the eleventh century; and it was not only the people who were removed, but the bishops of the province as well, and the election was conducted entirely by the clergy of the cathedral church," 12.

58. Canon 6 of Nicea further developed the concept of metropolitans by delineating the jurisdictions of Alexandria, Antioch, and Rome; canon 7 recognized the dignity of Jerusalem.

59. Niebuhr and Williams, *Ministry*, 298, n. 8: "The fact that the word mob *(tois ochlois)* is used may mean that orderly election *(ekloge)* by the properly constituted *laos* is not expressly excluded, but this was a marked tendency from the beginning in the East with the metropolitan appointing or the emperor nominating as chief layman. Popular suffrage survives much longer in the West. Even pope Leo could exclaim, 'He who is to preside over all must be elected by all,' " Ep. 10 and Ep. 14.

60. Synod of Laodicea, *Seven Ecumenical Councils*, 131.

61. Chrysostom, *Homily 18* (on 2 Cor. 8:16-24).

62. Idem, *Homily 11* (on 1 Tim. 3:8-18), 1.

63. Ibid.

64. Chrysostom, *On the Priesthood*, 3:15, trans. Graham Neville, 89–93.

65. Ibid., in Joseph Lienhard, *Ministry* (Wilmington, Del.: Michael Glazier, 1984), 78–79.

66. Chrysostom, *Homily 86 on John* (John 20:10-23), 4, in Lienhard, *Ministry*, 96–97.

67. Gregory of Nyssa (Migne, PG 46, 581) cited by von Campenhausen, "Origins," 228–29. Von Campenhausen claims this is the first instance of sacerdotal endowments imparted sacramentally.

68. Von Campenhausen, "Origins," 221. In the West the idea of priesthood developed in reference to the sacrament, which the priest consecrated. In the East it is always related to the divine liturgy of the people. There is no objectivity of sacramental efficacy apart from the people.

69. Chrysostom, *Second Baptismal Instruction*, 26.

70. Jerome, *To the Presbyter Evangelus*, Letter 146, 1. "The presbyter is contained in the bishop. With the exception of ordinations, what does a bishop do that a presbyter does not do?" 146:2.

71. Ambrose, *To the Church at Vercelli*, Letters 46 and 66. Ambrose here refers to the new custom at Vercelli of clergy living in community according to a rule.

72. Chrysostom, *On the Priesthood*, 1:6–7.

73. Jerome, *Epistle*, 1:1.

74. Gregory of Nazianzus, *On My Life*, 345.

75. Sozomon, Ecclesiastical History, 8:19, 6:30, 3:16.

76. Augustine, *Against the Grammarian Cresconius*, 2:13: "Neque enim episcopi propter nos sumus, sed propter eos, quibus verbum sacramentum dominicum ministravimus." Cf. von Campenhausen, "Origins," 224–25. With Augustine, those outside the catholic church possessed valid but inefficacious sacraments; today it is said that those outside the

Roman communion clearly have efficacious sacraments, which are invalid.

77. Augustine, *On Baptism*, 3:15: "The baptism which is consecrated by the words of Christ in the Gospels is holy, even when conferred by the polluted, however shameless and unclean they may be. This holiness itself is incapable of contamination, and the power of God supports his sacrament, whether for the salvation of those who use it aright, or the doom of those who employ it wrongly. The light of the sun or of a lamp is not defiled by contact with the filth on which it shines; so how can Christ's baptism be defiled by the wickedness of any man?"

78. Von Campenhausen, "Origins," 226.

79. Justinian, *Corpus Juris Civilis*, 1:3:41, in Cooke, *Ministry*, 451, n. 12.

80. Cooke, *Ministry*, 429.

81. Ibid., 436.

82. Lindsay, *The Church and the Ministry*, 351. Cf. Hatch, *Organization*, 353.

83. *Didascalia Apostolorum*, 8:3, 9:1.

84. Jerome, *Letter to Evangelus*, 2.

85. Hippolytus, *The Apostolic Tradition*, 3:5, 6.

86. Cited in *The Sacrament of Orders* (Collegeville, Minn.: Liturgical Press, 1957), 123 (Migne, PG, 48:644).

Chapter 2: Pastor and People

1. Wayne A. Meeks, *The First Urban Christians* (New Haven: Yale University Press, 1983), 11.

2. Roland Allen, *Missionary Methods: St. Paul's or Ours?* (Grand Rapids, Mich.: Wm. B. Eerdmans, 1962), 13. The work of Adolph von Harnack, *The Mission and Expansion of Christianity in the First Three Centuries*, trans. James Moffat (New York, 1908), remains one of the best treatments of this topic.

3. William M. Ramsey, "Roads and Travel in New Testament," in Hastings, *Dictionary of the Bible*, vol. 5, 396.

4. Tertullian, *Apology*, 7:4, 8.

5. Eusebius, *Ecclesiastical History*, 6:36:1.

6. Socrates, *Ecclesiastical History*, 4:27.

7. Eusebius, *Ecclesiastical History*, 6:43:8.

8. Robert Grant, *Early Christianity and Society* (New York: Harper and Row, 1977), 6–7.

9. Eusebius, *Ecclesiastical History*, 9:7:9.

10. Meeks, *The First Urban Christians*, 73–74. Meeks states that we cannot draw up a statistical profile of the constituency of the Pauline communities nor fully describe their social level, but we have clues that lead to these impressions.

11. Grant, *Early Christianity and Society*, 11.

12. Eusebius, *Ecclesiastical History*, 5:21:1.

13. Tertullian, *Apology*, 1:7, 37:4.

14. Origen, *Commentary on Romans*, 5:1.

15. W. H. C. Frend, *The Rise of Christianity* (Philadelphia: Fortress, 1984), 413.

16. *Letter to Diognetus*, 5.

17. Eusebius, *Ecclesiastical History*, 10:5:8.

18. Jean Daniélou and Henri Marrou, *The First Six Hundred Years*, vol. 1 in *The Christian Centuries* (New York: McGraw-Hill, 1964), 293. Daniélou suggests that the presence of heresy indicates a vigorous church. If that is true, the fourth-century church was vigorous indeed.

19. Cited in F. Van der Meer, *Augustine the Bishop* (New York: Harper and Row, 1961), 190–91. Augustine, *Sermons*, 302:21, 19 and 73:4.

20. Cyril C. Richardson, *Early Christian Fathers*, vol. 1 in The Library of Christian Classics (Philadelphia: Westminster, 1953), 34.

21. Clement of Rome, *To the Corinthians*, 1, 2.

22. Tertullian, *Prescription against Heretics*, 7.

23. *Shepherd of Hermas*, Similitude 8:7:4.

24. Ibid., Vision 3:9:10.

25. Cyprian, *Letters*, 59:18.

26. "The Martyrdom of Saints Perpetua and Felicitas," in Anne Fremantle, *A Treasury of Early Christianity* (New York: Viking, 1953), 219.

27. Eusebius, *Ecclesiastical History*, 7:1:7.

28. Gregory of Nyssa, "On the Deity of the Son and Holy Spirit" (PG 46:557), cited in Frend, *Rise of Christianity*, 636.

29. Ammianus Marcellinus, 22:5:4.

30. Augustine, *Commentary on Ps. 88, Sermons*, 3:4.

31. Cf. Henry Chadwick, *The Early Church* (New York: Penguin, 1969), 126–27.

32. Ramsay MacMullen, *Christianizing the Roman Empire*, A.D. *100–400* (New Haven: Yale University Press, 1984), 78.

33. Athanasius, *Life of Antony*, 40, 41.

34. Tertullian, *Apology*, 23.

35. Origen, *Against Celsus*, 7:62, 8:21–24, 28, 33.

36. Cyril of Jerusalem, *Catechetical Orations*, 3:3.

37. Council of Arles (314), can. 9 (8).

38. Gregory of Nyssa, *Great Catechism*, 37; Ambrose, *On the Mysteries*, 9.

39. Origen, *Against Celsus*, 8:2, 8:17, 49, 55.
40. Stephen Benko, *Pagan Rome and the Early Christians* (Bloomington: Indiana University Press, 1984), 119.
41. Council of Laodicea, can. 35, 36.
42. Meeks, *The First Urban Christians*, 74–84. The four models for the church is that given by Meeks.
43. Meeks, *First Urban Christians*, 77.
44. Justin, *First Apology*, 67.
45. Ibid.
46. Nicetas of Remisiana, in Joseph Jungmann, *Christian Prayer through the Ages* (New York: Paulist, 1969), 34.
47. *Martyrdom of Polycarp*, 18.
48. *Martyrdom of St. Justin*.
49. Richard Krautheim, *Early Christian and Byzantine Architecture* (New York: Penguin, 1965), 25–26.
50. Justin Martyr, *First Apology*, 14.
51. Athenagoras, *Plea for Christians*, 35.
52. Tertullian, *On Idolatry*, 39.
53. Idem, *On the Apparel of Women*, 6.
54. Idem, *On Idolatry*, 20, 18, 19.
55. Hippolytus, *Apostolic Tradition*, 16.
56. Council of Elvira, can. 20, 15, 16, 26, 36, 48, 79, 67.
57. Ibid., can. 81.
58. Ibid., can. 21, 5, 77.
59. Quintillian, cited in W. Goodsell, *A History of Marriage and the Family* (New York: Macmillan, 1934), 151–52.
60. Seneca, *On Benefits*, 3:16:2.
61. Justin, *First Apology*, 15.
62. Synod of Laodicea, can. 1.
63. Tertullian, *To My Wife*, 2:6.
64. Ibid., 2:8.
65. Ibid., 2:4. See also Tertullian's description of the difficulties in being married to a pagan in *Apology*, 3.
66. Origen, *Against Celsus*, 8:55.
67. Jerome, *Letter*, 22:20.
68. Augustine, *Sermon*, 82:8:11.
69. Hippolytus, *Refutation of Heresies*, 9:12:22–23. Tertullian, *On Idolatry*, 24.
70. Basil of Caesarea, *Epistle*, 197.
71. F. Dvornik, *Early Christian and Byzantine Political Philosophy*, vol. 2 (Dumbarton Oaks, 1962), 608.
72. Justin, *First Apology*, 14.

73. Eusebius, *Ecclesiastical History*, 7:22:1ff.
74. Lucian, *On the Death of Pererinus*, 13.
75. Tertullian, *On Idolatry*, 39.
76. Cyprian, *On Works and Almsgiving*.
77. Cited in Frend, *Rise of Christianity*, 604.
78. Gregory of Nazianzus, *Oration*, 43:63.
79. J. W. C. Wand, *Fathers and Councils* (London: Faith Press, 1962), 34.
80. Frend, *Rise of Christianity*, 631.
81. Justinian, *Corpus Iuris Civilis*, 1:3:41.
82. E. A. Judge, *The Conversion of Rome: Ancient Source of Modern Tensions* (North Ryde, Australia: Macquarrie Ancient History Association, 1980), 7.
83. *Rule of Saint Benedict*, 53, 30–31.
84. Hippolytus, *Apostolic Tradition*, 20.
85. Chrysostom, *Homily on Matt.*, 46:2.
86. Chrysostom, *Homilies*, 1 Thess. 11:3, 1 Cor. 30:3.
87. Chrysostom, *Homily* on Matt. 46.
88. Henry Chadwick, *The Role of the Christian Bishop in Ancient Society* (The Center for Hermeneutical Studies in Hellenistic and Modern Culture, 35th Colloquy, 1980), 5. "The distribution of alms to the poor was a plentiful source of discontent among its recipients. Augustine confesses that he finds the problems of the administration of church finances altogether hateful" (Ep. 129:9).
89. Ignatius, *To the Ephesians*, 7–9.
90. Gregory, *Pastoral Care*, ed. and trans. Henry Davis, S.J. (New York: Newman, 1950), vol. 11 in *Ancient Christian Writers*, see pp. 45-88.
91. *Didascalia Apostolorum*, 8:3. Cf. chap. 4 passim.
92. Origen, *Homily 6* (on Lev. 7:35—8:13).
93. Jerome, *To Nepotian*, cited in Joseph Lienhard, *Ministry* (Wilmington, Del.: Michael Glazier, 1984), vol. 8 in Messages of the Fathers of the Church, 149–69.
94. Chrysostom, *Homily 3 on Acts* (Acts 1:12-26).
95. Gregory, *Pastoral Rule*, 2:7
96. Augustine, *Epistle*, 54:2:2.
97. F. Van der Meer, *Augustine the Bishop*, 173.
98. *Apostolic Constitutions*, 2:59.
99. See Chadwick, *The Role of the Christian Bishop*, 5, on the bishop's care for orphans.
100. Augustine, *Epistle*, 126:1, 6. Cf. 126:9.
101. Basil of Caesarea, *Oration*, 7; Chrysostom, *Homily*, 23; Jerome, *Epistle* 121; *Comm.* on Ps. 38:12.

102. *Didascalia Apostolorum*, 2:47; *Apostolic Constitutions*, 2:47.
103. Augustine, *Commentary* on Ps. 118:24.
104. Henry Chadwick, *Role of the Christian Bishop*, 11.
105. Tertullian, *Exhortation to Chastity*, 13.
106. Charles A. Frazee, "The Origins of Clerical Celibacy in the Western Church," *Church History* 41/2 (June 1972): 151. Frazee's article has become a standard in the literature of clerical celibacy in the West, and I have followed his argument here.
107. H. Richard Niebuhr and Daniel D. Williams, *The Ministry in Historical Perspectives* (New York: Harper and Row, 1956), 28.
108. Ex. 19:15; Lev. 7:19–20; 15-16; 22:4; 1 Sam. 21:4, Ezek. 44:9.
109. Tertullian, *Exhortation to Chastity*, 7:5.
110. Cassian, *Institutes*, 11:18.
111. Siricius of Rome, *Letter 1* (to Himerius) 7:8.
112. Basil of Caesarea, *Epistle*, 199:27.
113. Frazee, "Origins of Clerical Celibacy," 157, citing P. Delhaye, "Celibacy," *New Catholic Encyclopedia*, vol. 3, 374.
114. Bernard Cooke, *Ministry to Word and Sacraments* (Philadelphia: Fortress, 1976), 558: "There is not a situation which could justifiably be called universal clerical celibacy (i.e., celibacy of bishops, presbyters, and deacons) prior to the reform movement directed by Gregory VII in the eleventh century."
115. Gregory of Nazianzus, *Funeral Oration* (18), in Philip Schaff, *Nicene and Post-Nicene Fathers* (Grand Rapids, Mich.: Wm. B. Eerdmans, 1st. pub. 1899), vol. 7 (second series), 254–69, passim.

Chapter 3: Pastor and Proclamation

1. Origen, *Against Celsus*, 3:9.
2. Chrysostom, *On the Priesthood*, 4:8.
3. *Apostolic Constitutions*, 8:1:5. It appears that 1 Cor. 14:23 indicates the possibility of pagans attending Christian assemblies.
4. Hippolytus, *The Apostolic Tradition*, 17.
5. Council of Elvira (306), can. 42. "He who has a good name and wishes to become a Christian must be a catechumen two years, then he may be baptized," in Carl J. Hefele, *Conciliengeschichte* (Freiburg: 1879), vol. 1, 155; Justinian, *Novellae*, 144.
6. Augustine, *On Faith and the Creed*, 1.
7. Idem, *On Catechizing the Uninstructed*, 10.
8. Cyril of Jerusalem, *Procatechesis*, 6, 10.
9. Chrysostom, *First Instruction to Catechumens*, 1:2.

10. Gregory of Nyssa, *Great Catechism*, Preface.

11. Augustine, *On Catechizing the Uninstructed*, 15.

12. Ibid., 5, 9, 11. So also Chrysostom suggests that instruction should be kept simple: "Do not by saying everything at once confuse their minds," *First Instruction to Catechumens*, 1:5.

13. Augustine, *On Catechizing the Uninstructed*, 14.

14. Ibid., 18.

15. Chrysostom, *Second Instruction to Catechumens*, 3, 4.

16. Rufinus, *Commentary on the Apostles' Creed*, 10.

17. Ibid., 7.

18. Augustine, *On Catechizing the Uninstructed*, 15.

19. The edition here referred to is by M. L. W. Laistner, *Christianity and Pagan Culture in the Later Roman Empire together with an English Translation of John Chrysostom's Address on Vainglory and the Right Way for Parents to Bring up Their Children* (Ithaca, N.Y.: Cornell University Press, 1951).

20. Hippolytus, *The Apostolic Tradition*, 20.

21. Cyril of Jerusalem, *Catechetical Orations*, 3:12.

22. Ibid., 4:2:3.

23. Clement of Alexandria, *The Tutor*, 1:1. Nevertheless, the early church offers no better example of an intellectual Christian than Clement, who distinguished between "simple believers" and the more advanced "gnostic" Christians.

24. Hippolytus, *Apostolic Tradition*, 39.

25. Yngve Brilioth, *A Brief History of Preaching*, trans. Karl E. Mattson (Philadelphia: Fortress, 1965), 3.

26. Justin Martyr, *1 Apology*, 67.

27. Martin R. P. McGuire, "Introduction," *Funeral Orations of St. Gregory Nazianzen and St. Ambrose*, vol. 22 in Fathers of the Church (New York, 1953), vii.

28. Clement of Rome, *To the Corinthians*, 25. Lactantius composed an entire poem, *De ave phoenice* in 85 verses on this myth, which is first found in Herodotus, 11:73. See Lactantius, *The Divine Institutes*, trans. Sr. Mary Frances McDonald, vol. 19 in Fathers of the Church (New York, 1964), xv.

29. Thomas K. Carroll, *Preaching the Word*, vol. 11 in Message of the Fathers of the Church (Wilmington, Del.: Michael Glazier, 1984), 37.

30. Melito of Sardis, *On the Pasch*, 72.

31. Cicero, as cited by Carroll, *Preaching the Word*, 174.

32. Origen, *Homilies on Jeremiah*, 39:1.

33. Augustine, *Quaest. In Hept.*, 2, q. 73, cited by J. N. D. Kelly, *Early Christian Doctrines* (New York: Harper and Brothers, 1958), 69.

34. Origen, *On First Principles*, 4:2:4.
35. Kelly, *Early Christian Doctrines*, 73.
36. Origen, *Homilies on Genesis*, 6:1.
37. Carroll, *Preaching the Word*, 61.
38. Tertullian, *On Purity*, 8:9.
39. Diodore of Tarsus, *Praef. in pass.*, cited in Kelly, *Early Christian Doctrines*, 76.
40. *Homily of Clement* (commonly known as 2 Clement), 8.
41. Ibid., 9.
42. Melito of Sardis, *On the Pasch*, 26.
43. Berthold Altaner, *Patrology*, trans. Hilda C. Graef (New York: Herder and Herder, 1961), 215.
44. Clement of Alexandria, *Who Is the Rich Man Who Can Be Saved?* 6:3.
45. Johannes Quasten, *Patrology*, vol. 2 (Utrecht, 1960), 37.
46. Socrates, *Ecclesiastical History*, cited by Carroll, *Preaching the Word*, 42.
47. Origen, *Homilies in Ezekial*, 4:3.
48. Idem, *Homilies in Genesis*, 12:1.
49. Idem, *Homily on Ps. 36*, 5:1.
50. Idem, *Homily on Luke*, 36:6.
51. Idem, *Homily on John*, 28:7.
52. Idem, *Homily on Jeremiah*, 18:7-10.
53. Ibid., 4:3.
54. Idem, *Homily on Genesis*, 10:1.
55. Idem, *Homily on Exodus*, 12:2.
56. Ibid., 13:3.
57. Idem, *Homily on Leviticus*, 8:3.
58. Idem, *Homily on Romans*, 2:7.
59. Ibid., 4:1.
60. Eusebius, *Ecclesiastical History*, 7:30.
61. Edward Gibbon, *Decline and Fall of the Roman Empire*, 20:6, cited in Thomas Jackson, *Curiosities of the Pulpit and Pulpit Literature* (New York: Virtue and Yorston, 1868), 22–23.
62. Brilioth, *A Brief History of Preaching*, 43.
63. Zeno of Verona, as cited in Carroll, *Preaching the Word*, 151.
64. Ambrose, *On the Death of Theodosius*.
65. Idem, *Epistle 41*, "To Marcellina."
66. Idem, *On the Mysteries*, 9:54.
67. Jerome, *Homily 88*, "On the Nativity of the Lord."
68. Idem, *Homily 1* on Ps. 1.
69. Idem, *Epistle 52:8*, "To Nepotian."
70. Athanasius, *On the Incarnation*, 54.

71. Gregory of Nazianzus, *On St. Basil the Great*, 71.

72. Idem, *Oration on Caesarius*, 7:18.

73. Idem, *Oration* 31:8.

74. Idem, *Epistle 130*.

75. Idem, *Epistle 16*, "Letter to Carmina."

76. Basil of Caesarea, *Homily 7*.

77. Idem, *Homily 1*, 6–7.

78. Idem, *Homily 8*, 5.

79. Ibid., 6.

80. Idem, *Homily 9*, 1.

81. Gregory of Nyssa, *Sermon 1 on The Lord's Prayer*.

82. Idem, *Sermon 3 on The Lord's Prayer*.

83. Idem, *Sermon 1 on The Beatitudes*.

84. Hans von Campenhausen, *The Fathers of the Greek Church* (New York: Pantheon, 1959), 144.

85. Hugh Thomson Kerr, *Preaching in the Early Church* (London: Fleming H. Revell, 1942), 175.

86. Chrysostom, *On the Priesthood*, 5:8. The citations from this work are from the translation by Graham Neville, *St. John Chrysostom—Six Books on the Priesthood* (New York: St. Vladimir's Seminary Press, 1984).

87. Chrysostom, *Homily on Earthquake*, cited in Carroll, *Preaching the Word*, 107.

88. Chrysostom, *On the Statues*, 21.

89. Idem, *Homily on Penance*, 3:4.

90. Idem, *On Genesis*, 6:3.

91. Idem, *Homily on John*, 11:1.

92. Idem, *Homily on Romans*, 14:6.

93. Idem, *Homily on 1 Timothy*, 12.

94. Idem, *Homily on the Psalms*, 47.

95. Idem, *Homily on Romans*, 18.

96. Chrysostomus Baur, *John Chrysostom and His Time*, vol. 1 (Westminster, Md.: Newman, 1958), 217.

97. Chrysostom, *Sermon on the Mount*, 5:1.

98. Socrates, *Ecclesiastical History*, 6:21:2.

99. W. H. C. Frend, *The Rise of Christianity* (Philadelphia: Fortress, 1984), 750.

100. Chrysostom, as cited by Carroll, *Preaching the Word*, 127.

101. Augustine, *On Christian Learning*, 4:5.

102. Ibid., 12:27.

103. Ibid., 4:19.

104. Ibid.

105. Brilioth, *A Brief History of Preaching*, 54.

106. Ibid., 55.
107. Augustine, *Sermon on Psalm 72*, 24.
108. Idem, *On Christian Learning*, 4:29.
109. Ibid., 4:15.
110. Ibid., 4:29.
111. Brilioth, *A Brief History of Preaching*, 48.
112. Augustine, *On Catechizing the Uninstructed*, 7:11.
113. Idem, *Sermon on Matthew and Luke's Account of Christ's Genealogy*.
114. Idem, *Sermon on John*, 8:13.
115. Idem, *Tractate on the Epistles of John*, 4:4.
116. Idem, *Sermon on Matthew and Luke's Account of Christ's Genealogy*.
117. Idem, *Sermon 229*, "On the Sacraments of the Faithful."
118. Idem, *Sermon 256*.
119. Idem, *Sermon 224*.
120. Brilioth, *A Brief History of Preaching*, 59.

Chapter 4: The Care of Souls

1. Gregory, *Pastoral Care*, 1:1.
2. William A. Clebsch and Charles Jaeckle, *Pastoral Care in Historical Perspective* (New York: Jason Aronson, 1964); John T. McNeill, *A History of the Cure of Souls* (New York: Harper and Row, 1951); H. Richard Niebuhr and Daniel Day Williams, *The Ministry in Historical Perspective* (New York: Harper and Row, 1956). Two other works commend themselves: Joseph T. Lienhard, *Ministry*, vol. 8 in Fathers of the Church (Wilmington, Del.: Michael Glazier, 1984). This work is focused primarily on ministry as office and not on pastoral care, although a few selections pertain to the category of care. See also Herbert T. Mayer, *Pastoral Care: Its Roots and Renewal* (Atlanta: John Knox Press, 1979). This work contains several case studies in pastoral care from the early church designed for parish discussion groups. They point to the similarities between modern parish concerns and those of the early church.
3. Thomas C. Oden, *Care of Souls in the Classic Tradition* (Philadelphia: Fortress, 1984).
4. Polycarp, *To the Philippians*, 6.
5. Chrysostom, *On the Priesthood*, 3:12, 13.
6. Ibid., 6:4.
7. Ibid., 3:18.
8. Ibid., 2:2.
9. Ibid, 2:2, 3.

10. Ibid., 2:4.
11. Gregory of Nazianzus, *Oration 2*, 18, "In Defense of His Flight to Pontus."
12. Ibid., 19.
13. Origen, *Homily on Ps. 37*, 2:6.
14. Jerome, *Letter 52*, "To Nepotian," 14, 15.
15. Ambrose, *On the Office of Ministry*, 1:3:13.
16. *Didascalia Apostolorum*, 7.
17. Pseudo-Eusebius of Alexandria, *Sermon 5:5*.
18. Bernard Cooke, *Ministry to Word and Sacraments* (Philadelphia: Fortress, 1976), 351.
19. Chrysostom, *On the Priesthood*, 2:2.
20. Gregory of Nazianzus, *Oration 2*, 71, "On Defense of His Flight to Pontus."
21. Kenneth E. Kirk, quoted by John T. McNeill, *History of the Cure of Souls*, 105.
22. F. Homes Dudden, *The Life and Times of St. Ambrose* (Oxford: Clarendon Press, 1935), vol. 2, 529. An English translation, *On the Office of Ministry,* can be found in Philip Schaff and Henry Wace, *A Select Library of the Nicene and Post-Nicene Fathers of the Christian Church* (New York: Christian Literature, 1896), vol. 10, 1–90.
23. Chrysostom, *On the Priesthood*, 2:3.
24. Clebsch and Jaeckle, *Pastoral Care in Historical Perspective*, 13–21.
25. *Martyrdom of Polycarp*, 19:1.
26. *The Martyrs of Scilli in Africa Proconsularis*.
27. Ignatius, *To the Romans*, 5:2, 3.
28. *The Martyrdom of Justin and His Companions*, 5.
29. *The Martyrs of Lyons and Vienne*, 11.
30. Tertullian, *To the Martyrs*, 1:3.
31. Cyprian, *Epistle 58*, 1, "To the People at Thibaris."
32. Ignatius, *To Polycarp*, 5:2.
33. L. Duchesne, *Christian Worship: Its Origin and Evolution* (London: S.P.C.K., 1904), 428ff., offers a short history of the early Christian nuptial blessing.
34. Siricius of Rome, *Letter 1*, 4:5, "To Bishop Himerius."
35. Chrysostom, *Address on Vainglory and the Right Way to Bring up Their Children*, in M. L. W. Laistner, *Christianity and Pagan Culture in the Later Roman Empire* (Ithaca, N.Y.: Cornell University Press, 1951), 88.
36. Chrysostom, *Homily 20 on Ephesians*.
37. Augustine, *City of God*, 19:6.
38. Victorinus Afer, *Commentary on Ephesians*.
39. Augustine, *Letter 262*, "To Ecdicia."
40. Ibid.

41. Augustine, *Sermon 392*, 4, 5.
42. Idem, *Epistle 259*, 3.
43. F. Van der Meer, *Augustine the Bishop* (New York: Harper and Row, 1961), 184.
44. Chrysostom, *Address on Vainglory and the Right Way to Bring up Their Children*, in M. L. W. Laistner, *Christianity and Pagan Culture in the Later Roman Empire* (Ithaca, N.Y.: Cornell University Press, 1951).
45. *Apostolic Constitutions*, 4:11.
46. Hippolytus, *Apostolic Tradition*, 34.
47. Chrysostom, *On the Priesthood*, 3:16.
48. Hippolytus, *Apostolic Tradition*, 15.
49. Ibid., 5.
50. For an elaboration of physical cures, see Bernard Cooke, *Ministry to Word and Sacraments*, 356.
51. Chrysostom, *On the Priesthood*, 3:18.
52. Ambrose, *Epistle 51*, 4, 5, "To Theodosius."
53. Ibid., 12, 13.
54. Ambrose, *Epistle 19*, 4, "To Vigilius."
55. Augustine, *Epistle 189*, "To Boniface."
56. Basil of Caesarea, *Epistle 109*, "To Count Helladius"; *Epistle 116*, "To Firminius"; *Epistle 46*, "To a Fallen Virgin"; *Epistle 66*, "To Athanasius"; *Epistle 126*, "To Atarbius"; *Epistle 170*, "To Glycerius."
57. Augustine, *Sermon 209*.
58. Jerome, *Epistle 39*, "To Paula."
59. Ibid.
60. Idem, *Epistle 60*, "To Heliodorus."
61. Idem, *Epistle 66*, "To Pammachius."
62. Idem, *Epistle 108*, "To Eustochium."
63. Gregory of Nazianzus, *Epistle 197*, "Condolences on the Death of Theosebia."
64. Chrysostom, *Letter to a Young Widow*. References are to the English translation in Schaff and Wace, *A Select Library of Nicene and Post-Nicene Fathers of the Christian Church*, series one, vol. 9, 121–28.
65. Ambrose, *Two Books on the Death of His Brother, Satyrus*. References are from the English translation in Schaff and Wace, *A Select Library of Nicene and Post-Nicene Fathers of the Christian Church*, series two, vol. 10, 161–97.
66. Ambrose, *Sympathy at the Death of Valentinian*, 51.
67. Ambrose, *Epistle 39*, "To Faustinus."
68. Ibid.
69. Ibid.
70. Hippolytus, *Apostolic Tradition*, 34.

71. *Martyrdom of Polycarp*, 18.

72. Tertullian, *On Repentance*, 5.

73. Ibid., 9.

74. Ibid., 12.

75. Hippolytus, *Refutation of All Heresies*, 9:12, 20–26.

76. Cyprian, *Epistle 55*, 20. Regarding idolatry, his *Testimonia*, compiled before the outbreak of the Decian persecution, clearly show that at that time it was still considered an irremissible sin (*Testimonia*, 3:28). In 251, however, at a council held when the persecutions had died down, the policy approved was more merciful. *Libellatici*, who had satisfied the state by producing certificates that they had fulfilled its requirements, should be readmitted at once, while *sacrificati* who had actually offered the sacrifices should undergo lifelong penance and be readmitted at death.

77. Basil of Caesarea, *Epistle 188*.

78. Epiphanius, *Panarion*, 59:1.

79. Socrates, *History of the Church*, 5:19. Duchesne, *Christian Worship*, writes: "Just as there was a *doctor audientium*, or head catechist, assisted by a staff of exorcists, so there was, in certain churches, at all events, a penitentiary priest, with clerks under him, who were entrusted with the care of the penitents, and were responsible for the sincerity of their expiation," 436. Bernard Cooke, *Ministry to Word and Sacraments*, writes: "By the sixth century it is quite clear that the bulk of the ministry of reconciling has been assigned to presbyters, particularly in the countryside. . . . In the East it seems that penitential discipline had been entrusted to certain designated presbyters as early as the late third century. In the West the designation of presbyters to receive people's confession of sin, assign penance, and then reconcile them probably helped prepare for the spread of private confession," 437.

80. Ambrose, *On Repentance*, 1:1.

81. Augustine, *Sermon 351*, 2:2.

82. See also Ambrose, *On Repentance*, 2:5:35: "He who exercises repentance ought not only to wash away his sins with tears but also to hide and cover his greater offenses by better works, so that sin may not be imputed to him."

83. Augustine, *Sermon 355*, 4:7.

84. Idem, *Epistle 56*.

85. Idem, *Sermon 351*, 7.

86. Origen, *Sermon on Lev.*, 2:4.

87. Duchesne, *Christian Worship*, 439–45.

88. Victor Vitensis, *On the Persecution of the Vandals*, 2:2.

89. Caesarius of Arles, *Homily 18*.

90. Gennadius, *On Ecclesiastical Doctrine*, 53.

91. Julius Pomerius, *On the Contemplative Life*, 2:7:2.

92. Gregory the Great, *Sermon 26*.

93. Bernard Cooke, *Ministry to Word and Sacraments*, 424, n. 43.

94. See McNeill, *History of the Cure of Souls*, 133.

95. Hans von Campenhausen, *Ecclesiastical Authority and Spiritual Power in the Church of the First Three Centuries* (London: Adam and Charles Black, 1969), 252.

96. Ibid., 262.

97. Origen, *Sermon on Isaiah 17*, 2.

98. George H. Williams, in H. Richard Niebuhr and Daniel Williams, *The Ministry in Historical Perspective* (New York: Harper and Row, 1956), 76. "In the meantime, as bishop and metropolitan became involved in their new imperial assignments, many of the faithful felt estranged by clerical accommodation to the world; and monasticism developed with its own special ministry to the saints within and seekers without. Thus by the end of the patristic period the saintly or charismatic anchorite emerges as an alternative curer of souls; the abbot takes his place alongside the bishop and the parish priest as a third kind of chief pastor," 30.

99. Julius Caesar, *Gallic War*, 6:13.

100. Gildas, *Introduction to Penance*, 1.

101. *Poenitentials Vinniani* in H. Wasserschleben, *Die Bussordnungen der ablaendischen Kirche* (Halle, 1851), 109.

102. O. D. Watkins, *A History of Penance*, vol. 2 (London: 1920), 609.

103. Cooke, *Ministry to Word and Sacraments*, 437.

104. S. Donatus, *Rule for Virgins*.

105. See Edward E. Malone, *The Monk and the Martyr*, Studies in Christian Antiquity, 12 (Washington, 1950) on the replacement of martyrs by monks.

106. W. H. C. Frend, *The Rise of Christianity* (Philadelphia: Fortress, 1984), 569.

107. Van der Meer, *Augustine the Bishop*, 211.

108. Chrysostom, *On the Priesthood*, 6:5–7.

109. John Cassian, *Conferences*, 2.

110. Gregory, *Moralia in Job*, 26:28.

111. John Cassian, *Conferences*, 4.

112. Ibid., 14.

113. Maximus the Confessor, *Selected Writings*, trans. George C. Berthold (New York: Paulist, 1985). Selections are from *Four Hundred Chapters on Love*, 3rd century, 76, 82; 4th century, 19, 34, 94.

114. The text here used is that of Henry Davis, *St. Gregory the Great Pastoral Care* (New York: Newman, 1950), vol. 11 in Ancient Christian Writers.

115. Thomas C. Oden, *Care of Souls in the Classic Tradition*, 78. See Gregory's *Pastoral Care*, 3:8.

Chapter 5: The Pastoral Role of Women

1. Roger Gryson, *The Ministry of Women in the Early Church*, trans. Jean LaPorte and Mary Louise Hall (Collegeville, Minn.: Liturgical Press, 1972), 5.

2. Jean Daniélou, *The Ministry of Women in the Early Church* (London: Faith Press, 1961), 10.

3. Hans von Campenhausen, *Ecclesiastical Authority and Spiritual Power in the Church of the First Three Centuries* (London: Adam and Charles Black, 1969).

4. P. de Labriolle, *La crise montaniste*, Book III, "Tertullien et le Montanisme" (Paris, 1913), 34–105, as cited by Jean LaPorte, *The Role of Women in Early Christianity* (New York: Edwin Mellon Press, 1982), 57.

5. Barbara J. MacHaffie, *Her Story: Women in Christian Tradition* (Philadelphia: Fortress, 1986), 33.

6. Tertullian, *On the Soul*, 9:4.

7. Tertullian, *Against Marcion*, 5:8:11.

8. Ireneaus, *Against Heresies*, 1:13:5.

9. Elaine Pagels, *The Gnostic Gospels* (New York: Random House, 1979); Susanne Heine, *Women and Early Christianity: A Reappraisal*, trans. John Bowden (Minneapolis: Augsburg, 1988).

10. Pagels, *Gnostic Gospels*, 138.

11. N. Brox, *Die Pastoralbriefe* (Regensburg NT, 1969), 125, as cited by Pagels, *Gnostic Gospels*, 140. George H. Tavard, *Woman in Christian Tradition* (Notre Dame: University of Notre Dame Press, 1973), 75: "Meanwhile, the Christian principle of spiritual freedom contrasted sharply with the realities of life in the Hellenistic world. The Christian woman could be persuaded of her intrinsic value; yet the law, recognizing no such thing, placed her always under the power of a man. Some restrictions on her legal rights were removed very late by the Christian Emperor Justinian (527–65). In these circumstances the theologians had to take account of two sets of notions: Christian principles (baptismal equality of all; the biblical command to increase and multiply; the desire for spiritual fulfillment; the unreality of the present world as compared with the heavens; the true union, which is between

Christ and the soul) and the secular realities (the legal status of women; the normality of concubinage, adultery, divorce)."

12. 1 Timothy 5:4, 8, 16.
13. *Shepherd of Hermas*, Mandate 8:10, Similitude 1:8, 5:3, 9:26, 9:27.
14. Ignatius, *To the Smyrneans*, 6.
15. Polycarp, *To the Philippians*, 4.
16. Cornelius of Rome to Fabius of Antioch, in Eusebius, *Ecclesiastical History*, 6:43; Chrysostom, *Homily on Matt. 66*, c. 3 (PG 57:630).
17. Polycarp, *To the Philippians*, 4:3.
18. Hippolytus, *Apostolic Tradition*, 11.
19. Ibid., 23.
20. Tertullian, *Exhortation to Chastity*, 13:4.
21. Idem, *On Monogamy*, 11:1.
22. Clement of Alexandria, *The Instructor*, 3:12; *Ante-Nicene Fathers* vol. 2 (Grand Rapids, Mich.: Wm. B. Eerdmans, 1962), 294.
23. Origen, *On Prayer*, 28:4; *Homily on Luke*, 17.
24. Idem, *Commentary on Romans*, 10:20.
25. *Didascalia Apostolorum*, 14.
26. Ibid., 15.
27. Ibid.
28. LaPorte, *Role of Women*, 64.
29. Clement of Alexandria, *Who Is the Rich Man That Shall Be Saved?*, 34; Tertullian, *On Monogamy*, 11; *On Penitence*, 9-10.
30. Gryson, *Ministry of Women*, 40–41.
31. Jerome, *Epistle 234*, "To Ageruchia."
32. Idem, *Epistle 54*, "To Furia."
33. *Apostolic Church Order*, cited in Gryson, *Ministry of Women*, 45, n. 2.
34. C. H. Turner, "Ministries of Women in the Primitive Church," *Catholic and Apostolic: Collected Papers by C. H. Turner*, ed. H. N. Bate (London: A. R. Mowbray, 1931), 325.
35. Daniélou, *Ministry of Women*, 18. Gryson questions this conclusion: "It is impossible to understand what permits J. Daniélou this opinion," Gryson, *Ministry of Women*, 46.
36. *Canons of Hippolytus*, can. 9.
37. Synod of Laodicea, can. 11 in *Nicene and Post-Nicene Fathers*, series 2, ed. Henry R. Percival (Grand Rapids, Mich.: Wm. B. Eerdmans, 1962), vol. 14, 130.
38. Gryson, *Ministry of Women*, 53–54.
39. *Apostolic Constitutions*, 8:12, 43–44; 8:13:14; 8:30:2.
40. Ibid., 3:3:1.
41. Daniélou, *Ministry of Women*, 19.
42. *Testamentum Domini Nostri Jesu Christi*, 23.

43. Ibid., 40.

44. Ibid.

45. Ibid., 42. Daniélou, *Ministry of Women*, 20, in commenting on the *Testamentum* claims that the widows of this document are, in fact, deaconesses, because they do the work of deaconesses. "They retain the name [of widows] but are, in fact, deaconesses." This appears to be an arbitrary judgment, and I am inclined to believe that when the document refers to them as widows, that is what they were. Furthermore, the *Testamentum* specifically places deaconesses under the guidance of widows, and it seems unlikely that the author would have meant the opposite.

46. *A Dictionary of Christian Antiquities*, ed. W. Smith and S. Cheetham (London: John Murray, 1880), vol. 2, 2035.

47. Gryson, *Ministry of Women*, 3.

48. Ibid., 4.

49. Ibid.

50. *Didascalia Apostolorum*, trans. and ed. R. Hugh Connolly (Oxford: Clarendon Press, 1929), 146.

51. Ibid., 146–47.

52. Gryson, *Ministry of Women*, 42.

53. LaPorte, *Role of Women*, 113. See also *Apostolic Constitutions*, 3:14.

54. *Didascalia Apostolorum*, 25; Connolly, 88.

55. Clement of Alexandria, *Miscellanies*, 3:6:53, 3–4.

56. Ibid.

57. Origen, *Commentary on Romans*, 10:17.

58. Gryson, *Ministry of Women*, 30–34, reference is to 32.

59. *Council of Nicea* (325), can. 19.

60. Turner, "Ministries of Women," 337.

61. *Apostolic Constitutions*, 6:17.

62. Ibid., 3:2:19.

63. Gryson, *Ministry of Women*, 61, citing *Apostolic Constitutions*, 2:58, 4–6.

64. *Apostolic Constitutions*, 3:1:8.

65. Ibid., 2:4:26.

66. Ibid., 8:3, 19–20.

67. Gryson, *Ministry of Women*, 62.

68. This is found in an essay on the ordination of deaconesses as an appendix in Gryson, *Ministry of Women*, 115–20.

69. *Apostolic Constitutions*, 3:1:11.

70. Basil of Caesarea, *Epistle 199*.

71. Turner, "Ministries of Women," 341.

72. Ibid. Turner cites Basil, *Epistle 105*, and Theodoret, *Ecclesiastical History*, 3:14 and 19.

73. Chrysostom, *Homily 30 on Romans 15, Homily 31 on Romans 16.*
74. Idem, *First Homily on "Salute Priscilla and Aquila,"* 16.
75. Ibid.
76. Chrysostom, *Homily 31 on Romans 16,* 6.
77. Ibid.
78. Ibid.
79. Chrysostom, *On the Priesthood,* 3:9.
80. Chrysostom, *To Olympia,* 1.
81. As cited by W. R. W. Stephens, *Nicene and Post-Nicene Fathers,* series one, vol. 9, 287.
82. *Life of Olympias the Deacon,* 8, as cited by Elizabeth Clark, *Women in the Early Church, Message of the Fathers of the Church,* vol. 13, ed. Thomas Halton (Wilmington, Del.: Michael Glazier, 1987), 228.
83. Ibid., 230–31.
84. Theodore of Mopsuestia, *Commentary on 1 Timothy,* 3:11, 5:9, 5:3-16.
85. Ibid., 3:11.
86. *Council of Chalcedon* (451), can. 15.
87. Justinian, Novellae, 3:1:1, as cited in Gryson, *Ministry of Women,* following the edition of R. Schoell and G. Kroll (5th ed., Berlin, 1928), 21:3–12.
88. Ibid., 6:6.
89. Ambrosiaster, *Commentary on 1 Timothy,* 1 Tim. 3:11.
90. Pelagius, *Commentary on Romans,* Rom. 16:1.
91. Gryson, *Ministry of Women,* 101.
92. *First Council of Orange* (441), cited by Smith and Cheetham, *Dictionary,* 534.
93. *Council of Epaon* (517), can. 21.
94. *Second Council of Orange* (533), can. 18.
95. Ignatius, *To Polycarp,* 5.
96. Polycarp, *To the Philippians,* 5.
97. Justin Martyr, *First Apology,* 15.
98. Hippolytus, *Apostolic Tradition,* 13.
99. Tertullian, *On the Veiling of Virgins,* 9.
100. Tertullian, *On the Resurrection of the Flesh,* 61.
101. Cyprian, *On the Dress of Virgins,* 3.
102. Methodius of Olympas, *The Banquet of the Ten Virgins, Ante-Nicene Fathers,* vol. 6, 309–55, passim.
103. Although LaPorte, *Role of Women,* 70, writes, "They did not constitute an order or rank in the church before the second half of the third century," such an ordering does not appear likely until the fourth century.

104. Cyprian, *On the Dress of Virgins*, 20.

105. Ibid., 14.

106. Chrysostom, *On the Priesthood*, 3:17.

107. Ibid.

108. Ibid.

109. *Council of Nicea*, can. 3.

110. *Apostolic Constitutions*, 2:26:8, 2:57:12.

111. Ibid., 4:14.

112. Sozomon, *Ecclesiastical History*, 2:2; Socrates, *Ecclesiastical History*, 1:17.

113. Ibid.

114. Cyril of Jerusalem, *Catechetical Lectures*, 4:24.

115. Jerome, *Epistle 128*, "To Gaudentius"; *Epistle 147*, "To Sabinianus," 5.

116. Basil of Caesarea, *Epistle 46*, "To the Lapsed Virgins," 5.

117. Augustine, *Letter 150*, "To Proba and Juliana." The treatise, *On the Lapse of Consecrated Virgins*, sometimes attributed to Ambrose, offers a vivid account of the ceremonies which had taken place when the lapsed (i.e., married) sister had taken her vows.

118. Basil of Caesarea, *Canonical Epistle 2*, "To Amphilocus," 18; Ambrose, *On Virginity*, 7: *Theodosian Code*, "Novellae" tit. 6, c. 1:1–2.

119. *Testamentum Domini Nostri Jesu Christi*, 1:22.

120. Tertullian, *On the Veiling of Virgins*, 2.

121. Palladius, *Lausiac History*, 32–33.

122. Gregory of Nyssa, *Life of Macrina*, 6.

123. Ibid., 17.

124. Jerome, *Epistle 108*, "To Eustochium," 20.

125. Ibid., 14.

126. Jerome, *Epistle 127*, "To Principia," 7.

127. Ibid.

128. Palladius, *Lausiac History*, 46 and 54.

129. Paulinus of Nola, *Epistle 129*, "To Sulpicius Severus."

130. Palladius, *Lausiac History*, 141–44.

131. Jerome, *Epistle 77*, "To Oceanus," 6.

132. Ibid., 11.

133. Etheria, *Diary of a Pilgrimage*, 3.

134. Ibid., 36.

135. Clark, *Women in the Early Church*, 204–5.

INDEX